Sortedams Sø
Kastellet
Den Hirschsprungske Samling
Statens Museum
ROSENBORG SLOT AND AROUND
pages 14–15
THE AMALIENBORG AND AROUND
pages 16–17
BOTANISK HAVE
Rosenbaorg Slot
ROSENBORG HAVE
Amalienborg Plads
Operahuset
STRØGET AND AROUND
pages 8–9
KONGENS NYTORV AND NYHAVN
pages 12–13
CHRISTIANSHAVN AND HOLMEN
pages 20–21
SLOTSHOLMEN
pages 10–11
Christians kirke
Vor Frelsers Kirke
USPLADSEN
D TIVOLI
ages 6–7
KLØVERMARKEN
AMAGER
0
200
400m

INSIGHT GUIDES

COPENHAGEN

smart guide

Discovery CHANNEL

APA PUBLICATIONS
Part of the Langenscheidt Publishing Group

Contents

Areas

Copenhagen 4
Rådhuspladsen and Tivoli....................6
Strøget and Around..........8
Slotsholmen 10
Kongens Nytorv and Nyhavn................12
Rosenborg Slot and Around 14
The Amalienborg and Around................16
Vesterbro and Frederiksberg.............18
Christianshavn and Holmen 20
Copenhagen's Suburbs.....................22
Sjælland 24

Below: proudly displayed, the red and white flag of the Danes.

A–Z

Architecture....................26
Cafés and Bars...............28
Children..........................34
Churches and Synagogues...............36
Danish Design 40
Environment 44
Essentials 46
Festivals 48
Film 50
Food and Drink...............52
Gay and Lesbian 56
History............................58
Hotels.............................62
Language 70

Left: the popular quayside of Nyhavn is lined with outdoor cafés and bars.

Literature
and Theatre 72
Monuments
and Fountains 78
Museums and
Galleries 82
Music and Dance 100
Nightlife 104
Palaces 106
Pampering....................110
Parks, Gardens
and Beaches...........112
Restaurants..................116
Shopping......................126
Transport......................130

Below: seasonal treats.

Atlas

Nørrebro, Østerbro
and Kastellet 134
Frederiksberg, Vesterbro
and Amagerbro........136
Centre and
Christianshavn 138

Inside Front Cover:
City Locator
Inside Back Cover:
Copenhagen Transport
The Nationalmuseet
Floorplan: p.92
The Glyptotek
Floorplan: p.94

Street Index: 140–1
General Index: 142–4

Copenhagen

Copenhagen, capital of Denmark and once head of Sweden and Norway too, is a pretty, seaside city with a a thriving nightlife, the gastronomic and cultural offerings of a far larger city, and a visible history going back to the 12th century. It now also supports plenty of big business and is the world's ninth richest city in terms of gross pay per head.

Copenhagen Fact and Figures

Population: **503,699 (1.21 million in metropolitan Copenhagen)**
Area: **91.3sq. km**
GDP per capita: **35,798 euros**
Unemployment: **3.8 per cent**
Inflation: **1.8 per cent**
Annual average rainfall: **630mm**
Longest pedestrianised street: **Strøget, 1.6km**
Total length of bicycle tracks: **316km**
The most books: **Royal Library, 2.5 million volumes**
Oldest boat: **the 2,000 year-old Hjortespring boat in the Nationalmuseet**
Largest brewery: **Carlsberg, probably**

Small but Densely Populated

Copenhagen (*København* in Danish), the capital of Denmark, is located on the eastern side of Sjælland, the largest of Denmark's 406 islands, with only the Øresund (Sound) separating it from Sweden. It was founded by Bishop Absalon in 1167 and originally made its living from the vast herring stocks in the Sound. These days it is home, including its greater metropolitan area, to about 1,210,000 of the country's estimated 5.45 million population. With a land area of just 43,000 sq km. Denmark is the smallest, yet most densely populated nation in northern Europe. In Denmark there are over six times as many people per square kilometre as in neighbouring Sweden.

Strategic Link to Europe

Connected by the south of Jutland to Germany, Denmark is the only Scandinavian country physically joined to the European mainland and, as such, it is the bridge between Scandinavia and the rest of the continent; quite literally with the opening of the Øresund bridge in 2000. Consequently, Denmark shares many of the characteristics of its Nordic neighbours: liberal welfare benefits coupled with a high standard of living, and a style of government that aims at consensus and the avoidance of petty bureaucracy. But Denmark is also more 'European' and accessible than the rest of Scandinavia.

Cultural Centre... and Shops

Copenhagen, with its strategic location at the mouth of the Baltic Sea, has always been an important crossroads. It boasts a fine historic centre with a lovely old harbour, cobbled streets, open spaces, a Renaissance castle as well as cutting-edge modern architecture and design, international museums and art galleries, good (though expensive) shopping, plenty of cultural events (it's home to one of the best opera houses in the world), a reputation as one of northern Europe's jazz capitals and excellent restaurants – 10 Michelin-starred restaurants with 11 stars between them.

Below: the Marble Bridge at Slotsholmen was built in 1745 and has survived two fires.

The Delightful Danes

In addition, Copenhagen can offer its inhabitants as an appeal in themselves – law-abiding, socially responsible (just look at their generous social security system), gregarious, and, at one and the same time, charming and sarcastic.

They are skilled at enjoying life, especially when it comes to the combination of family, friends, food and copious amounts of alcohol.

Hygge is a word that you will often come across; it loosely translates as a combination of warmth, well-being and intimacy. You will sense it in every candlelit café that provides shelter from the rain, any Danish home you visit and even on warm, sunny days in parks and open spaces where people congregate.

Hygge may be physically represented by warm lighting, candles and simple, welcoming designs, but it succeeds here thanks to the Danes spirit of inclusiveness; an inherent need to keep friends and families, especially children, close by their side.

Despite the long periods of dark and grey weather, *hygge* keeps the Danes' spirits up. In 2007, a European study revealed that when asked to rate thier long-term life satisfaction and happiness, Danes scored the highest in Europe.

This contentedness is infectious, even to the short term visitor, and it's difficult to not want to bring part of the Danish spirit home when you return.

Highlights

▲ **Danish design** is the main attraction of any shopping expedition in Copenhagen.

▶ **The Little Mermaid** has become Copenhagen's symbol and the top site for a pilgrimage along the city's waterfront.

▲ The docks at **Nyhavn** are a pleasant place to go for bustling outdoor cafés and bars, or to watch the sunrise.

▶ **Tivoli** is more than just an amusement park, with a selection of popular restaurants and fireworks every night.

▲ **Slotsholmen** (Castle Island), with its monumental architecture, is the historic heart of the capital.

▶ **Roskilde**'s cathedral and Vikingskibsmuseet make it the day trip of choice.

Rådhuspladsen and Tivoli

Rådhuspladsen, a huge square surrounded by busy streets and flanked on one side by København Rådhus (City Hall), is home to the city's main bus terminal and a place you're likely to get to know well if you're travelling around the city. Tivoli, the world-famous pleasure park, runs along one side of it, a romantic and leafy enclave amid the bustle of bikes, buses and cars. It's amazing to think that until the early 1840s, this area was empty land outside the city walls.

Rådhuspladsen

Rådhuspladsen, while in itself not much to look at, is adjacent to the heart of the city, and is the capital's administrative and transport hub. It is close to the main station **Hovedbanegård** and a good place to stay, well within easy reach of Copenhagen's major sites and not far from the city's pretty reservoirs and more quirky, residential areas of Nørrebro and Vesterbro. Its main point of interest, unless a concert or public event is happening in the square, is its **Rådhus** or City Hall where every Saturday you are bound to see happy couples standing on the steps having just plighted their troth.

Before 1892, when work began on the Rådhus, the road now leading up past the station into the square was the road to the western gate of the city, where the old town begins. It was on one of these streets, Vester Kvarter 146, that a fire began early on the morning of Wednesday 20th October 1728 in the home of one Peder Rasmussen and his wife, Anne Iversdatter. Unnoticed at first, it soon spiralled out of control, raging for three days, razing to the ground just over a quarter of the city and almost half of its medieval quarter. Over 1,600 houses were destroyed as well as the University Library, which contained thousands of irreplaceable texts. Twenty per cent of the population, that is 15,000 people, were made homeless.

Delightfully mock Gothic, the Rådhus is worth a visit for the pseudo-Italian decorations of the entrance hall, the extraordinary cleverness of Jens Olsen's astronomical world clock and the view from the clock tower.

SEE ALSO ARCHITECTURE P.26

Museums and Monuments

To the left of the Rådhus clock tower, you will see a splendid neo-Gothic statue, **Lurblœserne**, two horn-blowers high up on a column. and in the centre stands the **Dragon's Leap Fountain**.

Despite the rumble of the surrounding traffic, the square is pedestrian-friendly, with pavement cafés filling its wide open space during the summer. It is also the site of Christmas and New Year's Eve festivities, and it's a fun and lively place at weekends and holidays.

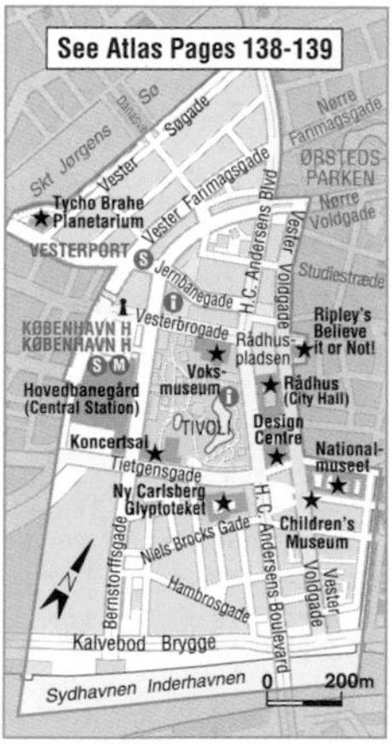

Rådhuspladsen is the spot from which any signpost or milestone in Sjælland measures its distance to the capital, and most streets in the city have their lowest house numbers at the end closest to the square.

Nearby attractions include the macabre

Tivoli started with just one horse-drawn carousel and a roller coaster and was named Tivoli and Vauxhall after the 18th-century Jardins de Tivoli in Paris and the Vauxhall Pleasure Gardens on the banks of the Thames in London.

Left: Tivoli is a collage of architectural styles, *à la* Disney World, that includes Chinese pagodas, Moorish palaces and everything in between.

Ripley's Believe it or Not! museum and the sophisticated **Dansk Design Centre**, just opposite Tivoli; a little further along is one of Copenhagen's cultural highlights: the **Ny Carlsberg Glyptotek**.

SEE ALSO DANISH DESIGN P.40; MONUMENTS AND FOUNTAINS P.79, 81; MUSEUMS AND GALLERIES P.85, 95, 96

Transport Hub

Not only is Rådhuspladsen convenient for its proximity to the central rail station, but it is also the location for the city's main bus station. It's hard to find a bus that doesn't eventually lead to the stop at the end of the pedestrianised Strøget.

This location becomes even more vital at night as everyone from clubbers to theatre goers congregates on the neon-lit square to wait for the night bus that will take them home.

SEE ALSO TRANSPORT P.130

Tivoli

Tivoli (spell it backwards), now a rainbow of gardens, open-air amusements, restaurants, cafés, theatres, an open-air stage and a major concert hall, did not come into existance until 1843. Originally part of the fortification and demarcation area surrounding the city, its original 15 acres were leased in 1841 for five years by an enterprising journalist, Georg Carstensen, who convinced King Christian VIII that if people were well entertained they were less likely to talk politics and sedition.

A FLATTERING IMITATION

Now drawing over five million visitors a year, its popularity is undiminished with tourists and locals alike and in the 1950s it even inspired film maker Walt Disney to think about creating an amusement park of his own, one that could make Tivoli's popularity seem modest in comparison.

SEE ALSO MUSIC AND DANCE P.100; PARKS, GARDENS AND BEACHES P.115

Below: a peaceful night on Rådhuspladsen.

Strøget and Around

If Rådhuspladsen is the head of Copenhagen, then Strøget, the 1.6-km pedestrianised shopping street, is its spine. It has interesting shops, street vendors and buskers galore; workshops, cellar galleries and the biggest of the Danish design stores. All year round, street musicians play classical, rock, jazz and folk tunes to entertain you in mid-spending spree. There is even more free music during the two-week jazz festival in June–July. Not only is it central to Copenhagen's vibrancy, it is also a fascinating historical area, which grew up around the island of Slotsholmen from the 12th century onwards.

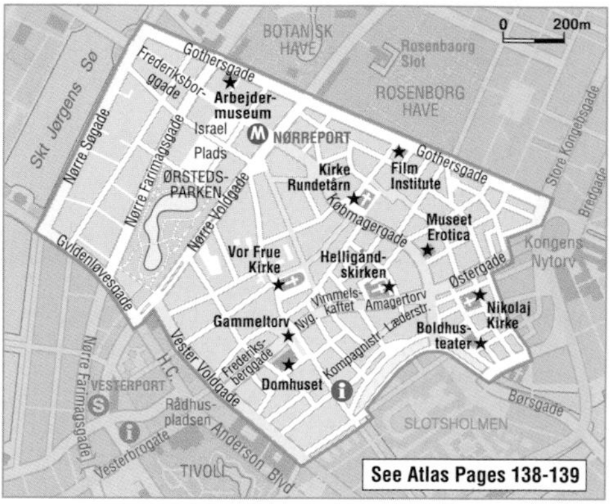

Strøget

Strøget is a combination of five separate streets: Frederiksberggade, Nygade, Vimmelskaftet, Amagertorv, and Østergade. The name, pronounced 'stroll', means 'stripe' and is sometimes called the 'Walking Street'.

At the southwestern end, closest to Rådhuspladsen, are **Frederiksberggade** and **Nygade**, the more lively part of Strøget, with many small clothing stores, record shops, snack stands and burger bars. Nygade begins at a large open area made up of two squares, Gammeltorv and Nytorv (the Old and the New Square).

Before the second fire in 1795, a block of houses separated the two, but new fire regulations required more space between buildings and the houses were never rebuilt.

Below: Bishop Absalon.

GAMMELTORV

Copenhagen's oldest marketplace, Gammeltorv dates back to the Middle Ages, when it was the scene of jousting tournaments. Peep inside the gate of no. 14 to see a relief depicting the history of the square.

The **Caritas Fountain** in the centre dates from 1608; it was donated to the town by Christian IV, who thought it would make a contribution to the water supply, as well as enhance Copenhagen's beauty. On royal birthdays golden apples are placed on the jets to dance on the water.

The Neoclassical **Domhuset** or Courthouse stands on Nytorv, designed by C.F. Hansen after the 1795 fire. It was also the town hall until the Rådhus was built in the late 19th century.

SEE ALSO MONUMENTS AND FOUNTAINS P.78

AMAGERTORV

This, the widest part of Strøget, usually has street musicians. It dates from the 14th century but became especially busy from the 17th when a law was passed stipulating that all the fresh produce grown on the island of Amager had to be sold here.

The 14th-century **Helligåndskirken** (Church of the

Left: street performers draw big weekend crowds to Strøget.

Holy Spirit), stands on its west side. A monument to the Danes who died in concentration camps during World War II stands at the church's gate nearest Strøget. It was designed by Kaare Klint, the furniture designer.

Further down, on the same side are the shops most often visited by tourists: **Illums Bolighus** and the flagship stores of **Royal Copenhagen Porcelain** and **Georg Jensen** silver.

Ostergade is the Bond Street end of Strøget, which opens out on to the 17th-century square Kongens Nytorv, which in turn leads down to the harbour area at Nyhavn.
SEE ALSO CHURCHES P. 37; DANISH DESIGN P. 41–3

Strøget's Sister Streets

The streets parallel with Strøget are equally historic and perhaps more interesting in terms of shopping, with more independent boutiques.

VESTERGADE

In the Middle Ages, before Copenhagen grew into a city, Vestergade to the west was the village street. The rows of Neoclassical houses in Vestergade are the best example of rebuilding after the fire in 1795: merchants' houses stand behind several gates.

FARVERGADE

This street, east of Strøget, runs into **Kompagnistraede** and **Laederstraede** and is one uninterrupted pedestrian street, lined with shops dealing in oriental rugs, antique furniture, silverware, china and curios. The prices are not exactly low, but on a good day it's possible to find a fair deal. The streets are more popular than Strøget among Copenhageners and the cafés are always full of people.

KOBMAGERGADE

To the west of Amagertorv is Købmagergade, yet another pedestrian shopping street. To the east is **Højbro Plads**, with the equestrian statue of **Bishop Absalon**, Copenhagen's founder, standing proud *(see picture opposite)*. Look past Absalon to the canal which surrounds Christiansborg on Slotsholmen. To the right is **Gammel Strand** (Old Beach) where the fishwives used to sell their wares.
SEE ALSO MONUMENTS AND FOUNTAINS P.78; SHOPPING PP.126–7

The Latin Quarter

The Latin Quarter lies in the streets northwest of Strøget and is one of the city's oldest areas. So-called because Copenhagen's ancient university used Latin was the language of education from the 15th century onwards. The medieval buildings were all destroyed in the fires of 1728 and 1795 and most of what you see now is 17th century.

Behind Helligandskirken is **Grabrødretorv**, a 13th-century square that takes its name from the Grey Brothers, the order of monks who built Copenhagen's first monastery here in 1328.

On Frue Plads is the **universitet**: the current Neoclassical building and library are from the 19th century. However, the old Bishop's Palace, *c.*1420, is in the courtyard. Disorderly students were once put in its cellar as a punishment.

Many street names reflect their medieval roots in which trades tended to stick together: Købmagergade used to be the butchers' street, Læderstræde was the furriers' street, and textile merchants sold their silks and linens at Silkegade.

Slotsholmen

Slotsholmen, or Castle Island, is where Copenhagen's history begins; the place where the village of *Havn* (Harbour) grew up on the banks of the Øresund in about 1000 AD. Here the herring fishing was plentiful and access to the Baltic was easy. Over the centuries, it has been attacked by pirates, been the site of royal power and court intrigues, and devastated several times by fire. It is no longer the centre of Copenhagen life, but it still wields power as the seat of the Danish Parliament. A good way to get your bearings is to take a harbour tour (from Nyhavn) that will take you along the Frederiksholm canal, which encircles the island.

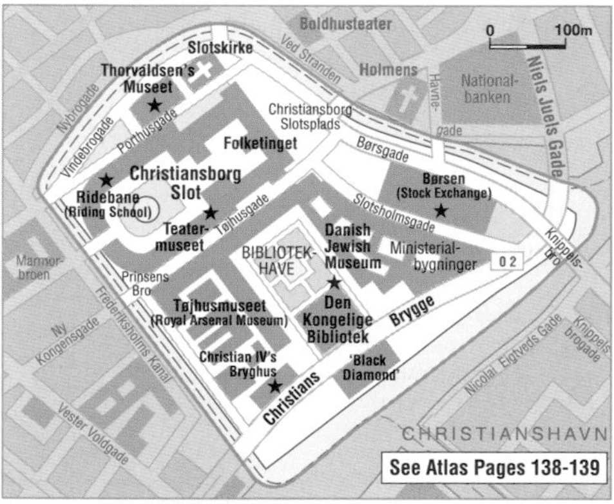

Bishop Absalon's Fortress

Bishop Absalon, regarded as the founder of Copenhagen, was given Slotsholmen, then known as *Strandholmen* (Beach Island) by his brother King Valdemar I in the 1160s. By this time, Havn had caught the attention of German Wendish pirates. It needed defending, so Absalon – a cleric as at home with a sword in his hand as when saying Mass – built a castle here in 1167. His simple stone fort was ringed by a thick wall of limestone.

Over the next century, Havn flourished and became a successful trading centre. This threatened the Hanseatic league, an alliance of German trading guilds, which monopolised trade in the Baltic and Northern Europe. After several attacks, they destroyed the castle in 1367.

The First Castle

A new castle was built eight years later. In 1417, it gained more importance when the king, Eric of Pomerania, took up residence here. Havn, now Kjøbmandehavn (Merchants' Harbour), was a major economic centre, and the **Børsen** (stock exchange) was added to the complex in the early 17th century.

The castle was added to over the years but by the mid 18th century was beginning to fall down. The new king, Christian VI, mindful of his position and perhaps the unflattering comments of visiting dignitaries, razed it to the ground.

SEE ALSO ARCHITECTURE P. 26

The Second Castle

This splendid building, begun in 1731 and finished in 1745 was a Baroque palace suitable for the grandeur of an absolute monarch. However, it did not last long; a fire in 1794 destroyed the entire complex, with the exception of the grand stables and the lovely red and gold palace theatre (now both museums).

As a result of the fire, the Royal family were homeless and took refuge in the aristocratic mansions of Amalienborg.

SEE ALSO AMALIENBORG P.16; MUSEUMS AND GALLERIES P.97, 98

The Third Castle

Alas, despite a magnificent rebuild, Frederik VI and the royal family preferred their new quarters in Amalienborg and, to this day, the royals have never returned.

The new palace, built in 1803–28 and designed by C.F. Hansen in French Empire style, was used for entertainment purposes and housed

Left: the Borsen's unique spire represents four entwined dragons' tails.

the **Parliament** and administrative departments.

In 1884 it suffered the fate as its predecessors, the only part to survive being the **Slotskirke** and riding ground.

The Current Castle

The current neo-Baroque castle was built between 1907 and 1928 by Thorvald Jørgensen. With its predecessors' fates in mind, **Christiansborg Slot** (Palace) is built of reinforced concrete with a granite façade. It contains the **Royal Reception Rooms** used to entertain foreign dignitaries and the Folketinget, the elected parliament, the **prime minister's office** and the **supreme court**.

SEE ALSO PALACES P.107–8

The Folketinget

Denmark has had a national parliament since 1849 when Royal Absolutism (instated in 1660) was dissolved. Initially one of two elected chambers, it became the sole parliamentary body in 1953. The monarchy now shares its legislative power but international policy can only be implemented with the Folketinget's consent, which is democratically elected every four years.

Slotsholmen in a Day

Start with a tour of the **Royal Apartments**, before visiting the **ruins** under the palace. Do not miss the charming **Theatre Museum** and the **Royal Stables** next door and, if it is open, **Christiansborg Slotskirke** is also interesting and one of the few parts of the older palaces that still remain.

The **Thorvaldsen's Museum** displays the work of Denmark's great sculptor, Bertel Thorvaldsen (1770–1844) as well as his tomb. On the other side of the island, the **Tøjhusmuseet** is full of weaponry.

The **Royal Library**, which dates back to 1482, is the largest library in Scandinavia. Most of the collection is now in the '**Black Diamond**', a black polished granite building constructed on the water's edge in 1999.

The area where the **Library Garden** now stands was once a naval harbour, and you can still see mooring rings on the walls of the old buildings along its side. This peaceful garden is a nice place to take a little time out and the only place you will find greenery on the island.

The small **Jewish Museum** has received international acclaim for its innovative design by the well-known American-Jewish architect Daniel Libeskind.

SEE ALSO ARCHITECTURE P.26; MUSEUMS AND GALLERIES P.88, 97, 98; LITERATURE AND THEATRE P.77

Anyone can listen to debates from the public gallery of the Folketinget.

Below: taking a break outside the Black Diamond.

Kongens Nytorv and Nyhavn

Spacious and stately Kongens Nytorv is complemented by its neighbour, Nyhavn, a lively dockside district of sunny outdoor bars and cafés. In the Middle Ages, the square was the site of the town gallows and stood beyond Copenhagen's medieval east gate. Historically, Nyhavn used to be where sailors on shore leave went drinking, picking up prostitutes and getting tattooed. Today's drinking dens are more civilised, but tattoos (on the side streets) are still popular.

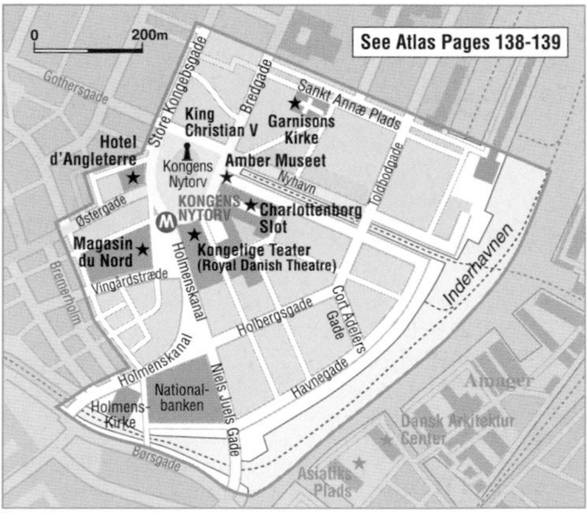

Kongens Nytorv

'King's New Square' is one of Copenhagen's most cherished spots. This large, elegant roundabout is full of Neoclassical palaces and mansions.As a tract of land between the eastern city gate and the seedy harbour area, it was not always so salubrious. Its present incarnation was planned by Frederik III (1648–70), who also had built the canal that forms today's **Nyhavn** waterway to enable ships putting into port to unload and transport their cargoes more easily. Inadvertently, he also created a centre along the quayside for the sailors to satisfy their desires brought from too much time aboard ship, namely women and drink.

Kongens Nytorv was finished by Christian V (1670–99), and follows the French model of a *palais royale* with an equestrian statue in the middle. These days, it is one of Copenhagen's smartest areas, a stone's throw from the upmarket area around the Amalienborg to the north.

The grand old hotel of the city, the **Hotel d'Angleterre**, stands on the corner of Østergade and Kongens Nytorv, offering first-class suites to the rich and famous, and a good restaurant.

Opposite the hotel is another venerable old building with a fine façade: the **Magasin du Nord** department store, dating from 1894.

The central statue shows **King Christian V**, dressed as a Roman emperor, astride his horse. The original, dating from 1687, was recast in 1946 as the gilded lead original,

Below: a free City Bike for tourists rests on the quayside.

Hans Christian Andersen always lived in and around Nyhavn, it is thought, for its proximity to the theatre, which he loved: a plaque marks his residence at no. 67 during the 1860s, and for shorter periods at nos. 18 and 20.

Left: the crowds fill Nyhavn after sundown.

made before such large bronze castings were possible, was quietly collapsing.
SEE ALSO MONUMENTS AND FOUNTAINS P.78–9; HOTELS P.65; SHOPPING P.127

Palaces and Theatre

The square is dominated by the **Kongelige Teater** or Royal Theatre, which stands on its south side. The present theatre was designed in the 1870s, taking the Paris Opéra as its model.

To the east (have a look at the mosaic ceiling of the archway as you walk that way) is the **Charlottenborg Slot**, an early example of Danish Baroque style, built by Frederik III's illegitimate son Ulrik in 1672–83. It has been the home of the Royal Academy of Fine Arts, where painters, sculptors and architects receive their formal training, since 1754. **Thotts Palace**, at no. 4 Kongens Nytorv, was built in 1680 and today houses the French Embassy.

The small square with the statue and surrounding garden is called **Krinsen**. In late June every year, students dance around the garden to celebrate the end of their final examinations. Every winter, things liven up even more at Christmas time when an outdoor ice-skating rink is opened here.

On the corner of Kongens Nytorv with Nyhavn, you will find the **House of Amber** (Amber Museet).
SEE ALSO LITERATURE AND THEATRE P.77; SHOPPING, P.129

Nyhavn

Nyhavn, the canal and promenade that runs down to the Sound, literally means 'new harbour' and you will notice the nautical flavour of this one-time sailors' street. It gives you a taste of old Copenhagen with 18th-century merchants' houses and warehouses – some now hotels – and plenty of vessels at anchor. Nyhavn is now a popular meeting place, filled with bars and restaurants with outside terraces for summer and cosy, candlelit interiors in the winter. This is also the main place from which you can take a worthwhile **harbour tour** up the Sound as far as the Little Mermaid, along the canals of Christianshavn and around Slotsholmen.
SEE ALSO CAFÉS AND BARS P.31; RESTAURANTS P.121; TRANSPORT P.133

Below: the statue of Christian V stands in the middle of the vast Kongens Nytorv, Copenhagen's main roundabout.

Rosenborg Slot and Around

One of Copenhagen's greenest districts, Rosenborg is home to Christian IV's favourite royal palace, as well as the bountiful Botanical Gardens and two world-class art galleries. The King's Garden is a favourite place for Copenhageners to escape the hubbub and relax, play games or practise *tai chi* under the trees on the green lawns. The Botanical Gardens close by are more sedate but very pretty and are renowned for their immaculate plants and a huge conservatory.

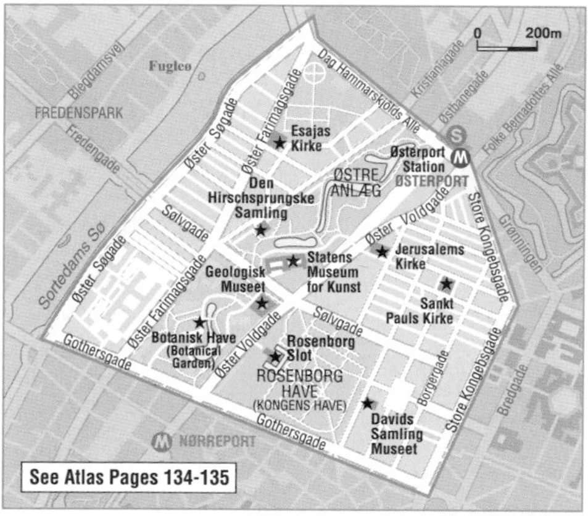

Above: tropical blooms at the Botanical Gardens.

Rosenborg Slot

Rosenborg Slot is one of Copenhagen's most attractive sights, especially on a sunny day when the park is busy. Although now close to the inner city, when Christian IV built the palace in 1606–34, it was outside the city walls and was his small country retreat from the oppressive officialdom of Christiansborg.

He expanded it into the three-storey fairytale, turreted, Dutch Renaissance-style castle that you see today, and, never having suffered a fire, it is much as it would have been in the 17th and 18th centuries.

It was Christian's favourite home and he died here (he insisted on being carried here from Frederiksborg) in 1648; you can still see his bedroom.

Since 1838 it has housed the **Royal Danish Collections**, a museum of considerable grace, and home to the crown jewels. It is well worth a visit; highlights include the Knights' or Long Hall with one of the world's largest collections of **silver furniture** and the '*rosen*' antechamber. In many ways it is a very homely palace (Frederik IV's bathroom is remarkably pretty), and the displays include all sorts of fascinating oddities, including a 17th-century 'trick' chair in which the unsuspecting victim was grasped and soaked with water from the seat.

The **crown jewels**, guarded by soldiers and held behind massive steel doors in the basement, are as sparkly and impressive as you would expect, and the exhibition includes additional royal treasures.

SEE ALSO PALACES P.109

Christian IV is fondly remembered by the Danes, but he is also renowned for his pleasure-loving nature that made him prone to excess. Needless to say this resulted in his family life being rather 'full-blooded': his first marriage produced three sons, his second (a morganatic union with a young noblewoman) another son and six daughters. When the second wife was banished for adultery, he consoled himself with her chambermaid.

Left: Rosenborg Slot was built as a country retreat for Christian IV.

Den Hirschsprungske Samling, a delightful small art gallery in an old mansion, devoted to 19th-century Danish painting, sculpture and decorative art, can be found across Østre Anlaeg park, at Stockholmsgade 20. It is especially worth a visit for the lovely collection of paintings by the Skagen School of painters, Denmark's answer to the Impressionists.

West of Rosenborg, on pretty Kronprincessegade, is the **Davids Samling Museum** (under renovation at time of writing), specialising in Asian and Islamic art. It is atmospherically housed in a 19th-century mansion.

SEE ALSO MUSEUMS AND GALLERIES P.86, 87, 97, PARKS, GARDENS AND BEACHES P.112–3

The barracks of the Royal Life Guard are next to Rosenborg Slot and the changing of the guards is rehearsed beside the barracks each morning. Wait outside the gates at 11am to accompany the guards through the city to the Amalienborg.

Kongens Have

This park – the King's Garden – which lies beside Gothersgade, is Denmark's oldest royal garden. It was laid out by Christian IV as the grounds for his new castle. Converted into an English-style garden in 1820, with its tall, old trees, statues, grassy lawns and shady walks, it is now an important breathing space in the densely populated city and offers lots of entertainment, including a puppet theatre, in summer.

SEE ALSO PARKS, GARDENS AND BEACHES P.114

Around Rosenborg Slot

There are several places near Rosenborg that are worth a visit. On the other side of Østergade are the **Botanical Gardens and Museum**, a delightful environment for a relaxing stroll, with water features, bridges, benches, a lovely palm house and the **Geological Museum**. There is a café just behind the conservatory, or you can take a picnic. Sit on a bench as you're not allowed to sit on the grass.

To the north is the **Statens Museum for Kunst**, Denmark's charming national art gallery, with a strong collection spanning from the 14th century to the present day.

Below: at the north end of Store Kongensgade, the Nyboder district forms a contrast to sophisticated Rosenborg. It was built in the 1730s to house navy officers and their families.

The Amalienborg and Around

Amalienborg is all about royalty: there are the palaces, there's a regal statue in a huge square, and there's the pomp and boot-polish of the changing of the Royal Life Guards. Yet it is only a short walk south to the formerly seedy dockside and rough characters of Nyhavn and an equally short distance north to Kastellet, the old fortress that defended the Øresund, and the Little Mermaid, a symbol that has caught the popular imagination since its creation almost a century ago.

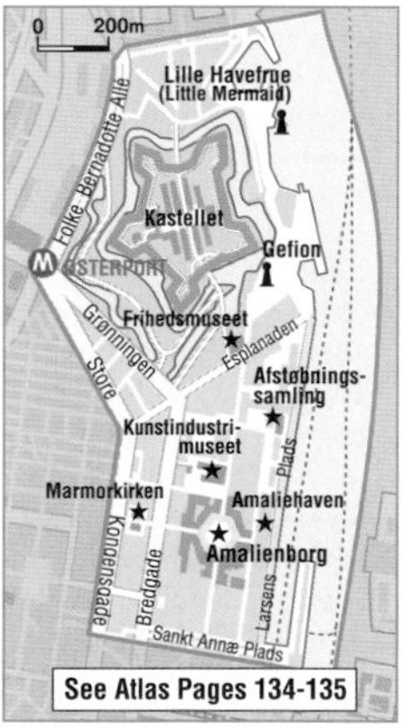

The Amalienborg and Frederiksstaden

The **Amalienborg** and the surrounding mansions were not built as a royal palace. A century after Frederik III started building his palaces a short distance away on Kongens Nytorv, his great, great grandson, Frederik V, decided that another aristocratic area should be developed to celebrate 300 years of rule by the Royal House of Oldenborg, incidentally a period that coincided with an economic boom in Denmark and flourishing overseas trade.

In 1749, a year after the tercentenary, he designated an area for this grand design on the grounds of two older palaces, the Sophie Amalienborg Palace, which was accidentally burnt down in 1689, and another, a replacement started by Frederik IV, which was incomplete. It stood just outside the city walls on the banks of the Sound and was to be called **Frederiksstaden**. The king's master architect Nicolas Eigtved began work in the early 1750s.

Central to the plan were three things: the magnificent Marble Church (Marmorkirken), the Amalienborg complex, now known as the palace, and the so-called **Golden Axis**; the lining up of the first two on a short axis with a view of the Sound. Around these, other stately mansions were built.

Palace and Square

The palace is made up of four mansions round an octagonal 'square'. Today, these are considered to be one of the finest Rococo ensembles in Europe. They were originally the homes of important aristocratic families but, aware of their duty, they sold to the king when the royal family became homeless after the Christiansborg fire in 1794.

Four roads converge at right angles on the square, and bearskin-clad soldiers from the **Royal Life Guard** patrol each of the palaces and corners. In the centre stands the huge **equestrian statue of Frederik V**, unveiled in 1771.

When the queen is in residence, a popular attraction is the daily changing of the

> The imperial statue of Frederik V in Amalienborg square is by the Frenchman Jacques Saly. He took 18 years to complete it, owing, it is said, to his liking for parties and the fact that his expenses were paid by the Danish Asiatic Company.

Above: a member of the Royal Life Guards patrols Amalienberg.

Left: based on H.C. Andersens' fairy tale, the Little Mermaid has become a symbol of Copenhagen.

guards at about midday; when replacement soldiers march from the Rosenborg barracks to take their turn in guarding the monarch.
SEE ALSO MONUMENTS AND FOUNTAINS P.80; MUSEUMS AND GALLERIES P.82; PALACES P.106–7

Marble Church

To the west (on the Golden Axis) is the **Marmorkirken** (Marble Church). It took nearly 200 years to take its place within the overall plan, as it was abandoned in 1770 due to spiralling costs, and remained half built until 1894.
SEE ALSO CHURCHES P.38

Around the Amalienborg

There is plenty to see and do in this seaside area. At the end of the short axis are the pretty **Amalienborg Gardens** with a view across to the Opera House. To the right, you can walk along the Sound, taking in the view and visiting the **Afstøbningsamling**, home to the royal cast collection, the **Kunstindustrie Museet**, the Museum of Decorative Art, the **Frihedsmuseet**, which documents the activities of the Danish Resistance Movement during the German occupation of World War II, and the **Kastellet**, the 17th-century star-shaped fortress that guards the harbour's entrance.

At the far end of the waterfront, past the statue of the goddess **Gefion** with her four sons transformed into oxen ploughing up the island of Sjælland, you will find Copenhagen's **Lille Havefrue**, or Little Mermaid, who has stared out to sea from here since 1913. She has recently been joined by a rather strange younger sister.
SEE ALSO MONUMENTS AND FOUNTAINS P.79, 80; MUSEUMS AND GALLERIES P. 86, 87, 89 -90

The Danish Royal family is very popular and even republicans admire Queen Margrethe's diplomatic skill. Unsurprisingly the family's personal life receives great attention, with the press covering every angle of Crown Prince Frederik's marriage to an Australian citizen in May 2004 and the birth of their children, Christian in 2005 and most recently their daughter in 2007.

Below: the legendary goddess Gefion turned her sons into oxen and in one night ploughed up the land that is now known as the island of Sjælland.

Vesterbro and Frederiksberg

Vesterbro and Frederiksberg are on the edges of Copenhagen, to the southwest and west of the inner city. Multicultural Vesterbro, formerly poor, seedy and home to the city's red-light district, has been partially regenerated and, while still quite edgy, now has a reputation for its cafés, nightlife and young designer fashion. Adjacent Frederiksberg is leafier and more upmarket, with extensive parkland within its boundaries. Until the 19th century, both were outside the city walls.

Vesterbro

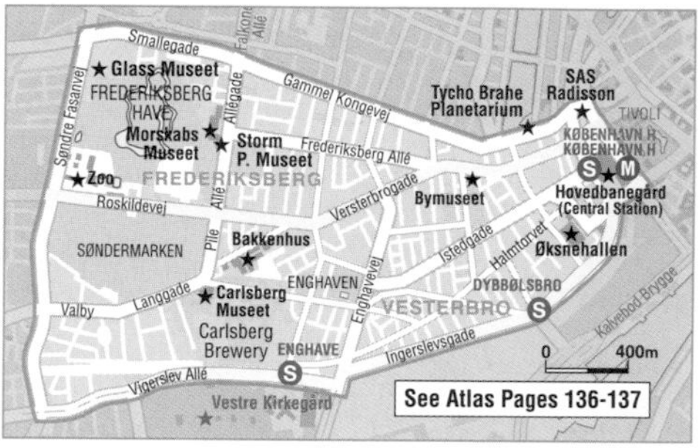

Vesterbro starts just west of Hovedbanegård station, in the opposite direction from Rådhudpladsen. It's an interesting place to walk around and, if you are shopping, offers a pleasing blend of old-fashioned food and clothing stores, independent shops, trendy cafés, and shops filled with the exotic scents of imported fruits, vegetables and spices. Unlike some other parts of Copenhagen, the businesses in Vesterbro are not aimed squarely at the international visitor.

For a good walk, start at the obelisk outside Hovedbanegård. This is the **Frihedstøtten** or 'pillar of freedom', donated by the city in 1792 in recognition of new legislation that allowed farm workers to live in the city, thus ending a legal form of enforced slavery of the peasants.

The 1950s design icon, the **Radisson SAS Hotel** designed by Arne Jacobsen, stands on the corner of Hammerichsgade. Close by, on Gammel Kongevej, is one of the city's architectural novelties, the **Tycho Brahe Planetarium**.

SEE ALSO ARCHITECTURE P.27; HOTELS P.63–4; MONUMENTS AND FOUNTAINS P.80; MUSEUMS AND GALLERIES P.98–9

ISTEDGADE

Heading the other way is Istedgade – formerly the main red-light district and now home to some very good bars and boutiques – and **Halmtørvet**, which used to be Copenhagen's cattle market.

The large building is **Øksnehallen**, the old cattle auction house, and now

Left: once a design icon, the SAS is starting to show its age.

Left: Vesterbro is fast becoming quite the place for Copenhagen's younger crowd.

Vesterbro's biggest cultural exhibition space. The square is full of busy cafés and restaurants.

Nearby, the houses on **Skydebanegård** date from the 19th century. The wall at the end, dating from 1887, separated the inhabitants from what is now the **København Bymuseet** (City Museum); you enter through the door in the wall.

This late-18th-century building was constructed for the Royal Shooting Society and the Danish Brotherhood, which dated back to the Middle Ages; its members did target practice in the gardens.

Now a museum detailing Copenhagen's history, it's worth a visit to get your historical bearings – don't miss the model of the medieval town outside.

SEE ALSO MUSEUMS AND GALLERIES P.89, 95; SHOPPING P.127–9

Twenty floors high, the SAS Radisson is the tallest building in Copenhagen. It was vilified when it was first built and even its architect Arne Jacobsen agreed that it looked like the so-called 'punch card' or 'glass cigar box' as described by his detractors.

VESTERBROGADE

Absalonsgade is pretty, with original cobblestone pavements and old street lamps, and connects Istedgade to Vesterbrogade. Off Vesterbrogade, check out **Vaerdamesvej**, a street recommended for its food shops and restaurants.

Towards Frederiksberg (take the 6A bus), you can visit the **Bakkehusmuseet** on private home reflecting the tastes of its 19th-century literary owners, friends of Hans Christian Andersen. The street feels pleasantly countrified.

Not far from here, you will also find the **Carlsberg Brewery**, interesting for both its architecture and visitor centre detailing the history of the famous brand and its workers.

SEE ALSO MUSEUMS AND GALLERIES P.84

Frederiksberg

Frederiksberg was a country village, which from the 18th century onwards, became increasingly popular as the middle and upper classes began to appreciate and revel in the countryside.

The attractions here are **Frederiksberg Have**, formerly a royal residence (closed at present) and garden dating from 1802, where you can also find the atmospheric underground **glass museum**, and the **zoo**, which is a delight; it opens late in the evening in the summer, so it's a nice place to visit towards the end of the day.

SEE ALSO CHILDREN P.35; ; MUSEUMS AND GALLERIES P.85; PARKS, GARDENS AND BEACHES P.113–4

Below: once run-down Vesterbro is filling up with the best in designer fashion, such as Design Zoo pictured here.

Christianshavn and Holmen

Christianshavn bears little relation to anything else in Copenhagen – an impression enhanced by having to cross the wide Øresund to get to it. It has a strong maritime feeling of yesteryear, reminiscent of Amsterdam, with narrow canals lined with houseboats, trees and 17th-century townhouses standing back from the cobbles. Holmen, to the north, was built as the naval dockyard in 1690, a role it retained until 1989 when the navy moved out and rejuvenation set in.

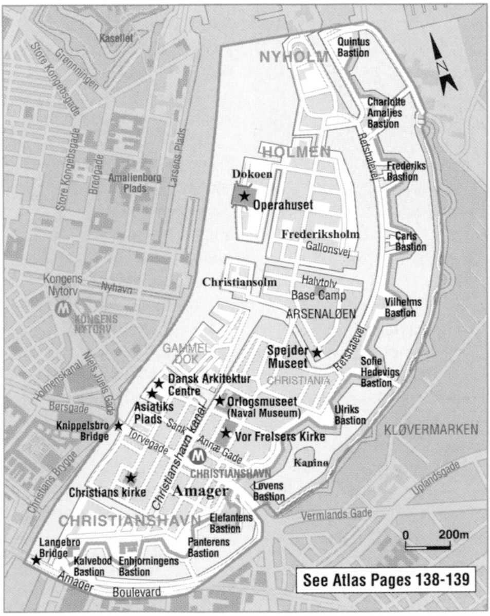

Above: the maritime way of life at Christianshavn is still there for all to see.

Christianshavn

One of Copenhagen's oldest and most colourful areas, Christianshavn was built in 1639 by Christian IV on the island of Amager as a harbourside merchant town. This was part of his plan to make the town the cultural, religious and business centre for the whole of the Nordic region.

Formerly a marshy swampland, canals were built and earthworks and bastions raised to surround both Christianshavn and Copenhagen. The fortifications around the inner city and Kastellet have now disappeared but you can still see the **bastions** in Christianshavn. By the time Christian IV died in 1648 much of his dream had became a reality; Copenhagen was the naval and economic centre of the region.

VISITING THE ISLAND

There are two ways to reach the island: by harbour bus, getting off at Knippelsbro bridge or at the new opera house on Holmen; or by crossing the Knipplesbro bridge. You can also cross over on another bridge, Langebro, if you then turn left you can walk along the island's southern perimeter, taking in five bastions, before heading left up Sankt Annæ Gade – no. 32, built in 1622–4, is thought to be the oldest building on the island.

You can also catch a **harbour tour** from Nyhavn and see Christianshavn from the water, which is perhaps the quickest and prettiest way of seeing the sights. It will take you up to the Opera House and down Christianshavns Kanal, with Overgaden Van-den Vandet, 'upper street

Left: a dramatic day on the quayside.

Since the new right-wing government came to power in 2001, Christiania's free status and the liberties its inhabitants enjoy have become restricted. Rumours persist that the government is slowly trying to 'normalise' the district and protests are becoming frequent.

below the water' and Overgaden Neden Vandet, 'upper street above the water', on either side, before crossing the Sound to Slotsholmen.

But nothing really beats wandering Christianshavn's cobbled streets, checking out the cafés and shops, popping in and out of churches, wandering along the fortifications and gawping at the Opera House. While life in Copenhagen does not exactly feel frenetic to your average European city dweller, it's even more gently paced on this side of the Sound.

Things to do in the area include visiting **Vor Frelsers Kirke** and **Christians Kirke**, two churches dating from Christianshavn's early days, both built for the merchant community. The former has a spiral tower from which you can get a marvellous view of the city *(see picture page 39)* and the latter designed with a gallery running around the walls as if it were a theatre.

Otherwise, there is the charming **Orlogsmuseet** (Naval Museum) or, if you are so inclined, you can visit the Free State of **Christiania**, set up by free-thinking hippies in 1971 in a former 19th-century military barracks – though, frankly, it's not terribly interesting to walk around.

SEE ALSO CHURCHES P. 36–7, 39; MUSEUMS AND GALLERIES P. 95–9

Holmen

For those interested in the rejuvenation of this quarter, the **Dansk Arkitektur Centre**, formerly an abandoned warehouse in Gammel Dok (Old Dock), is now used as a venue for exhibitions. Also visit **Asiatlks Plads**, which dates from the start of the 18th century when the city's trading links were developing – note the marble façade of the elongated Rococo warehouse (designed by Nicolai Eigtved in 1750) on the north side of the square. The **Operahuset**, Copenhagen's smart new Opera House, which opened in Dokoen (Dock Island) in 2005 is also here.

SEE ALSO ARCHITECTURE P.27; MUSEUMS AND GALLERIES P.85; MUSIC AND DANCE P.102

Below: Christiania is filled with psychedelic murals like this one, a reminder of its hippy origins.

Copenhagen's Suburbs

None of Copenhagen's suburbs lie very far from the centre. To the east, over the Øresund, is the island of Amager (home to Christianshavn), but thereafter heading to the outskirts of town, the airport at Kastrup, a surprisingly peaceful nature reserve and forest, Amager Strand park and the pretty seaside town of Dragør, which is enjoying a revival. To the northwest are the quiet residential districts of Nørrebro and Østerbro, both 19th-century additions to the city located just beyond the reservoirs, but still very close in. In days past these popular districts were little more than farmland beyond the city walls.

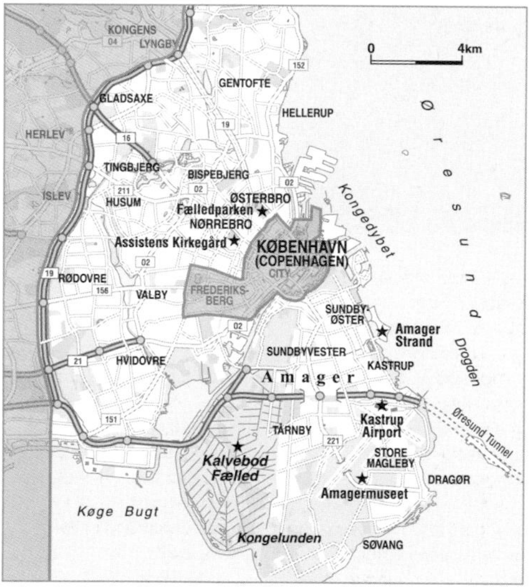

Nørrebro

Nørrebro may not have any conventional tourist attractions, but along with the neighbouring Vesterbro it is the hippest area of the city, for its buzzy cafés, trendy boutiques and vibrant nightlife.

Much of the action focusses around **Sankt Hans Torv** and the surrounding streets. Get there by crossing the Dronning Louises Bro (Queen Louise's Bridge). If you are in search of 'sights', the **Assistens Kirkegård Cemetery** is home to many a famous deceased Dane, including Søren Kierkegaard, Christen Købke and Hans Christian Andersen. It's also a nice place to stop for a rest. Because space was at a premium during the 18th century, the cemetery (1760) was laid out beyond the ramparts.

In 2007 Nørrebro was the unlikely site of the worst riots in Copenhagen's recent history. When authorities evicted squatters and tore down the popular Youth House on Jagtvej, rioting continued for three nights and hundreds of people were arrested. The Youth House had long been a centre for left-wing groups.

SEE ALSO MONUMENTS AND FOUNTAINS P.81; PARKS, GARDENS AND BEACHES P.112

Østerbro

Østerbro, slightly northeast of Nørrebro, has been an uncluttered suburban residential area since the 19th century. It was built near the site of Copenhagen's eastern fortified gate and the train station, **Østerport**, was built in 1894–7 so workers could travel to the centre.

Small, speciality shops characterise the area. There are no big attractions here but the big park **Fælledparken**, formerly common land where executions used to take place, is popular and has plenty of sports facilities.

SEE ALSO PARKS, GARDENS AND BEACHES P.113

The Dutch farmers who settled around Dragør introduced a lively Shrovetide custom still practised today: men in fancy dress ride horses at full speed, lances outstretched, to spear a barrel suspended over the course and split it in half.

Left: leaving the city behind and heading for Amager Island.

Since the opening of the Øresund Bridge, the southern area of Amager has become known as Ørestad. The former fields have given birth to housing, a university annexe and infra structure for the 14,000 commuters who use the bridge.

Amager Island

Don't be put off by the fact that this is home to **Kastrup airport**. Amager is an up-and-coming area, home to an idyllic **nature reserve** and the artificial city **beaches** on the banks of the Sound, the nearest beach to the city, at **Amager Strand**.

Get there by crossing Langebro, at the end of H.C. Andersen Boulevard by Rådhuspladsen. Bus no. 33 covers most of the area and the metro stop is **Orestad**.

Otherwise rent a bike, so you can spend the day riding and walking around the whole area. The nature reserve, **Kalvebod Fælled**, is in the west, teeming with bird life. You can then take the coastal path from Søvang to Dragør.

Søvang, south of Dragør, has a beach that is popular with Copenhageners escaping the city in summer, whilst **Dragør** is am attractive seaside town with pretty yellow cottages. Once a busy fishing and commercial port, it is now almost a living museum. The oldest house (1682), is now the **Dragør Museum of Local History**.

SEE ALSO PARKS, GARDENS AND BEACHES P.112; TRANSPORT P.130–1

FORESTS AND FARMS

Just west of Dragør is **Støre Magleby**, home to the Dutch farmers – noted for their agricultural expertise – who were brought to the island in the 1520s by Christian II, in an effort to ensure that Copenhagen was always well supplied with produce.

The **Amagermuseet**, housed in two old thatched farmhouses gives you a taste of life on a Dutch farm in 1900.

Southwest of Dragør is the **Kongelunden**, a forest planted in 1818 to grow the timber and firewood that was lacking on the island. The land passed to the king in 1836, and he set up wild pheasant farms so that wealthy Copenhageners could enjoy a day's shooting.

In 1920, the King's Forest was opened to the public, and walkers are still likely to encounter pheasants scratching around in the undergrowth.

SEE ALSO MUSEUMS AND GALLERIES P.82

Below: a night of skating in Nørrebro.

Sjælland

If you have a couple of weeks in Copenhagen you will have time to venture into its province, Sjælland. Or you can visit its attractions on day-trips from the capital. For more history, including a proper look at the Vikings, visit Roskilde Helsingør and Frederiksborg Slot; for art, the museums of Arken, Louisiana and Ørdrupsgaard are world-class; for literature, visit the Karen Blixen museum and, for, allegedly, the world's oldest funfair, you only need go as far as Klampenborg, also home to a nice beach. Several of these can be accessed on the same train line and possibly in one day – if you are being very efficient.

Above: a long boat at the Vikingskibsmuseet.

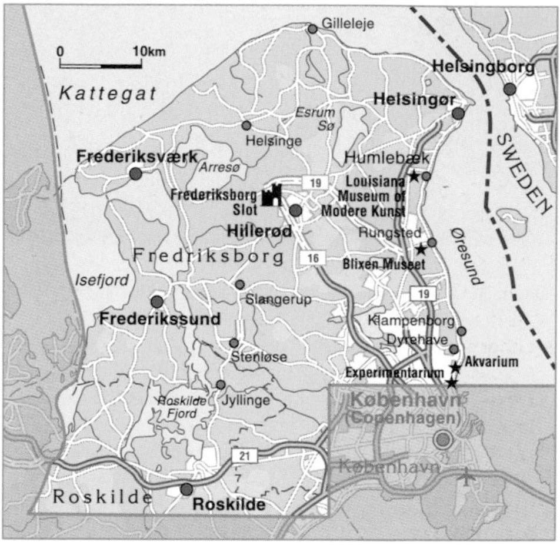

Roskilde

If you only do one day trip, this ought to be it. Easily reached by a train (only 25 mins) from **Hovedbanegård** or bus nos. 6a or 123 from Copenhagen, Roskilde is one of Denmark's oldest towns, older than Copenhagen and, until the 14th–15th centuries, much more important.

According to legend, it was founded by the Viking king Roar around AD 600. Other sources disagree and say that it was founded by the charmingly named Harald Bluetooth in the 990s. Either way, it grew rapidly and became important to both the Crown and the Church and was made a bishopric in 1020.

Its main claims to fame are its cathedral and the Vikingeskibsmuseet (Viking-ship Museum). The **cathedral** was commissioned by none other than the founder of Copenhagen, Bishop Absalon, in 1170, and is full of **royal Danish tombs**.

The **Vikingskibsmuseet**, not only has a splendid display of ships, but also working shipwrights and artisans on the harbour using authentic Viking methods. You can even help to row a Viking longship of their creation if you book ahead.

SEE ALSO MONUMENTS AND FOUNTAINS P.81; MUSEUMS AND GALLERIES P.99

Helsingør

One of Denmark's most historic towns, with entire streets of well-preserved, colour-washed buildings, Helsingør is, nevertheless perhaps best known as the ferry crossing to Sweden, which takes just

> In the dungeons of Kronborg Slot stands the statue of Holger Danske, a sleeping Viking chief who, according to legend, will awake and inspire the Danes when the country is in danger. His name was used as a code-word by the Danish Resistance during World War II.

Left: the fairytale façade of Frederiksborg Slot.

20min. But it's also famous for its massive Renaissance **Kronborg**, Hamlet's 'Castle of Elsinore'. It has provided a fabulous backdrop for many productions of Shakespeare's play.

There is also an interesting city museum, housed in a former 16th-century Carmelite convent and the **Tecknisksmuseum**, which has a marvellous collection of vehicles, gadgets and appliances, including over 30 aeroplanes, and is usually a hit with men… and kids.

For a flavour of the old town, walk down **Strandgade** and the streets off to the right, especially **Odernesgade**; no. 66 dates from 1459, nos. 70, 72 and 74 are late 16th-century, while nos. 76 and 64 date from 1579 and 1739 respectively.

The newly restored **cathedral** on Sankt Anna gade originally dates from 1200–*c.*1600 and has some lovely church furnishings

SEE ALSO PALACES P.108–9

Frederiksborg Slot

If you haven't had enough of fairytale castles, this is another turreted Renaissance confection surrounded by a moat. Take the train bound for Helsingør and get off at **Hillerød**. You are unlikely to manage both in one day though it might be worth a try.

SEE ALSO PALACES P.108

Arken Museet for Moderne Kunst

Opened in 1996 in **Ishøj Strandpark** by the Baltic coast (S-train to Ishøj station, then bus no.128), this marvellous building designed in the shape of a ship's hull, provides an ideal setting for the *avant-garde* works of art displayed here. As the museum's own collection is currently rather modest, special exhibitions are the main focal point of a visit. Check the listings in *Copenhagen This Week* to see what is showing.

SEE ALSO MUSEUMS AND GALLERIES P.83–4

A Busy Day

Take the train to Helsingør and get off at **Humlebæk** for the **Louisiana Museum for Moderne Kunst**, featuring work by the likes of Henry Moore, Alberto Giacommetti and Pablo Picasso. Take the train back three stops to **Rungsted** for the **family home of Karen Blixen**, the famous and controversial Danish writer, her family home is now open to visitors as a fascinating museum devoted to her life. Then, get back on the train and return to **Klampenborg** where you can visit **Bellevue beach**, **Bakken** funfair in **Jægersborg Dyrehaven**, the old deer park and, if it's not too late, **Ørdrupsgaard**, home to an excellent collection of Danish and European Impressionist paintings displayed in a lovely old house.

SEE ALSO CHILDREN P.34; LITERATURE AND THEATRE P.73–4; MUSEUMS AND GALLERIES P.88–9, 90–1, 95; PARKS, GARDENS AND BEACHES P.114

Below: the Louisiana Museum makes a great day out.

Architecture

Copenhagen is filled with beautiful buildings. In addition to the many churches and palaces which once served as symbols of royalty and religion, there are more 'functional' buildings, from stock exchanges to opera houses, that have allowed the architects of the day to express themselves. As a result, the city has an excellent selection of European architecture from Dutch Renaissance to Bauhaus; waves from all movements seemed to reach the banks of the Øresund eventually. Recent additions such as the Black Diamond and Operahuset have transformed the waterfront into a showcase of modern architecture.

Børsen

Børsgade, Slotsholmen; bus: 2a; map p.138 C2

Built in 1619–40 as a warehouse in Dutch Renaissance style, this is Europe's oldest Stock Exchange.

For Christian IV, a great lover of pomp and grandeur, the two-storey building was not grand enough, so in 1625 he commissioned the first of 18 striking gables and the 54m high spire, made up of four entwined dragons' tails. The three golden crowns on its top represent Denmark, Norway and Sweden.

In the mid-19th century, the currency and security dealers moved in, hence its name. The traders are now long gone, and the building is used as offices.

Copenhagen has suffered two devastating fires (in 1728 and 1794) which accounts for the small number of buildings dating from before this period. In modern times, Copenhagen has embraced some of the most innovative architectural designs of the 21st century.

Den Sorte Diamant (Black Diamond)

Christians Brygge 1; tel: 33 47 47 47; building: 8am–5pm, information and lending: Mon–Fri 10am–5pm, Sat 10am–2pm; bus: 47, 66; map p.138 B1–C1

This modern extension to the Royal Library, built by the architects Schmidtt, Hammer and Lassen, opened in 1999. If you just want a closer look at the outside, one of the best ways to see it is on a harbour tour. It is also home to the **National Museum of Photography** and the **Queen's Hall**.

SEE ALSO MUSIC AND DANCE P.100

Kastellet

Churchillparken; map p.135 E2–3

This star-shaped fortress with five bastions stands on the west bank of the Øresund and is a Unesco World Heritage Site.

It was begun by Frederik III in 1662, building continued until 1725 and today it is still used by the army; the church, prison and main guardhouse having resisted the assaults of time.

Above: the dramatic interior of the Opera House catches the natural light off the Øresund.

The Danish Nato headquarters are here and it's the home of Copenhagen's Defence Forces too. Nonetheless, it is a delightfully peaceful enclave; its charming **windmill** (1847) and some remains of the old ramparts are worth seeing.

Københavns Rådhus

Rådhuspladsen 1; tel: 33 66 25 82; Mon–Fri 8am–5pm, tours in English: Mon–Fri 3pm, Sat 10am and 11am; clock:

Left: the Black Diamond opened in 1999 and began a renaissance on the waterfront.

Mon–Fri 10am–4pm, Sat 10am–1pm; entrance charge, includes tower; bus: all Rådhuspladsen buses; map p.138 A2

This building replaced the Domhuset on Nytorv as the city hall in 1905. Architect Martin Nyrop created an eclectic design overlooked by Bishop Absalon who appears on a gilded statue above the main doorway.

You can also visit the **Jens Olsens Verdensur**, an astronomical clock with over 14,000 parts. According to the Guinness Book of World Records, it is the most accurate and complicated clock in the world.

Visitors can climb the 106-m **tower** and look over the city and across the Øresund to Sweden. There is also a pretty garden at the back.

SEE ALSO RÅDHUSPLADSEN AND TIVOLI P.6, 7

Operahuset (Opera House)

Ekvipagemestervej 10; tel: 33 69 69 69; boat: 901, 902, bus: 66, opera bus, metro: Christianshavns Torv then bus 66; map p.138 D3

When it opened in January 2005 this building transformed the banks of Holmen, formerly Copenhagen's naval dock yards, into a centre of culture. It took four years to build, has glass ceilings and a Sicilian marble floor as well as astonishing one-tonne **lamps** hanging in the foyer.

SEE ALSO MUSIC AND DANCE P.102

Rundetårn

Købmagergade 52a; tel: 33 73 03 73; www.rundetaarn.dk; Sept–May: Mon–Sat 10am–5pm, Sun noon–5pm, June–Aug: Mon–Sat 10am– 8pm, Sun noon–8pm; entrance charge; map p.138 D3

Built in 1642 as an observatory, the Round Tower is one of Christian IV's most imposing works. Inside there is a spiral walkway 209m long, which is wide enough to take a carriage (steps would have made it harder for transporting the heavy equipment needed at the top). The view from the 36-m tower takes in the whole of Copenhagen.

Radisson SAS

Hammerichsgade 1; tel: 33 42 60 00; bus: 6a, 26, S-tog: Vesterport, Hovedbanegård; map p.137 C3

This 1960s hotel was designed in its entirety, down to the cutlery and door knobs, by iconic Danish designer Arne Jacobsen. It has been redecorated several times over the years, but Room 606 has retained its original interior. If it's unoccupied, they might let you look.

Otherwise the foyer is 60s cool and the chairs, Jacobsen's famous Swan and Egg design, are there to sit on.

SEE ALSO HOTELS P.63–4

Below: the unique ramp inside the Rundetårn was built to allow access by horse and cart.

Cafés and Bars

Copenhagen has hundreds of cafés and snack bars, which are rapidly taking over from bars as the preferred places to go for a drink, many are open all day, while some stay open through the night, turning into nightclubs, with DJs, live music and dancing. Others – so-called fusion cafés – give you the opportunity to buy books, flowers or do your laundry at the same time. You can also eat well in cafés, and more cheaply than in most restaurants, with many places serving cheap snacks and light meals all day. The *dagens ret* (dish of the day), including coffee, is usually good value.

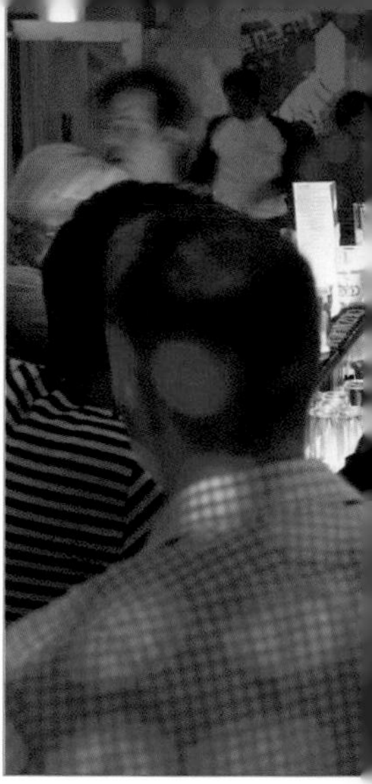

Rådhuspladsen & Tivoli

Café Glyptotek

Ny Carlsberg Glyptotek, Dantes Plads 7; tel: 33 41 81 28; Tue–Sun 10am–4pm, kitchen closes 3.45pm; entrance charge, for museum; map p.138 A1

The museum café offers reasonably priced lunch dishes, good coffee and a selection of cakes, but the real recommendation is the venue – in the middle of the wonderful palm-filled Winter Garden surrounded by world-class statuary.

SEE ALSO MUSEUMS AND GALLERIES P.95

Færgekroen

Tivoli; tel 33 75 06 80; *see p.115*; map p.138 A1–2

You have to pay your entrance to Tivoli, but if you are going anyway, this is a good, traditional microbrewery, offering two 'house' beers alongside Danish food. It's been going since 1934 so it must be doing something right.

SEE ALSO PARKS, GARDENS AND BEACHES P. 115

Fox Bar and Kitchen

Jarmers Plads 3; tel: 33 38 70 30; Sun–Thur 5pm–midnight, Fri–Sat 5pm–2am; bus: 67, 68, 69, 5a, 14; map p.138 A3

This stylish hotel prides itself on its alternative decor, but its relaxing, modern bar is surprisingly mellow and lit with traditional candles. The food and light snacks are Danish and the cocktails are recommended

Below: Råduspladsen is filled with open air cafés in summertime.

Strøget & Around

Absolut Ice Bar

Hotel 27, Løngangstræde 27; www.absoluteicebar.com; bus: 6a; map p.138 A2

Opening in 2007, this promises to be a unique experience. With a year-round indoor temperature of -5°C, guests will be given coats and gloves on entry so that they can enjoy a vodka cocktail in an ice-glass, in an interior filled with art and furnishings that are all made from crystal-clear ice. It is planned that the interiors will be redesigned and resculpted by different artists twice a year.

Barbarellah Bar

Nørre Farimagsgade 41, tel: 33 32 00 61; www.barbarellah.dk; Mon–Thur 4pm–2am, Fri–Sat 4pm–4am; bus: 40, S-tog: Norreport; map p.138 A3–4

Left: pouring them out at Barbarellah.

Coffee first arrived in Copenhagen in the 1600s and was usually brewed in a Madam Blue, a metal enamel coffee pot. More sophisticated methods have been created, but Madam Blues are still sold at antique shops.

Barbarellah is a keen attempt to make itself a one stop shop for trendiness in the heart of Copenhagen. There is a lounge to sip coffee in during the day, a bar to look beautiful in at night, clothes and jewellery are on sale and young artists display their works here.

Bar Rouge

Hotel Sankt Petri, Krystalgade 22; tel: 33 45 98 22; Sun–Thur 4pm–1am, Fri–Sat 4pm–2am; map p.138 A3

In the heart of the Latin Quarter, this is a swanky bar in a swanky 5-star modern hotel – definitely a good place to have an early- or late-evening cocktail. DJs playing jazz make for a relaxing experience in tasteful, artistic surroundings.

SEE ALSO HOTELS P.65

Café & Ølhalle 1892

Arbejdermuseet (Workers' Museum), Rømersgade 22; tel: 33 33 00 47; daily 11.30am–4.30pm; map p.138 A4

This 'Café and Beer Hall' is part of the Workers' Museum which is housed in the Workers' Building dating from 1879. The restaurant serves old-fashioned Danish fare and a selection of Danish and continental beer, including 'Stjerne (Star) Pilsner' as it was brewed at the cooperative 'The Workers' Brewery Stjernen' and still sporting the original label from 1947. Booking is advisable.

SEE ALSO MUSEUM AND GALLERIES P.82

Café Dan Turell

Store Regnegade 3; tel: 33 14 10 47; Mon–Wed 9.30am–midnight, Thur 9.30am–1am, Fri–Sat 9.30am–2am, Sun 10am–11pm; map p.138 B3

One of Copenhagen's oldest cafés (i.e. dating from the early 1990s), this Parisian-style café-restaurant attracts a trendy crowd full of fans of the Danish Poet. The food is generally speaking only middling.

SEE ALSO LITERATURE AND THEATRE P.76

Café Hovedtelegrafen

Post and Tele Museum Café, Købmagergade 37; tel: 33 41 09 86; Mon–Sat 10am–5pm, Wed 10am–8pm, Sun 11am–4pm, kitchen closes one hour before; free; map p.138 B3

This is a rather well-kept secret.The menu is good, standard fare, but the real reason for coming is the view out through the glass walls or from the balcony over the roof tops of the old town.

SEE ALSO MUSEUMS AND GALLERIES P. 96

Café Ketchup

Pilestræde 19; tel: 33 32 30 30; Mon–Thur noon–midnight, Fri noon–2am, Sat 11am–2am, café kitchen closes 10pm, restaurant 10.30pm; map p.138 B3

One of Copenhagen's first really stylish café-restaurant eateries (and nightclub) – the name is ironic. Expect a well-dressed crowd in a modern interior; food is a Danish-Oriental cross. There is another Café Ketchup in Tivoli.

SEE ALSO NIGHTLIFE P.104

Café Klaptræet

Kultorvet 11; tel: 33 13 40 38; Mon–Wed 10am–1am, Thur 10am–3am, Fri 10am–5am, Sat 11am–5am, Sun 11am–midnight; map p.138 B3–4

Below: sweet nibbles to accompany your coffee.

Above: service with a smile at Café Kys.

Overlooking the lively Kultorvet square, this is a popular place with the young crowd. Film posters and spotlights remain from its former days as an independent cinema. At weekends there is a disco and in summer you can sip your coffee out on the square.

Café Kys

Læderstræde 7; tel: 33 93 85 94; daily 10am–2am; map p.138 B2

In one of the pleasant little streets parallel with Strøget, this cosy café with very reasonable prices, is popular with students. The walls are covered with many movie kissing moments and the straight-forward menu offers filling sandwiches. There is also outdoor seating in the summer months.

Café Norden

Østergade 61; tel: 33 11 77 91; daily 9am–midnight; map p.138 B3

In the middle of Strøget, overlooking Amagertorv, this classic café is decorated in a French Art Nouveau style with chandeliers and wood panelling. Food is fairly standard – you are paying for its prime location.

Copenhagen's café revolution began in the 1990s and there is now a café on virtually every street corner, often with plenty of space to sit outside. Many places have tall outdoor heaters and if you ask, the staff will bring you a blanket to wrap up in.

Café Stelling

Gammeltorv 6; tel: 33 32 93 00; Mon–Thur 9am–11pm, Fri–Sat 9am–2am; map p.138 A2

Do not miss the chance to eat lunch in a historic setting. On the corner of Gammeltorv and Skindergade, this eye-catching building was created in 1937 by architect, Arne Jacobsen and retains its original cream and wood functionalist interior with lovely big windows and Jacobsen chairs.

Cafeen i Nikolaj

Nikolaj Plads 12; tel: 70 26 64 64; Mon–Sat 11.30am–5pm; map p.138 B3

In a wing of the Nikolaj Church, built in 1795 and now an arts venue, this is slightly hidden away and popular with the locals – including politicians from nearby Christiansborg. In summer you can sit outside under a parasol. Lunches tend to be Danish (lots of fish, especially herring) although there are other good choices if you are inclined to salads or red meat.

SEE ALSO MUSEUMS AND GALLERIES P.85

Illums

Østergade 52; Mon–Thur 10am–7pm, Fri 10am–8pm, Sat 10am–5pm; map p.138 B3

This is a good place to know about if you are travelling with children. There's an attractive, red-banquetted café on the top floor of this department store with a glass roof and views from the balcony. A section at the back is reserved for customers with children.

Krasnapolsky

Vestergade 10; tel: 22 35 43 00; Mon–Wed 10am–2am, Thur–Sat 10am–5am, Sun 2pm–midnight; map p.138 A2

In its early days in the 1980s, this was almost exclusively a hangout for a bohemian crowd. It's now much more mainstream and the food is interesting. Techno and House are played at weekends.

La Glace

Skoubogade 3, tel: 33 14 46 46; www.laglace.com; Mon–Thur 8.30am–5.30pm, Fri 8.30am–6pm, Sat 9am–5pm, Sun 11am–5pm; map p.138 A3

Copenhagen's oldest confectioner, La Glace is still very popular. Its tiny ground floor can get quite overbearing with people waiting to pick up their chocolates and cakes. Take a number and be

patient. There is more space upstairs, but it's a shame for some that the place is not very child friendly.
SEE ALSO FOOD AND DRINK P.54

Laszlo Café and Bar
Læderstræde 28; tel: 33 33 88 08; daily 11am–1am; map p.138 B2
This one always seems to be full and no wonder – decent, hearty portions of Meditrranean-style sandwiches and salads, lots of sundried tomatoes are involved. In summer, sit outside, drink, eat and watch the world go by on this appealing little street.

Thé à la Menthe
Kompagnistræde 29; tel: 33 33 00 38; Mon–Sat 10am–9pm; map p.138 B2
On the edges of the Latin Quarter, this is an unusual little place – a charming, basement Moroccan tea shop where you can settle down on a comfortable divan, surrounded by candles, waterpipes and kilims for a snack or a few meze.

Zirup
Læderstræde 32, tel: 33 91 31 51; www.zirup.dk; Mon–Thur, Sun 10am–midnight, Fri–Sat 10am–2am; map p.138 B2
Hangover brunches at the weekend are their speciality, presumably for those who had a bit too much of the café's golden decor late into the night before.

Above: the counter at La Glace is filled with a variety of Danish pastries.

Kongens Nytorv & Nyhavn

Badteåtret
Nyhavn; during performances only; map p.139 C3
In summer, the theatre boat is a more charming and usually less crowded Nyhavn option than one of the bars on the north side. It offers experimental theatre performances downstairs, but if your Danish isn't up to it, sitting on deck with a glass in your hand is a very enjoyable way to spend the evening. Prices are not above average either.

Café a Porta
Kongens Nytorv 17; tel: 33 11 05 00; Mon–Fri 8am–4pm, 5pm–10pm, Sat 11am–4pm, 5.30pm–10pm, kitchen closes 10pm; bus: 15, 19, 26, 1a, 999, S-tog: Kongens Nytorv; map p.138 C3
One of the city's oldest and most popular cafés, Café a Porta, then known as Mini's, used to be Hans Christian Andersen's local. It dates from 1788 and is a good place to stop for a meal, cake, coffee or cocktail. Nicely retro with old photographs on the wall and good views of the square. Prices aren't bad given its location.

Left: a quiet afternoon at Café Zirup.

Hviids Vinstue
Kongens Nytorv 19; tel: 33 15 10 64; Sun–Thur 10am–1am, Fri–Sat 10am–2am; bus: 15, 19, 26, 1a, 999, S-tog: Kongens Nytorv; map p.138 C3
Cosy, atmospheric and pub-like, Copenhagen's oldest wine bar, dating from 1723, has wooden panelling, pictures on the walls and a good drinks selection. In summer, it's nice to sit outside and watch the buzz on Kongens Nytorv.

Magasin du Nord
Kongens Nytorv 13; tel: 33 11 44 33; Mon–Thurs 10am–7pm, Fri 10am–8pm, Sat 10am–5pm; map p.138 C3
There are numerous cafés inside this splendid department store.
SEE ALSO SHOPPING P.126–7

There are plenty of restaurants on the north side of Nyhavn where you can also just have a drink. Sitting outside, there is not much to choose between them – in summer, if you find a seat, take possession immediately!

Above: laundry and lattes at the Laundromat Café.

Rosenborg & Around

Café Republic

Statens Museum for Kunst, Sølvgade 48; tel: 33 74 86 65; Thur–Tue 10am–5pm, Wed 10am–8pm; map p.135 D2

Thanks to new architectural design work, the museum now boasts an airy café decorated by artist Viera Collaro with large, floor-to-ceiling picture windows overlooking the water and green spaces of the park at the rear of the building. The menu offers an attractive selection of fresh food.

SEE ALSO MUSEUMS AND GALLERIES P. 97

Café Sommersko

Kronprinsensgade 6; tel: 33 14 81 89; Mon–Wed 9am–midnight, Thur 8am–1am, Fri 8am–4am, Sat 9am–4am, Sun 10am–midnight; map p.135 B4

A really cosy café with *boules* lamps hanging overhead, artwork and mirrors on the walls, a nice long bar with vases full of flowers, red leather banquette seating, candles on the table and a small art gallery running on a second level. You'd think you were in Paris. Serves good breakfasts, lunches and suppers.

Vesterbro & Frederiksberg

Bang & Jensen

Istedgade 130; tel: 33 25 53 18; daily 8am–2pm; bus: 10; map p.136 C3–B2

Intimate, trendy cafe in a former pharmacy in the lively part of Istedgade, with high ceilings, squashy sofas and a big mahogany counter. It's good for a late brunch and the Saturday night cocktail bar is lively.

Roccos

Istedgade 119; tel: 31 21 04 40; daily 9am–11pm; bus: 10; map p.136 C3–B2

This café-bar may be small but the locals say that it serves the best coffee in town. The owner selects and roasts all the beans himself and nothing is served that is over 12–14 days old; these beans are thrown away or given to a good cause. The atmosphere is charming with mosaic-top tables, old coffee grinders on shelves and a selection of vinyl records that you can choose and play on the café record player.

Christianshavn & Holmen

Bastionen and Løven

Lille Mølle Christianshavns Voldgade 50; tel: 32 95 09 40; daily noon–midnight, Sat–Sun brunch 10am–2pm; map p.139 D1

This is one of the most romantic places to settle down for a meal in the whole of Copenhagen, situated in an old mill on the ramparts in Christianshavn. It has a well-deserved reputation for a delicious and copious weekend brunch, Danish style.

Café Rabs Have

Ved Kanalen, Christianshavn; Wed–Sun 8am–11pm, L 11am–4pm, D Wed pm, daily specials 8am–8pm; map p.138 C1

Just around the corner from the main waterway, this is a lovely local pub that dates from the 17th century – set up on Christian IV's orders to provide beer and food for the sailors and soldiers on the bastions nearby. Staff are friendly, there's a garden out the back and the organic, Danish food is recommended

Café Wilder

Wildersgade 56, corner of Skt Annæ Gade; tel: 32 54 71 83; Mon–Fri 9am–2am, Sat–Sun 10am–2am; map p.139 C2

Café Wilder's youthful, casual atmosphere behind a glass façade. Popular with the locals; Sunday brunch is served 10am–2pm and the food is French-Italian fare.

Kontiki Bar

Takkelloftvej 1z v/operahuset; tel: 29 46 54 17; daily until late; map p.139 D3–E4

If the stylish bar at the opera house doesn't appeal, head for this rough-and-ready boat behind it. The menu is not extensive and changes at the chef's whim. Not sophisticated, but charming.

Luftkastellet

Strandgade 100b; tel: 70 26 26 24; summer only; map p.139 D2

Below: Café Republic at the Statens Museum for Kunst.

Left: harbour-side drinks in the summer.

Sand, a seat and beer: on a sunny day on the Øresund, nothing else is needed.

Sofiekælderen

Sofiegade 1; tel: 32 57 77 01; Tue–Wed noon–midnight, Thur–Sat noon–3am, Sun noon–10pm, L noon–5pm, D Tue–Wed 6–9.30pm, Thur–Sat 6–10pm, Sun 6–9pm; S-tog: Christianhavns; map p.139 C1

Set right by the canal, this is a pretty place to sit outside close to the water. It's fairly basic inside but is especially popular in the evenings when an alternative crowd pours in for beer and dancing; live music is a regular and popular feature.

The Suburbs

NORREBRO

Bodega

Kapelvej 1; tel: 35 39 07 07; Tue 10am–midnight, Wed–Thur 10am–2am, Fri–Sat 10am–4am, Sun 10am–11pm; bus: 5a, 350s, 12, 66, 69; map p.134 B2

Until recently known as Bar Starten, one of Copenhagen's coolest bar-restaurants when it opened in 2001, Bodega is a popular, cosy place with reasonable prices and good bar food. There is a small dance floor and live music Fri–Sat. Lunch choices are mainly sandwich related; evening meals are limited but a tad more solid.

Café Salonen

Peblinge Dossering 6; tel: 35 35 12 19; Tue–Fri 9am–5.30pm, Sat 9am–1pm; map p.134 B1

On the edge of Nørrebro, this waterside café with French-Danish decor is cosy in winter and charming in summer when you can eat on the water on a pontoon – surrounded by swans if you are lucky. Food is standard fare, but fine. Don't expect to nip in and out quickly, service is variable.

Laundromat Cafe

Elmegade 15; tel: 35 35 16 72; Mon–Thur 8am–midnight, Fri–Sat 8am–2pm; bus: 3a; map p.134 B2

This orange, book-lined café has become very popular and rightly so. Good food, relaxed atmosphere, books and newspapers are on hand and to cap it all, you can do your laundry out the back at the same time. There is another location in Østerbro (Århusgade 38; tel: 35 55 60 20).

Pussy Galore's Flying Circus

30 Skt Hans Torv; tel: 35 24 53 00; Mon–Fri 8am–2am, Sat–Sun 9am–2am; bus: 3a; map p.134 B2

This is the café everyone mentions in Nørrebro – less for its food, which is acceptable but not outstanding, but more for its location on Nørrebro's most popular square and its ability to attract a cool crowd, drawn no doubt by the minimalist interior and Arne Jacobsen chairs. During the day, it's also family-friendly. If you can't find a table, the Sebastopol next door is less cool, but just as good for lunch and sitting in the sun.

ØSTERBRO

Amokka

36–40 Dag Hammarskjölde Allé; tel: 35 27 63 00; Mon–Wed, Sat 11am–11pm, Thur–Fri 11am–midnight, Sun 11am–10pm; bus: 1A, 14; map p.135 D3

An excellent restaurant and coffee house (which also serves a selection of teas) close to the north end of Sortedams Sø. Food is Danish-International fusion, cakes are heaven, coffee exceptional and staff friendly and helpful. Not surprisingly, the locals love it – especially at the weekends. It's also child friendly and you can sit outside in clement weather.

Park Café

Østerbrogade 79; tel: 35 42 62 48; Mon–Fri noon–midnight, Sat 10am–midnight, Sun 10am–10pm; bus: 1A, 14; map p.135 C4

If you are on this side of town, this is one of the best places to be for the well-dressed twenty-something crowd, late on Thur–Sat nights with live contemporary music verging on the cutting edge. There's a balcony with a view out over the sports stadium, which is nice in summer, day or night.

Children

Copenhagen is a great city to visit with your children. There are countless attractions, such as amusement parks, playgrounds, interactive museums and children's theatre events to keep them happy. The Danes genuinely like children and are keen that they should be involved in culture from an early age – Denmark is probably the only place you will see a bunch of five-year-olds happily trotting around an art gallery looking at pictures. It's also a safe and easy place to get around, with many pedestrian areas and traffic-free squares, as well as a good range of family-friendly restaurants and cafés.

Bakken

Dyrehavevej 62, Klampenborg; www.bakken.dk; Mar–May: variable, June: 2pm–midnight, July–Aug: noon–midnight; Sept: 2pm–midnight; free; S-tog: Klampenborg

Not far on the train, this funfair (cheaper though less magical than Tivoli) is in a deer park, which is nice for a picnic. You are also near Bellevue beach or on the same train line as several other attractions if you wish to combine activities.

Danmarks Akvarium

Kavalergården 1, Charlottenlund; tel: 39 62 32 83; www.danmarksakvarium.dk; open Nov–Jan: 10am–4pm, Feb–Apr: 10am–5pm, May–Aug 10am–6pm, Sept–Oct: 10am–5pm, touch-pools Sat–Sun, holidays, feeding Wed 2pm, Sat–Sun, holidays 11.30am–2pm; entrance charge, under-3s free; bus: 14, 166, S-tog: Charlottenlund

This long-established aquarium is considered one of the finest in Europe, with everything from sharks to piranhas and electric eels. As well as huge, landscaped tanks, it also has some very popular 'touch tanks' for children.

Above: a clown entertains the crowd at Bakken.

Hotel DGI-Byens

Tietgensgade 65; tel: 33 29 81 40; Mon–Thur 6.30am–noon, Fri 6.30am–7pm, Sat– Sun, holidays 9am–5pm; entrance charge; bus: 1a, 65e, S-tog: Hovedbanegård; map p.138 A1

Just behind Hovedbanegård station, this hotel and sports centre offers great swimming facilities, including a climbing and diving pool, a kids' pool and a warm spa pool.

SEE ALSO PAMPERING P.111

Experimentarium

Tuborg Havnevej 7, Hellerup; map p.24

This superb science museum just outside Copenhagen in Hellerup has more than 300 experiments that bring to life the wonders of science to enquiring young minds, and hands. It also contains the Kid's Pavilion, a fun area for 3–6 year olds.

SEE ALSO MUSEUMS AND GALLERIES P.86–7

Guinness World Records Museum

Østergade 16; map p.138 C3

This attraction is very popular and, although getting a bit tired, its 13 galleries are still fun for kids.

SEE ALSO MUSEUMS AND GALLERIES P.88

Nationalmuseet

Ny Vestergade 1, Frederiksholms Kanal 12; map p.138 B2

Left: up, up and away at Tivoli.

If you have kids in tow and plan to see a lot of sights, the CPH Card is very good value; it allows free transport and entry to sights for up to two children under the age of ten for every adult card. There are also children's cards available for 10–15 year-olds.

The National Museum has a large interactive area for kids where they can dress up in grandma's clothes, see what it would have been like to sit in an old Danish classroom and find out about castles, among other educational activities. There are usually holiday events, ring or check their website for details.
SEE ALSO MUSEUMS AND GALLERIES P. 93

Statens Museum for Kunst

Rosenborg palace gardens, Østre Anlæg; tel: 33 74 84 94; www.smk.dk; tour: Sat–Sun 1pm, workshop: Sat–Sun, holidays 10.30am–4.30pm; tours: free, workshop: entrance charge; map p.135 D2
The museum is keen to involve children and offers one or two exhibitions a year for 6–12s. Artist-led workshops also allow children to respond to art they have seen in the galleries. Children's weekend guided tours put an emphasis on telling good stories.
SEE ALSO MUSEUMS AND GALLERIES P.97

Tivoli

Vesterbrogade 3; map p.138 A1–2
The best time to take children is during the day.
SEE ALSO RÅDHUSPLADSEN AND TIVOLI P. 6; PARKS, GARDENS AND BEACHES P.115

Tyco Brahe Planetarium

Gammel Kongevej 10; tel: 33 12 12 24; map p.136 C3
Named after the world-famous Danish 16th-century astronomer, this attraction bristles with the latest computer technology, including an interactive space theatre and space store. There's also a huge IMAX cinema.
SEE ALSO MUSEUMS AND GALLERIES P.98–9

The Wonderful World of Hans Christian Andersen

Rådhuspladsen 57; tel: 33 32 31 31; entrance charge; bus: all Rådhuspladsen buses; map p.138 A2
Tableaux with light and sound effects of Hans Christian Andersen's life and stories with recordings of some of his fairytales.
SEE ALSO LITERATURE AND THEATRE P. 72–3

Zoo København

Roskildevej 32, Frederiksberg; tel: 72 20 02 00; Nov–Mar: daily 9am–4pm, Apr–May, Sept: Mon–Fri, 9am–5pm, Sat–Sun 9am–6pm, 1–16 June, 14–31 Aug: daily 9am–6pm, 17 June–13 Aug: daily 9am–10pm; bus: 4a, 6a, 18, 26, 832, S-tog: Valby
In the southwest corner of the Frederiksberg Gardens, this is a lovely zoo with a children's zoo as well as all the perennial favourites. In spring expect lots of babies. The new elephant house and enclosure, due to open in 2008, is being built by famous London architect Norman Foster.

Below: a Royal Life Guardsman with two admirers in tow.

Churches and Synagogues

Danes are not, generally, regular churchgoers, but the fabric of the Evangelical Lutheran church and the nation's cultural inheritance are fiercely guarded. Copenhagen's churches are well worth visiting, boasting a variety and history that is hard to beat. The fire of 1728 put paid to many medieval buildings but there are fine examples of the Rococo and Baroque. Several also reflect Denmark's maritime culture with votive ships hanging from the ceiling, remembering the sailors who worked in dangerous conditions so far away.

Alexandr Nevsky Kirke

Bredgade 53; tel: 20 76 16 47; Wed 11.30am–1.30pm; bus: 1a, 15, 19; map p.139 C4

This Russian orthodox church, topped with three golden onion domes, was built in 1883 as a gift from Tsar Alexander III to mark his marriage to Christian IX's second daughter Marie Dagmar, whom he had married in St Petersburg in 1866.

Marie Dagmar (known as Maria Feodorovna) had four sons and two daughters, including Tsar Nicholas II and the Grand Duke Michael, both murdered during the Russian Revolution in 1918.

A widow from 1894, she took refuge in London in 1919 with her sister Alexandra, wife to Queen Victoria's son, Albert. She never acknowledged the murder of her sons and their families.

The tsarina died in Denmark in 1928 aged 81. Her funeral was held at Alexandr Nevsky Church and she was buried in Roskilde Cathedral. In 2005, she was reburied in St Petersburg, next to her husband, as she had wished.

Left: Alexander Nevsky Kirke marks ties between a Russian tsar and a Danish king.

Christiansborg Slotskirke

Christiansborg Slot, Christiansborg, Slotsplads; tel: 33 92 64 51; www.ses.dk/christiansborg palace; Sun noon–4pm; bus: 2a; map p.138 B2

Just over the road from the royal palace, this building has seen its own fair share of drama. Originally built in the 18th century to the Rococo designs of Nicolai Eigtved, it was destroyed by fire in 1794 when the whole palace went up in smoke.

Rebuilding began in 1813, using the old foundations and remaining masonry, but this time designed in the Neclassical style by C.F. Hansen with a lovely light interior and dome. It took 13 years to finish and was inaugurated in 1826 to mark the thousandth anniversary of the introduction of Christianity into Denmark.

In 1992, almost 200 years after the first fire, it was once again immolated and the roof and dome caved in. It has since been reconstructed to international acclaim.

Christianskirke

Strandgade 1, Christianshavn; tel: 32 96 83 01; Mar–Oct: daily 8am–6pm, Nov–Feb: daily 8am–5pm; map p.138 C1

One of two splendid churches on Christianshavn, this elegant Rococo church was built in 1755–59 by Nicolai Eigtved, Frederik V's master architect, who designed many of

Left: the monumental interior of Grundtvigs Kirke.

Copenhagen's superb 18th-century churches. It is notable for its unusual, theatrical layout, in which seating galleries run around the walls at a second level, the royal pew in the centre opposite the altar, technically in the position of the 'stage'.

The church was first named for Frederik V (Frederiks Kirke) but in 1901 was changed to reflect the importance of Christian IV who founded this part of Copenhagen. The tower was added in 1769 by Eigtved's son-in-law G.D. Anthon.

Domkirke

SEE VOR FRUE KIRKE, P. 39

Grundtvigs Kirke

På Bjerget 14B; tel: 35 81 54 42; Mon, Wed–Fri 9am–1pm, Tue 4–6pm; bus: 6a, 171e, S-tog: Emdrup

Outside the centre, this impressive, yellow-brick church dedicated to Nikolai Frederik Severin Grundtvig (1783–1872), a renowned educationalist, austere parson and prolific hymn writer was built between 1921 and 1940.

Helligåndskirken

Niels Hemmingsensgade 5; tel: 33 37 65 40; www.helligaands kirken.dk; Mon–Fri 12–4pm, music and prayers Sept–June: Mon–Fri 12pm; map p.138 B3

In the heart of the Latin Quarter, the Church of the Holy Ghost originated in 1238 as a monastery and hospital, when this area made up most of Copenhagen. With the exception of Helligåndshuset (now used for markets and exhibitions), Christian IV's Baroque portal (1630, main door) and Griffenfeld's Chapel (the round burial chapel on the north side), the original buildings were burnt down in the 1728 fire. The present building dates from 1732.

Holmens Kirke

Holmens Kanal; tel: 33 13 61 78; Mon–Fri 9am–2pm, Sat 9am– noon; bus: 1a, 350s; map p.138 C2

Almost opposite Christiansborg, this is another of Christian IV's building projects. A naval forge in 1562, it was converted into a church in 1619 and finished in 1641. Dedicated to the navy, it has a pretty whitewashed interior with Rococo plasterwork and a large votive ship hanging from the ceiling. Queen Margrethe was married here in 1967.

Don't miss Denmark's tallest pulpit and altarpiece dating from 1661, the exotic iron font with four legs with human feet made by a local blacksmith in 1646, or the external east doorway,

Below: Grundtvigs Kirke was built by Peder Jensen-Klint in a style that has been described as 'neo-Gothic Functionalism'.

Above: Marmorkirken's dome measures 31m and is beaten in size only by St Peter's in Rome.

brought from Roskilde Cathedral in the 1800s.

Marmorkirken (Marble Church)

Frederiksgade 4; tel: 33 15 01 44; www.marmorkirken.dk; Mon–Thur 10am–5pm, Wed 10am–6pm, Fri–Sun noon–5pm; bus: 1a, 15, 19; map p.139 C5

Properly called Frederiks Kirke, after Frederik V, this circular church was designed by Nicolai Eigtved in 1740 as part of the smart Frederiksstad area around the Amalienborg. However, work was so expensive that it was halted in 1770 and did not recommence until 150 years later when the Danish industrialist Carl Frederik Tietgenit financed it. Inauguration took place on 19 August 1894.

It is especially remarkable for its dome, which stands on 12 pillars and is covered in paintings of the 12 apostles, with light flooding in from 12 skylights. Outside, at ground level, there are 14 Danish 'Fathers of the Church' and higher up, 18 figures of prophets, apostles and figures from Church history, finishing with Martin Luther.

SEE ALSO AMALIENBORG P.17

Old Synagogue

Krystalgade; map p.138 A3

Near the university is the Old Synagogue dating from 1833. Notable for surviving the Nazi invasion of World War II, it is still supporting the Jewish community that has lived in Copenhagen since the 17th century.

Roskilde Domkirke (Cathedral)

SEE SJÆLLAND P.24 AND MONUMENTS AND FOUNTAINS P.81

St Alban's

Churchill Parken, Langelinie; tel: 39 62 77 36; www.st-albans.dk; services Sun, Wed 10.30am; map p.135 E2

To the north, on the banks of the Øresund, near Kastellet, this pretty neo-Gothic church looks like it has been lifted from the English countryside. It was built in 1885 for the English Anglican population and consecrated in 1887.

Sankt Ansgar's Kirke

Bredgade 64; tel: 33 13 37 62; Tue–Fri 10am–4pm; bus: 1a, 15, 19; map p.139 C4

Built in 1841, this is Copenhagen's oldest Catholic church. Dedicated to St Ansgar, who brought Christianity to Denmark in the 9th century (and founded the original cathedral in Ribe on Jutland) it was built by CF Hansen, the architect in charge of rebuilding Copenhagen after the fire of 1794 and the British bombardment in 1807. It is noted for its patterned brickwork and brightly painted apse.

Sankt Petri Kirke

Sankt Pedersstræde 2; tel: 33 93 38 76; www.sankt-petri.dk; Tue–Sat 11am–3pm; bus: 6a; map p.138 A3

Thanks to surviving the fire of 1728, Skt Petri, the centre for the city's German-speaking population since 1585, is Copenhagen's oldest church, though it did sustain some damage during Nelson's bombardment of 1797.

The tower, nave and choir date from the 15th-century, the north and south transepts (site of the organ and main entrance) date from 1634, while the 'Christian V salen' is an 18th-century addition. The sepulchral chapels were built between 1648 and 1740 and the church spire was added in 1757.

Below: the dramatic interior of Roskilde Cathedral provides a lesson in Danish history.

St Alban, England's first martyr, died in 303 AD and was buried in Ely in Cambridgeshire. His remains are now in Odense – moved there in1075 by Canute of Denmark, nephew of Canute the Great, King of England.

Above: the view from the top of the Vor Frelsers Kirke.

Trinitatis Kirke

Købmagergade 52A, Landemærket 12; tel: 33 37 65 40; www.trinitatiskirke.dk; Mon–Sat 9.30am–4.30pm; map p.138 B3

Founded by Christian IV in 1637, this lovely church, built for the university, was finished in 1657 under Frederik III. Damaged in the 1728 fire, the interior dates from 1731 and has a gilded Baroque altar, a three-faced Rococo clock, a vaulted roof picked out in gold, galleries running down both side walls and a fabulous gold- and silver-coloured organ. If it is closed when you visit, go into the Rundetårn and look down the nave through the glass panel at the start of the ramp.

Vor Frelsers Kirke

Sankt Annæ Gade 29; tel: 32 54 68 63; www.vorfrelserskirke.dk; daily, spire Apr–Aug: 11am–4.30pm, Sept–Oct: 11am–3.30pm; S-tog: Christianshavn; map p.139 D3

The magnificent, Baroque Church of Our Saviour is particularly well known for its spiralling tower, twisting 90m skywards *(see picture on page 4)*. It affords one of the best aerial views of the city, but climbing it is not for the weak of limb or anyone who dislikes heights.

Built by Christian V for his new harbour district between 1682 and 1696, the church originally had a square tower – the current one was not added until 1749–52. Inside is a lovely, light-filled, white-walled church with tall windows.

The wishful cherub-covered font has a sad history, it was given by Frederik IV's then childless morganatic wife in 1702; she died in childbirth in 1704, her only baby following her nine months later.

The altarpiece, inspired by the altar in the Roman church of *SS Domenico e Sisto*, shows God, represented by the sun, and the events of Maundy Thursday when Christ prayed that he should be spared the crucifixion.

Christian V's insignia can be seen on the entrance, the ceiling and the three-storey organ, which rests on two elephants, the emblem of Denmark's most prestigious order, the Order of the Elephant, founded in 1450. The figures on the wooden pulpit represent the apostles and dates from 1773.

Vor Frue Kirke

Nørregade 8; tel: 33 37 65 40; daily 8am–5pm; bus: 6a; map p.138 A3

The site of this church, also known as St Mary's Cathedral or simply Domkirke, dates back to Copenhagen's earliest days in the 12th century and was the most important church in the city, founded by Bishop Absalon and hosting many important royal occasions over the centuries; the earliest, the marriage of Margrethe I, aged nine, to Håkon VI of Norway in 1363 and the most recent, the wedding of Crown Prince Frederik and Australian Mary Donalson in 2004.

Twice destroyed by fire, the present Neoclassical church (with the exception of the medieval tower, which survived and is home to both Denmark's oldest bell, dating from 1490, and its heaviest, weighing four tons) dates from 1829, designed by C.F. Hansen.

It has a light and bright interior dominated by the massive statues of Christ and his apostles (Paul has been substituted for the traitor Judas) created by Bertel Thorvaldsen specifically for this church in the 19th century. The font and two reliefs are also by Thorvaldsen.

Though Danes do not attend church regulary, they feel the church is an important part of their national character and visit during holidays such as Easter and Christmas as well as for christenings, weddings and deaths.

Danish Design

What we consider to be Danish design today was born from the Danish Modern movement that peaked in post-war Denmark. This movement concentrated on making objects beautiful by virtue of their respect for materials, often wood and silver, and removing unnecessary elements from the design. It built upon a tradition of craftsmanship and embraced ideals of rationalism and humanism. Their diverse output included everything from ceramics to jewellery, but its innovative furniture and lighting now fills museums across the world, and many shops in Copenhagen.

Design in the Home

For all its elegance, Danish design is not something limited to galleries and museums. It is found everywhere: hotels, restaurants, cafés, offices, and most importantly, homes. Nearly every Dane, it seems, has some sort of sleek designer lamp hanging over the dinner or coffee table.

For special occasions, such as weddings and birthdays, Danes give arty salad sets, candle holders, salt and pepper grinders, pot holders – even mixing bowls. It seems impossible to find anything for the home that hasn't been designed with a sense of syle in mind. Even cupboard handles and other household fittings are part of the Danish design world. Look out for 1930s silver cutlery designed by Kay Bojesen, and Ebbe Sadolin's plain white tableware.

> Many of Denmark's most famous designers worked primarily as architects with a keen sense for efficient designs. One example is Arne Jacobsen who designed the SAS Radisson in the 1960s. His famous Egg Chair was tailored for its lobby. They are still there, if you fancy judging the comforts of his style for yourself.

The shops below are, at best, a discrete selection. Shops selling quality houseware appear throughout the city.

Casa

Store Regnegade 2; tel: 33 32 70 41; www.casagroup.com; Mon–Thur 10am–5.30pm, Fri 10am–6pm, Sat 10am–3pm; bus: 350s; map p.138 B3

In many cities a store like Casa would stand out, but with Normann and Illums doing a similar cross-section of designer wares, it is against stiff competition and does not quite measure up, though as it's only just off Strøget, it's worth a quick visit.

Dansk Design Centre

27 H.C. Andersens Boulelvard; map p.138 A2

Despite it's impressive, glass-fronted building designed by Henning Larsen, some of the larger retail outlets on Strøget or the Klassik Moderne Mobelkunst on Bredgade seem to better represent the past and future of the country's design tradition.

SEE ALSO MUSEUMS AND GALLERIES P.85–6

Above: there is a little gift shop full of designer goods and a functional café at the Dansk Design Centre.

Designer Zoo

Vesterbrogade 137, Vesterbro; tel: 33 24 94 93; www.dzoo.dk; Mon–Thur 10am–5.30pm, Fri 10am–7pm, Sat 10am–3pm; bus: 6a; map p.136 A3–B3

Get eight Danes together in the same house and they form a club, or in this case a

Left: the warm tones of wood play a large part in Danish design.

store showcasing their work which includes furniture, jewellery, clothing, glass and metalwork. It's all beautifully stylish of course, and fits in perfectly with Vesterbro's new, trendy atmosphere.

Kunstindustrie Museet

Bredgade 68; museum: entrance charge, library, Design Studio: free; map p.139 D4

A tourist can see so much of Danish design, both old and new, from visiting the shops around the city and especially along Bredgade. But for the more serious student, this museum offers a research library and a more comprehensive overview of Danish design's beginnings. It's extensive collections also focus on older periods in industrial design and decorative and applied arts.

SEE ALSO MUSEUMS AND GALLERIES P.89–90

Montana Mobile

Bredgade 24; tel: 33 12 06 90; www.montanamobile.dk; Mon–Fri 10am–6pm, Sat 10am–3pm; bus: 1a, 15, 19; map p.139 C3

This off-shoot of the Montana shelving and storage company specialises in office storage and furniture in bright, fruit-stripe colours that would definitely brighten up any dull clerk's grey areas.

Rosendahl

Bremerholm 1; tel: 33 91 50 57, www.rosendahl.dk; map p.138 B3

A small shop on the corner of Strøget that has a great selection of kitchenware created by some of the country's finest living designers. It is also one of the best value in the area.

Royal Copenhagen

Amagertorv 6, Strøget; tel: 33 13 71 81; www.royalcopenhagen.com; Mon–Thur 10am–6pm, Fri 10am–7pm, Sat 10am–5pm; map p.138 B3

Royal Copenhagen has a distinguished history and is still the supreme porcelain producer in Denmark. Many may find their styles rather dated compared to other designer houseware, but there is the famous Flora Danica collection, some outstanding crystal and an antiques section (next door at no. 4) that those in the know would probably find worth a visit in its own right.

SEE ALSO MUSEUMS AND GALLERIES P.96

Electronics

Bang & Olufson

Kongens Nytorv 26; tel: 33 11 14 15; www.bang-olufsen.com; Mon–Thur, Sat 10am–6pm, Fri 10am–7pm; bus: 1a, 15, 19, 26, 999, S-tog: Kongens Nytorv; map p.138 C3

The visually striking sound systems designed by Bang & Olufsen are praised worldwide, and are found in many Danish homes. They have several shops in Copenhagen; the flagship store is on Kongens Nytorv.

Below: simple household items, smartly designed, feature greatly in Danish homes.

Poul Henningsen (1894–1967) has made a dramatic impact on the Danish home. Before designing his first lamps, he reflected 'When, in the evening, from the top of a tram car, you look into all the homes on the first floor, you shudder at how dismal people's homes are. Furniture, style, carpets, everything in the home is unimportant compared to the positioning of the lighting. It doesn't cost money to light a room correctly, but it does require culture.' Now one rarely sees flats in Copenhagen without sophisticated lighting. Mass production has enabled most people to be able to afford stylish lights.

Furniture

Danish homes are filled with two types of furniture: warm, rustic pieces that would not seem out of place in a log cabin and sophisticated, often minimalist pieces that look as much art object as a place to sit.

Hans J. Wegner is considered one of the most influential furniture designers in the world, with his Round Chair still being emulated today. Other great designers, many of whom studied under Kaare Klint at the Royal Academy of Architecture, went on to create modern classics in the 1950s include Mogens Koch, Børge Mogensen and Nanna Ditzel and Poul Kjaereholm.

The best place to see Wegner chairs, as well as many other famous designers' works, including Kaare Klint and Verner Panton, is at the Klassik Moderne Mobelkunst, at Bredgade 3. In fact the whole of Bredgade is probably the best place in the city to view Danish design.

Hay Cph

Pilestræde 28–31; tel: 99 42 44 00; www.hay.dk; Mon–Fri 10am–6pm, Sat 11am–4pm; map p.138 B3

This small shop's ambition is to encourage young designers to expand on the ideas of classic Danish design. Though their stock is limited their designers make a strong impact by using bright colours and innovative materials.

Illums Bolighus

Amagertorv 10, Strøget; tel: 33 14 19 41; www.royalshopping.com; Mon–Thur 10am–6pm, Fri 10am–7pm, Sat 10am–5pm; map p.138 B3

Considered the city's main temple of design chic. Here you can buy everything from beds to bottle openers – all of it high quality, but its sheer size and department store layout detracts from its products.

Klassik Moderne Mobelkunst

Bredgade 3; tel: 33 33 90 60; www.klassik.dk; Mon–Fri 11am–6pm, Sat 10am–3pm; bus: 1a, 15, 19, S-tog: Kongens Nytorv; map p.138 C3

This is an institution in Danish design and more of a museum than a shop, especially for those who don't have 20,000 krøner to spend on a single Poul Henningsen lamp.

It specialises in vintage furniture and lamps dating from the 1920s to 70s. Their large showroom is consistently stocked full of original pieces by Hans J. Wegner, Børge Mogensen, Arne Jacobsen, Kaare Klint and other famous designers. They also have a wide selection of Danish modern art.

Normann

Østerbrogade 70; tel: 35 27 05 40; www.norman-copenhagen.dk; Mon–Thur 10am–6pm, Fri 10am–7pm, Sat 10am–3pm; bus: 1a, 14, 15; map p.135 D4

Normann Copenhagen City

Magasin Kogens Nytorv, Kongens Nytorv 13, 3rd floor; tel: 33 18 20 27; Mon–Thur 10am–7pm, Fri 10am–8pm, Sat 10am–5pm; bus: 1a, 15, 19, 350s, 47, 66, S-tog: Kongens Nytorv; map p.138 C3

Opened in 1999, this enormous menagerie of designer chic inhabits the old Triangel

Theatre on the edge of the reservoir in Østerbro.

The store's 1700 sq m now showcases lighting, furniture, clothing, and other elements of interior décor from the Norman range and other international designers. The room you enter through also serves as a 20-m catwalk, used to show off their latest fashions. There is another, smaller location on Kongens Nytorv.

Paustian

Kalkbrænderiløbskaj 2, Østerbro; tel: 39 16 65 65; www.paustian.dk; Mon–Thur 9.30am–5.30pm, Fri 9.30am–6pm, Sat 10am–3pm

Quite a trek, or a short bus ride, from the city centre, this furniture emporium, designed by Jørn Utzon (the Danish architect who designed the Sydney Opera House), sells a wide selection of contemporary designers. It also has a reputable restaurant, in which to revive yourself.

Lighting

Perhaps it's the long winter nights, but something has inspired the Danes to create lighting that is as much warming as it is enlightening, whether it is the familiar modern style or a preponderance of lamps and lanterns, the Danes have definitely got a knack for warming the soul when they turn on the lights.

Le Klint

Store Kirkestræde 1; tel: 33 11 66 63; www.leklint.com; Mon–Fri 10am–6pm, Sat 10am–5pm; map p.138 B3

A tiny little oasis of lights, all of the pleated, white plastic variety made popular by the legendary architect and designer P.V. Jensen (also architect of Grundtvigs Church) who originally designed the shade for an oil lamp.

He named the design Le Klint for his presumably bright son Kaare Klint who went on to create the popular fruit lantern in 1944, still one of the company's best-selling lamps. Now made by a team of designers, these lamps truly are as transfixing as an open fire and the shop is worth a visit just to bask in their glow.

SEE ALSO CHURCHES P.37

Louis Poulsen

Gammel Strand 28; tel: 70 33 14 14; www.louis-poulsen.dk; Mon–Fri 10am–6pm; map p.138 B2

Selling lamps by such famous designers as Henningsen, Panton and Jacobsen, this is one of the finest showrooms for lighting in the city, though it seems a bit off the beaten track on Gammel Strand and should be on Strøget doing for lights what Georg Jensen does for silver.

Jewellery

Carré

Læderstræde 18, tel: 33 12 92 18; www.carre.dk; Mon–Fri 10am–6pm, Sat 10am–4pm; map p.138 B2

Sophisticated jewellery that looks like it's waiting to be worn by the daintiest of Danish princesses.

Georg Jensen

Amagertorv 4; tel: 33 11 40 80; www.georgjensen.dk; Mon–Thur 10am–6pm, Fri 10am–7pm, Sat 10am–5pm; map p.138 B3

Georg Jensen was Denmark's leading silversmith and architect, who designed some classically simple yet elegant silverware still produced today; and for our money, he's the best of Danish design, and that is saying quite a lot.

SEE ALSO MUSEUMS AND GALLERIES P.88

Halberstadt

Østergade 4; tel. 33 15 97 90; www.halberstadt.com; Mon–Fri 10am–6pm, Sat 10am–5pm; map p.138 B3

A jewel-encrusted toy train attracts strollers to their window at the beginning of Strøget. Perhaps they are relying too much on keen tourists to bite before exploring any further, as their inside selection is not as unique as Georg Jensen's shop further along.

Peter Hertz

Købmagergade 34; tel: 33 12 22 16; Mon–Fri 10am–6pm, Sat 10am–5pm; map p.138 B3

This shop has fabulous jewellery, but a very intimidating air to it (a bit unusual for this city). It also has a long history of providing jewellery to the royal family.

Below: Georg Jensen's silverwork is a timeless classic.

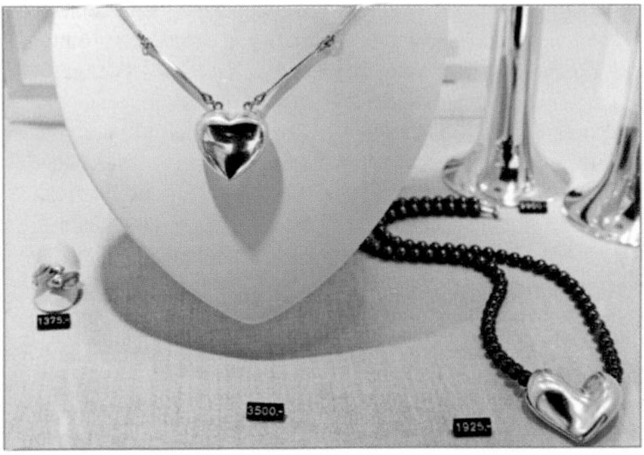

Environment

Be prepared. For Green tourists from the UK or US, a trip to Copenhagen is likely to mix equal parts admiration and exasperation. Copenhagen bills itself as the Environmental Capital of Europe. Gone are the 4x4s escorting a lone child on the morning school run. In their place are countless ruddy-cheeked parents employing various ways of strapping their phlegmatic tots to bicycles to navigate the city. Wind farms are visible from the coast, and the Øresund is so clean it has achieved Blue Flag status. All of this is terrific, and looks effortless; so why can't we all be so green?

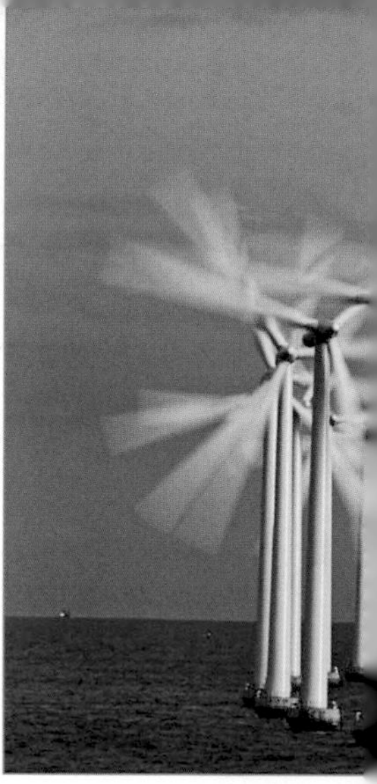

Wind Farms

One of the first things you'll notice whether you are arriving by air or sea is that wind farms play a vital role in Denmark's energy plans.

Isolated turbines dot the landscape as you approach Kalstrup airport and just off the coast of Copenhagen is the most visible of these farms: the **Middelgrunden wind farm**.

This project began in theory in 1993 and was finally completed in 2000 at a cost of €48 million after seven years of planning, designing and assessing its environmental impact.

The wind farm now consists of 20 turbines and produces a total of 40 megawatts, or enough to power 40,000 Copenhagen homes.

In an average wind year, this means Copenhagen avoids 81,000 tonnes of carbon dioxide pollution.

From 1982–2002 wind power has gone from a marginal contribution to Denmark's overall electricity consumption to providing over 14 percent.

Middelgrund is by no means the only wind farm in the country, nor the largest. Horns Rev and Rødsan off the west coast of Jutland and the south coast of Sjælland respectively both came online after Middelgrund and each produce four times as much electricity.

As a low-lying nation, Denmark has set the standard for harnessing nature to power the nation.

For those thinking the city is perfectly green, any visit to Tivoli will quickly banish this thought. With over 110,000 lights that consume 17,000 kilowatts per day, enough food waste to feed 1,460 pigs and an average of 440g of waste per guest, it struggles to just stay clean, much less green. Still, they do make an effort, being the first amusement park in the world to introduce eco-management. They have won several awards for measures including solar-powered rides and the lack of chemicals in the cleaning of equipment.

Above: Islands Brygge beach just south of Christianshavn is popular with families.

Clean Water

Despite the volume of transport that goes in and out of Copenhagen's harbour each year and the number of industries located alongside it, it is still clean enough for Copenhageners to swim in. This practice was banned in the 1950s, but in July 2002 the City of Copenhagen opened the baths at Havneparken on Islands Brygge. A new, sandy beach has also been established in the Port of Copenhagen, which is good news for sun-seekers and swimmers,

Left: the Middelgrunden wind farm.

In 2005, Copenhagen installed a geothermal plant which initially supplies the central heating water for about 4,000 households, or 1 per cent of the city.

which just about excuses the city's choice of name: Copencabana.

BEACHES

There are five more beaches just outside the city if you fancy dipping a toe in the clean, cold water. Bellevue is alone to the north, but south of the city the Beach Park along the Bay of Køge includes the popular Ishøj Beach and Brøndby, Vallensbæk and Hundige.

The city's very popular inner lakes, are not in as good shape as the Copenhageners who run and stroll along their shores. A predominance of fish eat water fleas and other small animals that would normally eat the algae in the water to keep the lakes clean. Since 2002 the city has begun a program of introducing pike into the lakes to control the trash fish and therefore help clean up the water.

SEE ALSO PARKS, GARDENS AND BEACHES P.112

Cycling

One in three Copenhageners ride their bicycle to work every day and that's just the beginning. Cyclists make up 35 per wcent of the city's traffic and it is immediately obvious that families view it as an easy means of transport for their days out. Specially designed bicycles can transport up to three small children in a box at the front.

As one of the city's green initiatives, more and more money is being spent on improving the cycle track infrastructure, which already covers over 300km.

Additionally there is a designated carriage for bicycles and baby buggies on all trains to assist cyclists trim time off longer journeys.

For the visitor there are several places to rent bicycles and the City Bike program which lets you borrow a bike for 20DKK, which is returned to you when you return the bicycle. There are over 100 city bike stands spread around the city.

SEE ALSO TRANSPORT P.132

Recycling

Copenhagen has a very ambitious program of recycling with plans to limit non-recycled materials to two per cent of household waste. Much of this occurs behind closed doors, in the inner courtyards of apartment blocks which have a collection of wheelie bins with a long list of instructions posted nearby. There are also frequent bottle collection points in squares in residential areas.

Below: to say that Copenhagen is a city of cyclists is a worn-out saddle of a cliché, but is true nonetheless.

Essentials

Visiting Copenhagen is a great pleasure, but inevitably, there are a few things it is handy to know in terms of getting information, dealing with emergencies or saving money. A visit to the tourist board to get listings, information or even book a hotel is never wasted; practically everyone speaks fluent English (and often French and German) and you will find locals and hotel staff also eager to help; American citizens should always travel with additional personal insurance to cover unexpected health problems; and lastly, although Copenhagen is an expensive city in comparison with many, there are ways to make it a bit cheaper.

CPH Card

The CPH Card, available from the Tourist Information Office, lasts for 24 (adult: 199DKK, 10–15: 129DKK) or 72 (adult: 429DKK, 10–15: 249DKK) hours and gives free or reduced admission to more than 60 popular museums and sights in the city. It also grants free travel on buses, S-tog, Metro and Waterbus and provides discounts on car hire and Scandlines ferry routes between Denmark and Sweden. Two children under 10 may accompany each card-carrying adult free of charge.

Embassies

British Embassy

Kastelsvej 36–40; tel: 35 44 52 00; Mon–Fri 9am–5pm; www.britishembassy.gov.uk; map p.135 D3

Embassy of the United States of America

Dag Hammarskjölds Allé 24; enquiries 2–4pm, tel: 33 41 71 00, emergencies, tel: 35 55 92 70; www.usembassy.dk; Mon–Tue, Thur–Fri 9am–noon; bus: 1a, 15; map p.135 D3

Canadian Embassy

Kristen Bernikowsgade 1; tel: 33 48 32 00; www.canada.dk; Mon–Fri 8.30am–4.30pm, consular office: Mon–Fri 9am–noon; map p.138 B3

Emergencies

For Ambulance, Police and Fire, tel: 112. Calls are free from phone boxes in the city.

English Listings

The English weekly newspaper, *The Copenhagen Post*, produces a useful weekly guide to what's going on, which comes out on Fridays; a free weekly magazine *Copenhagen This Week*, is also available at Tourist Information offices and most hotels. Also check out www.aok.dk and www.visitcopenhagen.com.

Health

Citizens of EU countries are entitled to free medical treatment in Danish hospitals on production of a European health card. For minor complaints, patients pay the doctor or dentist at the time of treatment and then claim the fees back from the local health service offices.

It is nevertheless advisable to take out a private medical and accident insurance policy to cover all eventualities. Contact the Tourist Information Office for information and guidance in choosing a doctor. Medicines are available from chemists *(apotek)*, and a prescription is not always necessary.

Steno Apotek

Vesterbrogade 6C; tel: 33 14 82 66; 24-hours; bus: 6a, 26, S-tog: Vesterport, Københavns; map p.138 2A

Money

The krøner (DKK) is the Danish currency. 1 krøne = 100 øre. You will find notes to the value of 50, 100, 200, 500 and 1,000 krøner, coins at 1, 2, 5, 10 and 20 krøner, plus 25 and 50 øre, but øre are usually rounded up or down.

Metric to Imperial Conversions
Metres–Feet 1=3.28
Kilometres–Miles 1=0.62
Hectares–Acres 1=2.47
Kilograms–Pounds 1=2.2

Left: the Danish Tourist Office is full of helpful information.

To phone abroad, dial 00, then the country code and the local phone number. Britain +44, Ireland +353, Ireland +353, Norway +47, Sweden +46, USA +1, Australia +61, New Zealand +64 and South Africa +27. To call Denmark from abroad, dial 0045 followed by the phone number.

Eight-digit numbers (without codes) apply in Denmark.

Banks are usually open Mon–Weds 10am–4pm; Thur 10am–6pm. Most have 24-hour cash machines (ATMs) – look for the word *Kontanten* – and you can draw out up to 3,000DKK, but expect to pay a commission whether you use the machine or cash a cheque at the counter.

Well-known traveller's cheques can be cashed in banks and at many hotels, restaurants and shops. There are no restrictions on importing and exporting currencies.

Not all outlets, especially smaller ones, accept credit cards.

TIPPING

Tipping is a nice gesture, but not regarded as necesary in hotels, restaurants and taxis, as service charges are included in the final bill.

Post

Post offices are generally open Mon–Fri 9am–5pm, Sat 9am–noon.

Main Post Office

Titgensgade 37; Mon–Fri 11am–6pm, Sat 10am–1pm

Central Railway Station

Mon–Fri 8am–9pm, Sat 9am–4pm, Sun 10am–4pm

Telephones

Coin- and card-operated telephone kiosks can be found all over the city, but most are open to the elements and it's not always easy to carry on a conversation. 1, 2, 5, 10 and 20DKK coins, and cards to the value of 30, 50 and 100DKK are accepted. The latter may be bought from post offices and pavement kiosks.

Tourist Information

Main Tourist Office

Vesterbrogade 4a; tel: 70 22 24 42; www.visitcopenhagen.com; May–June: Mon–Sat 9am–6pm, July–Aug: Mon–Sat 9am–8pm, Sun 10am–6pm, Sept–Apr: Mon–Sat 10am–4pm; bus: 5a, 30, 40, 47, 250s, S-tog: Hovedbanegård; map p.138 2A

Just outside Central Station, the tourist office is very efficient and most helpful.

Visa Regulations

Most visitors – including citizens of the UK, USA, Canada, Eire, Australia and New Zealand – only need a passport valid for at least three months at the time of entry.

Below: a vintage postbox in Dragør.

Festivals

Most of Copenhagen's annual festivals involve music, covering the complete spectrum, from classical and jazz, to rock and folk. Some, such as the Jazz Festival and Roskilde rock festival in June–July, attract international performers and are events for which people specifically book their visits; you need to book tickets a month or two in advance when they become available. It's also a good idea to book hotels ahead to avoid disappointment. Many festivals have their own websites, which become active a few months before the event; if you can't find what you want, check out www.visitcopenhagen.dk.

March

Copenhagen Catwalk
www.copenhagencatwalk.com
A new festival (2007), featuring fashion shows and offering make-overs and modelling auditions.

Night Film Festival
www.natfilm.dk
Watch quality, original language films from around the world. New, rep. and cult films are all shown.

May

Copenhagen Architecture and Design Days
www.cphadd.com
Visit show rooms, design attractions, lectures, workshops and auctions. There are special events such as guided city walks, as well as the international furniture fair in the Bella Center.

May/June

Copenhagen Architecture and Design Days
3 days in mid-May;
www.cphadd.com
A short, but intense celebration of the city's architecture, both old and new with special access to significant buildings.

Copenhagen Distortion
Wed before first Sun in June;
www.cphdistortion.dk
Five days and nights celebrating clubbing and nightlife.

Below: trying to find a friend at the Roskilde Festival.

Regular Summer Events

Hamlet Summer
www.hamletsommer.dk
Annual season of theatre held in the outdoor courtyard of Kronborg Castle in Elsinore.

Opera Concert
1st Sat in Aug;
www.kglteater.dk
Every year, the opera season opens with an open air concert at Fælledparken.

Royal Danish Ballet
www.kglteater.dk
The Royal Danish Ballet finishes its season (May–June) with an outdoor performance in 'Kastellet', the fortification by the Langelinie.

Wednesday Concerts
www.onsdagskoncerter.dk
Free classical concerts performed by students from the Royal Danish Academy of Music are held in the summer and autumn in churches and other venues across the city.

July

Father Christmas Congress
www.bakken.dk

Left: the annual Father Christmas Congress brings all manner of Santas, even Swedish ones.

For over 40 years, the world's Santa Clauses have convened at Bakken for the annual Father Christmas Congress in mid-July.

Jazz Festival
www.festival.jazz.dk; tickets available from May
450 jazz concerts take place indoors and out, with international stars such as Sonny Rollins, Ray Charles and Herbie Hancock.

The Roskilde Festival
www.roskilde-festival.dk
One of the world's biggest rock events, presenting artists such as U2, REM, Coldplay, Metallica and David Bowie; the average age rises considerably on the last days when one-day tickets are available (try and avoid the scumminess of four days in a tent).

August

Copenhagen Cooking
www.copenhagencooking.com
A week of gastronomic experiences from Denmark and the other Nordic countries takes place in restaurants, the Tivoli Gardens and public spaces across Copenhagen.

Copenhagen International Ballet
www.copenhageninternational-ballet.com
Three weeks of modern ballet and dance at the Arne Jacobsen Bellevue theatre at Klampenborg.

Copenhagen Summerdance
www.copenhagensummerdance.dk
Annual, free dance performances by Tim Rushton and the Dansk Dance Theatre in the inner courtyard of the Copenhagen Police headquarters.

Cultural Harbour
www.kulturhavn.dk
Four days of free dance, art, music, theatre and sporting events.

September

Copenhagen International Film Festival (CIFF)
www.copenhagenfilmfestival.com
A week of international films and film-related activities.

Golden Days in Copenhagen
www.goldendays.dk
A historical festival focusing on a different period in Copenhagen's history each year. Events include exhibitions, music, theatre, ballet and literature. The Danish Golden Age, the 19th century and the Bombardment of Copenhagen by the British Fleet in 1807 (the 2007 topic) have all been themes.

October

Gay & Lesbian Film Festival
www.cglff.dk
The oldest film festival in town, offering short films, feature films and documentaries. Also attracts a straight audience, as well as the city's media, cultural institutions and businesses.

November

CPH:DOX
www.cphdox.dk
Denmark's international documentary film festival aims to present new and innovative films and programmes and involves a range of activities such as seminars, directors' sessions, lectures, debates, music and club events.

Copenhagen Music Week
www.copenhagenmusicweek.com
In 2006 the city held its first Music Week to celebrate Danish music of all genres from dance to heavy rock. It was well received and is planned to be an annual event.

Other dates important dates are 16 April (the Queen's birthday), 1 May (May Day), 2nd weekend in May (Copenhagen Marathon), Whitsun weekend (Copenhagen carnival), mid-October (Kulturnaten – Culture Night) and mid November, (Tivoli reopens).

Film

Danish cinema returned to pre-eminence on the world scene with the launch of the Dogme 95 manifesto. The attention these low-production films attracted has kept modern Danish cinema firmly on the map, even a decade later. This burst of creativity did not occur through happenstance. The government, through the Danish Film Institute, invested heavily in the lagging film industry throughout the 1980s, providing enormous support for young artists. This position near the top of world cinema is nothing new; in the early 20th century, Denmark was a world leader in the new art of film.

Nordisk Film Company

Denmark's Nordisk Film Kompagni, founded in 1906, is the oldest film company on the planet still in operation. Its polar bear logo is familiar to all Danes. This is where Carl - Theodor Dreyer (1889–1968) began his career. The films of Dreyer, a master of psychological realism, are still shown at film festivals and schools the world over. His works include *The Passion of Joan of Arc* (1928) and *The Word* (1955). In the early 20th century, Denmark was a leader in the film industry, but from the 1920s onward, a lack of creativity led to its marginalisation.

Danish Film Institute

Today, Danish cinema revolves around the Danish Film Institute. Founded in 1972 to distribute public funds to feature films, the institute is a prime example of a successful government-sponsored art industry.

The organisation reads scripts and puts up half the funds for the movies. A quarter of its budget is allocated to productions made especially for children and young people. The Institute also manages the national film archive and the cinema on Gothersgade *(see Det Danske Filminstitute, opposite)*.

In 1982 the state increased its funding, and this, coupled with the establishment of the Danish Film School, jump-started the industry, which now churns out 15 or so productions a year.

The programme started paying off a few years later, when Danish films took Academy Awards for the best non-English language movies two years running. *Babette's Feast (pictured above)*, directed by Gabriel Axel and based on a story by Isak Dinesen (Karen Blixen), won in 1986, and *Pelle the Conqueror* triumphed the following year. Directed by Bille August it was based on a story by Martin Andersen Nexø.

SEE ALSO LITERATURE AND THEATRE P.73–5

Dogme 95 and Modern Danish Cinema

The 1990s heralded a new, edgier Danish cinema, and the prime mover was Lars von Trier *(see box left)*. A darling of the international film festival circuit and master of publicity, Lars von Trier manages to get the kind of funding that his Danish colleagues can only dream of. As the director-producer puts it, Danish film legislation 'has

Lars von Trier (b. 1956) was a key player in wresting Danish cinema out of the staid folk comedy and coming-of-age genres which had for so long held the country's cinema back. Von Trier broke through with the dystopian *Element of Crime* (1984), followed by *Zentropa* (1991), *Breaking the Waves* (1996) and *The Idiots* (1998). His popular breakthrough came with *The Kingdom I* and *II* (1994 and 1997), two television mini-series about oddballs at Copenhagen's main hospital. He also won new audiences in 2000 with *Dancer in the Dark*, starring the Icelandic singer Björk, and *Dogville* and *Manderley*, which were filmed in an imaginary setting consisting of chalk lines on the floor.

Left: *Babette's Feast*, directed by Gabriel Axel.

made it possible for me to direct films I would not have been able to make anywhere else in the world'.

Von Trier is part of the circle of Danish film-makers who formulated the Dogme 95 manifesto, a set of rules designed to turn movies away from the Hollywood bent. Featuring shaky hand-held cameras and all-on location shooting, the Dogme movies tell chilling, true-to-life stories.

Von Trier has helped to pave the way for all sorts of movies, including those of his 'Dogme' brothers, Thomas Vinterberg *(The Celebration)* and Annette K. Olesen *(Small Accidents)*, who have both won awards at major international festivals.

Urban crime dramas, like *Pusher* (1996) and *Bleeder* (1999), by film-maker Nicolas Winding Refn, feed off the tensions between Danes and immigrants.

Cinemas

Det Danske Filminstitut

Gothersgade and Landemærket; tel: 33 74 34 12; www.dfi.dk; film- and bookshop Tue–Sun noon–6pm, restaurant and café Tue–Fri noon–10pm, Sat–Sun 10am–10pm, screenings Tue–Sun; bus: 350s; map p.138 B3

This really is the heart of Danish cinema. Not only do they guarantee to be showing the latest Danish films, but they run extensive seasons of World and Rep. cinema that are sure to inspire the next generation of von Triers.

The fantastic café and restaurant, not to mention the film and bookshop that could serve as a research institution in some cities, could make this an all-day destination.

Empire Bio

Guldbergsgade 29F, Nørrebro; tel: 35 36 00 36; www.empirebio.dk; map p.134 B3

Tucked away down an alleyway only a short walk north of Nørrebro's main Skt Hans Torv, the Empire Bio shows a selection of Danish films and art-house movies from Europe and America.

The very intimate café makes a great place for a drink and other restaurants make the alley buzzy at night.

Grand Teatret

Mykkel Bryggers Gade 8; tel: 33 15 16 11; www.grandteatret.dk; map p.138 A2

The best cinema in the Strøget district. The interior is much more relaxed than the big brick façade suggests with six screens all well appointed with big cosy chairs. The bar-café is OK, but only for a quick drink.

Husets Biograf

Magstraede 14, 2nd floor; tel: 33 32 40 77; www.husetsbio.dk; map p.138 B2

A tiny little cinema located in the same complex as a popular gay club, the interior is not as lavish as the other options in the city, but the selection of films is unique.

Below: *The Idiots*, directed by Lars von Trier.

Food and Drink

The Danes like to think of themselves as the 'French of the North' – for their gastronomic expertise rather than other national characteristics. The plethora of fine restaurants, cafés and bars in Copenhagen support this belief. Plus, there are tempting bakeries, delectable delis, *smørrebrød* kiosks and many microbreweries for dedicated beer lovers. If you are looking for superior food shopping, the food halls in both Magasin du Nord on Kongens Nytorv and Illums on Strøget are both very good, and Copenhagen's gourmet food street can be found in Vesterbro on Værnedamsvej.

Smørrebrød

Visitors will soon discover that unique Danish creation, *smørrebrød* or 'bread and butter', but do not be misled by the over-simplification of these delicious open sandwiches. Rye bread, thickly-spread with butter or goose fat, forms the basis for open sandwiches topped with salmon, eel, plaice, herring, beef, liver *pâté*, ham, steak *tartare*, egg, cheese, chicken breast, turkey or seafood, and then garnished with sauces and vegetables, salads and herbs. *Smørrebrød* began as a hearty meal for agricultural workers who needed to top up their reserves at midday.

Below: the usual time for a *smørrebrød* is still midday, as a *frokost* or 'second breakfast'.

FROKOST

Copenhagen has several specialist *frokost* restaurants, which are usually open from 10am to 5pm. Many *frokost* restaurants prepare the toppings, and the guest selects the type of bread, topping, sauce or marinade from the spread at the bar by marking a list; a pair of skilful hands will then make up the snack. There are also self-service counters, where you can buy a ready-made *smørrebrød* to take away.

Café Food

If you want to eat well and cheaply, then go to one of the cafés, pubs or restaurants that serve hot meals at lunchtime. The choice of food will not be so great as in the evening, but it will be appetising and filling. The *dagens ret* (dish of the day), including coffee, is usually good value. Many newer cafés serve cheap snacks and light meals throughout the day. Copenhagen has many mobile snack bars, serving *pølser* (sausages) in a variety of ways.

SEE ALSO CAFÉS AND BARS P.28–33

Ida Davidsen's family have been producing *smørrebrød* for the locals for over a century and their restaurant is now something of a national institution, with over 250 fillings to choose from. Store Kongensgade 70; tel: 33 91 36 55; www.idadavidsen.dk.

Restaurant Food

Copenhagen is home to ten restaurants with 11 Michelin stars between them. You will find every kind of world food available – from *sushi* to Mexican, Italian to Indian. There are even dedicated Australian restaurants.

Fusion food, taking inspiration from many different areas of the world and combining them with local, Danish produce is especially popular,

Left: a traditional Danish lunch.

with Franco-Danish food being a particular favourite.

Prices vary but almost all restaurants, even some of the very smart ones, offer set prices, depending on how many courses you eat. So, in some instances, what might seem rather expensive for two or three courses, becomes somewhat more reasonable if you decide to splash out and go for four or five instead.

SEE ALSO RESTAURANTS P.116–25

Some Traditional Danish Dishes

Aeggekage
Rich omelette served with dark bread

Medisterpolse
Danish sausage often served with sautéed mushrooms

Flæskesteg med rødkål
Roast pork with red cabbage

Frikadelle
Home-made meatballs made from fried ground pork

Gravadlax
Cured or salted salmon marinated in dill and served with a mustard sauce

Husets platter
Traditional Danish platter

Kryddersild
Herring pickled in various types of marinade

Læskesteg
Roast pork, usually with crackling

Marineret sild
Marinated herring

Fish and Seafood

Fish (or small canapés) is the traditional first course of a full meal. It is also available as a main course, and a great variety of fish appears on the Danish menu. Herring is a firm favourite, and may be served pickled, marinated or fried, with various dressings.

Succulent red Greenland shrimps are also popular. Lobster is widely offered – though pricey – as is crab, cod and halibut. Plaice features frequently and is served boiled or fried with a garnish of shellfish or parsley. You'll see the Øresund *rødspætte* (red-spot plaice) on every menu.

One great Scandinavian delicacy is *gravad laks*, in which raw salmon is pressed with salt and a small amount of sugar, and then sprinkled generously with chopped dill. A creamy sauce of oil, mustard and sugar is traditionally served alongside it.

Chocolate

Alida Marstrand
Bredgade 14; tel: 33 15 13 63; www.alidamarstrand.dk; Mon–Fri 10am–5pm, Sat 10am–1pm; bus: 1a, 15, 19; map p.139 C1
This is Copenhagen's oldest chocolate shop and dates from 1930. Everything is still hand-made on site.

Amokka
Grønnegade 4; tel: 33 93 52 52; www.amokka.dk; Mon–Thur 10am–5.30pm, Fri 10am–6pm, Sat 10am–4pm; map p.138 B3
You can get chocolate everything here, from yummy chocolate pasta to body paint.

SEE ALSO CAFÉS AND BARS P. 33

Bojesen
Vesterbrogade 4a; tel: 33 91 46 00; www.bojesen.dk; bus: 6a, 26, S-tog: Hovedbanegård; map p.138 A2
Luxury chocolate maker, Bojesen trained in Paris under Michelin-starred chefs; his chocolates are

Below: though a tip is never refused, most bills include a service charge.

Left: fancy treats from La Glace, the perfect pudding after some *gravad laks* and *akvavit.*

known for their unusual flavours.

Frederiksberg Chokolade
Frederiksberg Allé 64; tel: 33 22 36 35; www.frederiksberg chokolade.dk; Mon–Thur 10.30am–5.30pm, Fri 10.30am–6pm, Sat 10am–2pm; bus: 26; map p.136 A3–B3
Seventy different types of hand-made chocolate are produced on the premises.

Løgismose
Nordre Toldbod 16; tel: 33 32 93 32; www.loegismose.dk; Mon–Fri 10am–7pm, Sat 10am–3pm
Gourmet supermarket that stocks a large assortment of Summerbird chocolates.

Peter Beier Chokolade
Falkoner Allé 43; tel: 38 33 18 01; ww.peterbeierchokolade.dk; Mon–Thur 10am–6pm, Fri 10am–7pm, Sat 10am–5pm; bus: 18; map p.136 A3–B3; **Nordrefrihavnsgade 20**; tel: 35 38 01 10; *see above*; bus: 3A; map p.135 D4; **Skoubogade 1**; tel: 33 93 07 17; *see above*, Sat 10am–4pm; map p.138 A3
Seventy percent cocoa products filled with truffles, creams, spices and nuts. The shop on Skoubogade has chocolate fountains playing in the window.

Summerbird Chocolaterie
Kronprinsessgade 11; tel: 33 93 80 40; www.summerbird.dk; Mon–Thur 11am–6pm, Fri 11am–7pm, Sat 10.30am–4pm; map p.138 B4
Delicious chocolates, often combined with marzipan or nougat; *flødeboller* is the house speciality featuring a dark chocolate outside, a traditional sweet filling, on a marzipan base – served up in the Michelin-starred Kong Hans Kælder restaurant.
SEE ALSO RESTAURANTS P.119–20

Pâtisseries and Confectioners

Emmerys
Vesterbrogade 34; tel: 33 22 77 63; www.emmerys.dk; Mon–Thur 7am–6pm, Fri 7am–7pm, Sat 7am–3pm, Sun 7.30am–3.30pm; bus: 6a, 26; map p.136 C3; **Bertram Hotel, Vesterbrogade 107A**; tel: 33 25 04 67; *see above*; bus: 6a, 26; map p.136 B3; **Nørrebrogade 8**; tel: 35 36 94 00; *see above*; bus: 5a, 350s; map p.134 B2; **Øster Farmiagsgade 39**; tel: 35 25 10 67; *see above*, Sat–Sun 7am–3pm; bus: 14, 40; map p.135 C2; **Østerbrogade 51**; tel: 35 25 12 10; *see above*, Sat–Sun 7am–3pm; bus: 1A, 14; map p.135 D4; **Store Strandstraede 21**; tel: 33 93 01 33; Mon–Thur 7.30am–6pm, Fri 7.30am–6.30, Sat–Sun 8am–5pm; map p.139 C3
This is Denmark's best and most well-known organic store. Its main claim to fame is its bread and pastries, but it sells plenty of other delicious goodies along the way.

Kransekagehuset Summerbird
Ny Østergade 9; tel: 33 13 19 02; www.kransekagehuset.net; Mon–Fri 10am–6pm, Sat 10am–4pm; map p.138 B3
Famous *pâtisserie* with eight confectioners making chocolates on the premises.

La Glace
Skoubogade 3; map p.138 A3
Heavenly cake shop dating back to 1870; serves excellent hot chocolate too.
SEE ALSO CAFÉS AND BARS P. 30–1

Beer and *Akvavit*

Carlsberg is a national institution – as a beer and also as a supporter of art and cul-

> You might never have thought about the origin of 'Danish pastries' before and although the Danes make no claim to them, calling them *wienerbrødd* (Viennese bread), they are readily available, delicious and very moreish, as you will have worked out if confronted with them in your breakfast buffet. Organic bread is increasingly popular and there are several lovely cake and chocolate shops that you might find a tad more than interesting.

Vodka is often drunk as a chaser after beer. For the more wary among you, it is advisable to eat something, even just a small piece of bread, before you knock it back.

ture. However, apart from Carlsberg, the Danes have become very interested in individual beers created by local microbreweries, of which there are now 25 in Denmark, five of which are in Copenhagen and another eight outside.

Apart from beer, the other national alcohol is akvavit, a fiery vodka that comes in several flavours, the most popular is made with caraway seeds.

Brewpub

Vestergade 29; tel: 33 32 00 60; www.brewpub.dk; restaurant: Mon–Sat noon–10pm, pub: Mon–Thur noon–midnight; Fri–Sat noon–2am; map p.138 A2

Run by a female-brewer who produces four in-house microbrews and seven 'guest brews'; you can also order a 10-cl sampler of five different beers.

Færgekroen

Tivoli; tel: 33 12 94 12; www.faergekroen.dk; ***see p.115*****; map p.138 A1–2**

Another microbrewery in Tivoli in an inn dating from 1834; two hand-brewed beers on offer alongside Danish fare from the kitchen

Nørrebro Bryghus

Ryesgade 3; tel: 35 30 05 30; www.noerrebrobryghus.dk; Mon–Wed 11am–midnight, Thur–Sat 11am–2am, Sun 11am–10pm; map p.135 D4

Makes its own Belgian white beer, New York pre-prohibition lager, Bombay pale ale and an English-style stout. There is also a modern Danish brasserie where you can drink beer to accompany your food.

Vesterbro Bryghus

Vesterbrogade 2; tel: 33 11 17 05; www.vesterbrobryghus.dk; Mon–Thur 11.30am–2am, Fri–Sat 11.30am–4am; bus: 6a, 26; map p.138 A2

Five beers brewed here from traditional Austrian recipes; atmospheric long bar and restaurant with open grill and beer-influence menu.

Coffee and Tea

Surprisingly perhaps, Copenhagen considers itself to produce a very good cup of coffee. It has several shops dedicated to superior beans. There's also an excellent tea shop.

AC Perch's Tea Shop

5 Kronprinsessegade; tel: 33 15 35 62; www.perchs.dk; Mon–Thur 9am–5.30pm, Fri 9am–7pm; Sat 9am–2.30pm; map p.138 B4

Delightful little tea importer that has been dispensing tea leaves and more since 1834; The shop is a charming time warp with knowledgeable, friendly staff. The tearoom upstairs offers 150 different blends and English high teas, including scones and clotted cream. They have just opened a franchise in Tokyo so they must be doing something right.

Baresso

This is the main coffee chain in the city and serves a decent cup. Bill Clinton nipped into the Vesterbro shop when he was in town in 1997.

Estate Coffee

Gammell Kongevej 1; tel: 38 11 12 11; www.estatecoffee.dk; Mon–Fri 8am–10pm, Sat–Sun 10am–10pm; bus: 14, 15; map p.136 C3

Winner of the 2006 Barista Championship, Estate coffee buys its beans direct from small growers worldwide and roasts them in its own micro roasting facility in Valby. The coffee house has a huge menu of coffees (hot and cold) tea and chocolate – and cakes, of course.

Sort Kaffe og Vinyl

Skydebanegade 4, Vesterbro; tel: 35 36 22 32; Tue–Fri 8am–6pm, Sat–Sun 11am–6pm; map p.136 C2

Part coffee house, part vinyl record store, the coffee comes from a local micro-roaster and if you like it, you can buy the beans.

Below: tea is well made in Copenhagen, though it is the poor relation to a cup of coffee.

Gay and Lesbian

Liberal, laid-back and politically active, Copenhagen finds itself as a hub for gay culture in northern Europe. The Danish National Association of Gays and Lesbians was one of the first such organisations to be founded on the continent, and since the end of World War II, it has pioneered the way for civil partnerships and adoption, and now provides the best up-to-the-minute information on their Gay Guide website. Nightlife is varied with everything from traditionally Danish cosy cafés to leather bars and a nightclub, PAN, that Swedes cross the Øresund to visit.

Advice and Information

Landsforeningen for Bøsser og Lesbiske
Teglgårdsstræde 13, Baghuset; tel: 33 13 19 48; www.lbl.dk, www.gayguide.dk; noon–4.30pm; map p.138 A3
The Danish National Association of Gays and Lesbians was founded in 1948, well before many of its European colleagues. In addition to their political works, they maintain the GayGuide website that provides up-to-date information on bars, accommodation and other establishments. Its library, café and offices occupy an entire building alongside the gay montly *Panbladet* and gay Radio Rosa.

Out and About
www.out-and-about.dk
A predominantly Danish magazine targeted at gay men; selected sections published in English to assist tourists.

Bars and Clubs

As Copenhagen is gay-friendly throughout, venues are spread all over the city centre. The main cluster is along Studiestræde and its side streets.

Boiz
Magstræde 12–14; tel: 33 14 52 70; www.boiz.dk; Sun–Thur 11am–2pm, Fri–Sat 11am–5am, reduced hours in winter; map p.138 B2
This restaurant, lounge and bar is next to an arthouse cinema, but provides its own entertainment with drag shows and art exhibitions.

Can Can
Mikkel Bryggers Gade 11; tel: 33 11 50 10; Sun–Thur 2pm–2am, Fri–Sat 2pm–5am; map p.138 A2
A friendly bar (mostly men) just off the Rådhuspladsen end of Strøget; nothing more than a jukebox and conversation for entertainment.

Centralhjørnet
Kattesundet 18; tel: 33 11 85 49; www.centralhjornet.dk; daily noon–2am; map p.138 A2
The oldest gay bar in Copenhagen, but a bit basic. They are happy for you to bring the neighbouring deli's sandwiches in if you order a drink. They have also created a long list of uniquely named alcoholic drinks to help you get the party started.

Chaca
Studiestræde 39; tel: 33 73 10 20; www.chaca.dk; Thur–Sat 4pm–*c.*4am; map p.138 A2–3]
At last, one for the girls' nights out. With the number of gay bars in Copenhagen it's a shame that this is one of the few that focuses on the women in town.

Jailhouse Copenhagen
Studiestræde 12; tel: 33 15 22 55; www.jailhousecph.dk; Sun–Thur 2pm–2am, Fri–Sat

> In 1989, Denmark became the first country in the world to recognise marriage between two persons of the same sex. In 1999, it became possible for married gays to adopt their partners' children – creating a broader legal definition of the term family.

Left: participants in the annual Gay Pride parade.

2pm–5am, restaurant Thur–Sat 6–11pm; map p.138 A2–3
A unique angle on upstairs/downstairs social divisions. Upstairs it's all white linen tablecloths, while downstairs it's more likely black leather that will influence the atmosphere and the bartenders dressed in police uniforms.

Masken Bar
Studiestræde 33; tel: 33 91 09 37; www.maskenbar.dk; Mon–Thur 4pm–2am, Fri–Sat 4pm–5am, Sun 3pm–2am; map p.138 A2–3
Divided over two floors, Masken hosts live music and drag shows.

Men's Bar
Teglgårdsstræde 3; tel: 33 12 73 03; www.mensbar.dk; daily 3pm–2am; map p.138 A3
As the name suggests, this isn't really the place for women on a night out, in fact women are banned. This is a place for men only; preferably men with a penchant for leather. There is also a popular free brunch on the first Sunday of every month when leather gives way to herring and *pâtés*.

PAN Disco
Knabrostraede 3; tel: 33 11 37 84; www.pan-cph.dk; Thur–Fri 11pm–5am, Sat 11pm–6am; map p.138 B2
This popular three-storey disco has a mixed gay and lesbian crowd and is one of Europe's largest gay clubs and the largest nightclub in the Øresund region. The main dance floor plays a mixture of house, whereas PAN2 gives in to high-pitched pop divas and late-night *karaoke*. There are chill out rooms and a courtyard for those that just want to get away from it all. A membership policy has been introduced, though all tourists are still welcomed.

Accommodation

Copenhagen Rainbow
4th Floor, Frederiksberggade 25C, Strøget; tel: 33 14 10 20; www.copenhagen-rainbow.dk; map p.138 A2
Five rooms in this guesthouse are for gays only. Each comes with a queen-size bed that can be made into two singles if so desired. Facilities are basic (no TV), but its location on Strøget is ideal. Prices start at 750 DKK per room, per night and include a continental breakfast. Two-night minimum.

Ebab
www.ebab.dk
A worldwide agency offering gay-friendly accommodation in guestrooms or apartments throughout the world.

Hotel Windsor
Frederiksborggade 30, tel: 33 11 08 30; www.hotelwindsor.dk; bus: 5a, 350s, S-tog: Nørreport; map p.138 A2
A more traditional hotel than the Rainbow; rooms have cable TV and wash basins. Showers and toilets are located in the corridors. Prices start at 525DKK for a double and includes breakfast.

Travel Agency

Out Scandinavia
Grønningen 15; tel: 33 18 92 74; www.outscandinavia.dk
Offering various tourist services including hotel packages, dinner cruises in Copenhagen harbour, sightseeing tours and information about gay life in Copenhagen.

Below: all dressed up....

History

c. AD 985	The Jelling Stones, runic inscriptions describing what is thought to be the first evidence of Denmark's conversion to Christianity.
c.1075	First appearance in Denmark of stone buildings.
c.1160	The foundations are laid for the first castle built on Slotholmen by Copenhagen's founder, Bishop Absalon. Considered the most interesting ruins in the capital today, you can see them now beneath Christiansborg Palace in the centre of Copenhagen.
c.1200	Some 1,200 churches had been built in Denmark by now. The churches are the main architectural survivors from the Middle Ages and their upkeep bears witness to the social bonds and coherence maintained through the centuries.
c.1250–1500	During the Gothic period, many churches were enlarged and vaults erected on earlier structures.
1254	The village of Købmandshavn, 'Merchants' Port', receives a charter. The Hanseatic League recognises it as an important post for Baltic trade.
1282	Erik V forced to sign a Great Charter at Nyborg, in which he rules with the nobles in the Council of the Danish Realm *(Danmarks Riges Råd)*.
1332–40	The Holstein dynasty rules Denmark.
1354	Valdemar IV restores the throne and unites the country after a period of civil war.
1369	Bishop Absalon's castle is demolished and replaced in 1376.
1397	Margrethe I sets up the Kalmar Union, an alliance with Norway and Sweden.
1417	Erik VII settles in Copenhagen and builds a palace in Helsingør.
1425–79	Copenhagen flourishes and grows; enriched by levies on ships passing through the Sound. Population rises from 3,000 to 10,000 and, in 1443 it becomes the capital of Denmark. In 1479 Copenhagen University is founded .
1523–34	The Kalmar Union ends with Gustav Vasa's coronation as King of Sweden. Norway remains part of Denmark.

8th century: Vikings began their exploration and invasion of Great Britain and Ireland.

10th century : the stones at Jelling were carved.

1397: a rare depiction of Queen Margrethe.

1536 Christian III makes Protestantism the official state religion.

1546–83 After six epidemics, sanitary conditions improve with the introduction of a new water supply to a well on Gammeltorv, now the Caritas Fountain.

1588–1648 Copenhagen booms during the Renaissance period, and many important buildings are erected, including Rosenborg Slot, Børsen, the Rundetårn and the new Kronborg Slot in Helsingør, built for King Frederik II (and the fictional home of Shakespeare's Prince Hamlet). Christian IV enlarges the town and harbour. The Thirty Years' War ends this prosperous period as Sweden gains much Danish land, and by 1648 the country is ruined.

1648–70 Frederik III rules, and plunges Denmark into war against Sweden. A third of the country is lost to Sweden. The gates of Oresund and Copenhagen become the border between the two countries; fortifications are strengthened.

1665 Frederik III strips the nobility of power and establishes an hereditary absolute monarchy.

1711–12 Plague strikes Copenhagen; 20,000 of its 65,000 population die.

1728 and 1795 Two fires destroy half of Copenhagen's housing, leading to major reconstruction work.

1732 Christian VI replaces København Slot with the palace of Christiansborg.

1754–1800s The Copenhagen Art Academy is founded (1754). Inspired by the internationally acclaimed sculptor Bertel Thorvaldsen (1768–1844), the subsequent creative output leads to Denmark's "Golden Age" of art, which flourished from 1815 through to the middle of the 19th century.

1783–1853 Christopher Wilhelm Eckersberg, painter and professor at the Art Academy, regarded today as the 'father of Danish painting'. He influenced a generation of young artists – the 'hard core of the Golden Age'.

1784–88 Crown Prince Frederik passes reforms allowing 60 per cent of Danish peasants to become landowners. In 1788 serfdom is abolished.

1801 The English fleet destroys much of the Danish navy in Copenhagen harbour, during the Napoleonic Wars. This forces Denmark to renounce its 1794 armed neutrality treaty with Sweden, Prussia and Russia.

16th century: *Dawn: Luther at Erfurt*, by Joseph Noel Paton.

1588: Christian IV's coronation day.

1732: Christiansborg Slot replaces the old fortress.

1768–1844: Thorvaldsen inspired Denmark's Golden Age.

1807–13 English fleet attack and destroy much of Copenhagen. The Danes join the continental alliance against England. By 1813 Denmark is bankrupt.

1807: a depiction of the Danish fleet at war by Carl Neumann.

1814 Treaty of Kiel cedes Norway to Sweden; Denmark keeps Iceland, the Faroe Islands and Greenland.

1847 Denmark's first railway links Copenhagen with Roskilde.

1848–9 Frederik VII abolishes absolute monarchy.

1857 Copenhagen's old ramparts are demolished to make way for new homes. Industrialisation draws in the poor from the countryside. By 1900, the population is nearly 400,000.

1864 After war with Prussia and Austria, the Danes cede Schleswig, Holstein and Lauenburg to Germany.

1865: a city street in Copenhagen.

Late 1800s The 'Skagen painters' – named after the artists' colony in northern Jutland – turned their backs on the traditional teachings of the Art Academy and like the French Impressionists concerned themselves with everyday life and natural light effects. Leading Skagen artists included Peter Severin Krøyer (1851–1909) and the artist couple Anna and Michael Ancher (1859–1935). A good selection of Skagen art is on display in Den Hirschsprunske Samling Museum.

1921–40 Construction of Grundtvig's Kirke (Grundtvig's Memorial Church), in memory of Nikolai Frederik Severin Grundtvig (1783–1872), a renowned educationalist, austere parson and prolific hymn writer. The church is a monument to 20th-century Danish architecture, designed by Peder Jensen-Klimt.

1783–1872: N.F.S. Grundtvig, priest, writer and pioneering educationalist.

1914–18 Denmark remains neutral during World War I and profits greatly from its position.

1915 Women gain the right to vote.

1924 Social Democrats elected to power for the first time. They are led by Thorvald Stauning.

1929–40 A welfare state is set up under the left-wing coalition dominated by the Social Democrats in response to the 1930s economic depression.

1940–45 Denmark invaded by Germany in 1940, retaining limited self-government. In 1943, the government resigns and Denmark joins the Allies. The Danish Resistance help 7,000 Jews to escape to Sweden. Denmark is liberated by the British on 5 May.

1940: German tanks enter Denmark.

1948 A group of artists set up the abstract movement CoBrA (Copenhagen-Brussels-Amsterdam), painting in a Baroque-like surreal style with emphasis on brushwork and colour. Its leading exponent was painter Asger Jorn (1914–73); others included Pierre Alechinsky and Karel Appel.

1914–73: Asger Jorn, Danish painter and leader of the CoBrA movement.

1968 onwards During the 1960s, the Experimental School of Art rose to prominence, in response to the CoBrA initiative. Its most prominent member was the Copenhagen abstract artist and sculptor Per Kirkeby (b.1938), who also enjoyed a successful career as an architect. Bjørn Nørgård (b.1947) gained notoriety in 1970 when he led a horse into a field and butchered it. He filmed the process and kept the pieces in jars.

1968–71 Following student unrest in Europe, squatters found the Free State of Christiania in Christianshavn, with its own schools and housing.

1968–71: Christiania founded after studen unrest.

1972 Margrethe II crowned the new Queen of Denmark. Denmark joins the EEC (today's EU).

1989 Denmark becomes the first country to recognise same-sex marriages.

1998 Denmark signs the Amsterdam Treaty, bringing the country closer to European integration.

2000 Denmark votes not to adopt the euro. The Øresund Bridge, a road and rail link, opens between Copenhagen and Malmo in Sweden.

2000: the Øresund bridge opens.

2001 A right-wing coalition, led by Anders Fogh Rasmussen, takes power in an electoral swing to the right. The new programme includes cuts in spending on environmental measures and promises to tighten immigration controls.

2002 Copenhagen's first metro line opens.

2004 Crown Prince Frederik marries Australian-born Crown Princess Mary in Copenhagen

2005 The Opera House opens.

2006 The *Jyllands–Posten* publishes 12 cartoons depicting the Prophet Muhammead, causing offfence in the Muslim community worldwide.

2005: the Opera House has led a renaissance on the waterfront.

2007 Nearly 700 protesters are arrested following three days of riots in Copenhagen's areas of Nørrebro and Christiania after authorities destroy the Youth House, a popular culture centre for leftist youth. Weeks later an international survey finds Copenhagen to be the happiest place in the EU.

Hotels

Many of Copenhagen's hotels are near Central Station, the cheaper ones are around the Vesterbro area and the more expensive ones on and around Rådhuspladsen, within a very short walk of the city's main sights. There are also several smart hotels in and around Kongens Nytorv and Nyhavn, but don't always expect a view. A little bit out of the way, but with good views, are the new hotels on Kalvebod Brygge, south of Slotsholmen. Alternatively, head away from the tourist centre and stay near Rosenborg or Amalienborg or even in the suburbs – they really are not very far away.

Tivoli and Rådhuspladsen

Danhostel Copenhagen City

H.C. Andersens Boulevard 50; tel: 33 11 85 85; www.danhostel.dk/copenhagencity, copenhagencity@danhostel.dk; €; bus: 33; map p.138 B1

This is very much a cut above your average youth hostel; five-star, bang in the centre, modern, comfortable and with plenty of family rooms (2–6 people). It also has great views over the city. You will need an international YHA card but the investment is made up by saving on the cost of a bed.

Hotel Alexandra

H.C. Andersens Boulevard 8; tel: 33 74 44 44; www.hotel-alexandra.dk; reservations@www.hotel-alexandra.dk; €€€; bus: 33; map p.138 A2

A lovely old hotel just off Rådhuspladsen in a building originating from 1880, it is stylishly decorated with plenty of 20th-century classics from Arne Jacobsen furniture (see room 223 in particular) to Kaare Klint chairs and Poul Henningsen lighting. Definitely one of Copenhagen's nicer hotels (of which there are many).

Hotel Astoria

Banegårdspladsen 4, tel: 33 42 99 00; www.dgi-byen.com; €€; S-tog: Hovedbanegård; map p.138 A1

A new member of the DGI-Byen group right by the Hovedbanegård station. The rooms were being updated to suit modern tastes at the time of writing, but the hotel is due to reopen during 2007.

Hotel Cab Inn City

Mitchellsgade 14, tel: 33 46 16 16; www.cab-inn.dk, city@cabinn.com; €; map p.138 A1

There are three of these attractive, functional budget hotels in Copenhagen *(see page 67 for the other two)*. Their decor is modern Danish, space is used effectively (many rooms have bunk beds – think of a ship's cabin, hence 'cab-inn') and the all-in breakfasts are healthy and copious. A good option for families and anyone not expecting to do much more than sleep here. This hotel is only a short walk from Tivoli.

Below: there is nothing bland about Hotel Fox.

Left: snug and stylish at Hotel Front.

A good location next to Vesterport Station and a few minutes' walk from Rådhuspladsen and Tivoli Gardens, this modern, stylish hotel is far more preopossessing on the inside than on the outside with well-appointed, elegant rooms, fine restaurants and on-site parking.

Le Meridien Palace Hotel
Rådhuspladsen 57; tel: 33 14 40 50, 33 42 85 21; www.palace-hotel.dk, booking@starwoodhotels.com; €€€€; bus: all Rådhuspladsen buses; map p.138 A2
An imposing historical landmark on Rådhuspladsen with its own rival clocktower. The Palace will remain open while it undergoes a radical renovation – due to be finished at the end 2007 – which will take it from four-star to five-star status.

Formerly a traditional hotel with Victorian decor, the public areas will retain their old-world grandeur while the bedrooms are being stylishly tarted up for a more modern designer-feel. The rooms are all a good size too.

Radisson SAS
Hammerichsgade 1; tel: 38 15 65 00; www.radissonsas.com, copenhagen@radissonsas.com; €€€€; bus: 6a, 26, S-tog: Vesterport, Hovedbanegård; map p.137 C3
This is Copenhagen's most iconic hotel; designed, down to the cutlery and the doorknobs, by the famous architect and designer, Arne Jacobsen. Although, only one

Hotel Danmark
Vester Voldgade 89; tel: 33 11 48 06, www.hotel-danmark.dk, hotel@hotel-danmark.dk; €€; bus: 6a, 12, 26, 29, 33; map p.138 A2
Adjacent to Rådhuspladsen and close to Strøget. Modern bright building has rooms tastefully furnished in subdued Scandinavian style. Underground parking.

Hotel Fox
Jarmers Plads 3; tel: 33 13 30 00; www.hotelfox.dk, hotel@hotelfox.dk; €€; bus: 2a, 5a, 14, 66, 67, 68, 173e, 250s; map p.138 A3
By the busy Ørstedsparken, a short walk from Rådhuspladsen, this is one of Copenhagen's most extreme hotels – it's either your cup of tea, or it isn't. All the rooms have been individually designed by 21 international artists and vary from startling white to crimson, green and fully-tiled. Check out rooms on the web before you check in. The bar and restaurant downstairs are good.

Hotel Kong Frederik
Vester Voldgade 25; tel: 33 12 59 02; www.remmen.dk, kongfrederik@remmen.dk; €€€; bus: 6a, 12, 26, 29, 33; map p.138 A2
Although named in 1898, its history as a hotel and inn dates back to the 14th century. Situated close to Rådhuspladsen and Tivoli, a recent renovation has retained its classic English atmosphere.

Imperial Hotel
Vester Farimagsgade 9; tel: 33 12 80 00; www.imperialhotel. dk, imperialhotel@arp-hansen. dk; €€€; bus: 12, 40; map p.137 C4

Below: the Palace Hotel's location on Rådhuspladsen is great for exploring the centre.

Prices for a standard double room in high season:
€ under 1000DKK
€€ 1000–1400DKK
€€€ 1400–1600DKK
€€€€ over 1600DKK

Above: Jacobsen's Swan and Egg chairs in the SAS Radisson were designed specifically for the hotel in 1960.

room (606) retains its original decor, this hotel is still popular with the rich and famous and has a nice retro/modern feel. There is also a very popular restaurant, Alberto K, on the top floor, with fabulous views over Tivoli Gardens and the city. Centrally located and just a short walk from Rådhuspladsen, Strøget and the University Quarter. There is also a sauna and private parking.
SEE ALSO ARCHITECTURE P.27; PAMPERING P.111

Scandic Copenhagen
Vester Søgade 6; tel: 33 14 35 35; www.scandic-hotels.com/copenhagen, copenhagen@scandic-hotels.com; €€€; map p.137 C4
A comfortable skyscraper hotel looking out over Copenhagen's reservoirs. It is popular with both business and leisure travellers and can offer non-smoking floors, free internet, friendly staff and a recommended breakfast.

Sofitel Plaza
Bernstorffsgade 4; tel: 33 14 92 62; www.sofitel.com, sofitel@accorhotel.dk; €€€€; bus: 5a, 30, 40, 47, 250s, S-tog: Hovedbanegård; map p.130 A2
Commissioned by Frederik VIII in 1913, this hotel has well-fitted rooms and lovely decoration throughout. The attractive Library Bar has been voted one of the five best bars in the world by *Forbes* magazine. Delicious buffet breakfast.

The Square
Rådhuspladsen 14; tel: 33 38 12 00; www.thesquarecopenhagen.com, thesquarecopenhagen@arp-hansen.dk; €€€€; bus: all Rådhuspladsen buses; map p.138 A2
In the heart of Rådhuspladsen, this air-conditioned hotel is converted from an office block and not much to look at on the outside. However, there are several grades of stylishly decorated rooms and a rooftop breakfast room with fine views and a good spread. Note that rooms with a view over the square can be a bit noisy if you open the window onto the balcony.

Strøget and Around

Ascot Hotel
Studiestræde 61, tel: 33 12 60 00; www.ascothotel.dk, hotel@ascot-hotel.dk; €€; map p.138 A2–3
Set in a distinguished old bathhouse building a few steps from City Hall (Rådhus) in the Latin Quarter, this pleasantly decorated hotel, with a mixture of antiques

> Many hotels include breakfast with the room; always ask as otherwise it usually costs between 1000 and 1700 DKK. This may seem a lot but a coffee and pastry will set you back 600–700 DKK in a café, so a hearty breakfast of all you can eat may well be a good investment.

and modern furniture, also offers suites, some with kitchenettes if you are into a bit of self-catering. It's very central and you won't be bothered by traffic.

Hotel Kong Arthur
Nørre Søgade 11; tel: 33 11 12 12; www.kongarthur.dk, hotel@kongarthur.dk; €€€€; map p.134 C1
Established in 1882, and situated beside Peblinge Lake, this hotel has retained much of its original charm and has a pretty conservatory-type inner court. A popular choice with both Danish and foreign visitors; it has a friendly and thoroughly Danish atmosphere. Some of the suites have jacuzzis.

Hotel 27
Løngangstræde 27; tel: 70 27 56 27; www.hotel27.dk, info@hotel27.dk; €€; bus: 6a; map p.138 A2–B2
Formerly an unremarkable hotel, Hotel 27 has been renamed and done up under new management – stylishly decorated to Danish taste – this is a reasonably priced 'life-style' hotel in the centre of town. It is also home to the upcoming Absolut Icebar, which will open when the last of the 200 rooms are renovated in 2007.
SEE ALSO CAFÉS AND BARS P.28

Left: the Astoria's narrow, carriage-like building dates from 1936 and is an excellent example of Functionalist style.

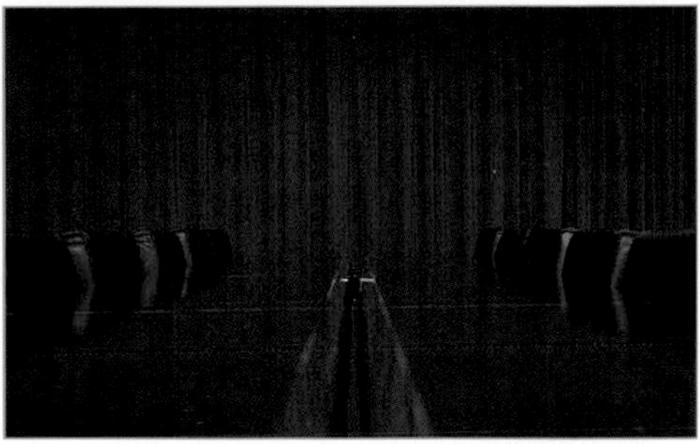

Above: the Sankt Petri hotel is Scandinavian chic at its best, with minimalist decor and Bang & Olufsen televisions in every room.

Ibsens Hotel
Vendersgade 23, tel: 33 13 19 13; www.ibsenshotel.dk; €€; map p.138 A4
In the same group as the Hotel Kong Arthur, this pleasant, comfortable three-star hotel is located between Nørreport Station and Peblinge Lake, about 15-minutes' walk from the city centre.

Sankt Petri
Krystalgade 22; tel: 33 45 91 00; www.hotelsktpetri.com, reservation@hotelsktpetri.com; €€€€; map p.138 A3
This fabulous and stylish five-star hotel is in the heart of the Latin Quarter by St Mary's Cathedral. Original art and orchids decorate every room, with designer modern décor and great bathrooms. There is also a good restaurant, a couple of excellent bars and a pretty atrium where live jazz plays or international DJs spin their discs. In summer, there is also an attractive outdoor area for drinks and dinner.
SEE ALSO CAFÉS AND BARS P.29

Kongens Nytorv and Nyhavn

Best Western Hotel City
Peder Skramsgade 24; tel: 33 13 06 66; www.hotelcity.dk; €€; map p.139 C2
Located in an elegant townhouse, the City has an international feel, clearly expressed in the hotel's striking modern décor. It has a hospitable and friendly atmosphere.

Copenhagen Strand
Havnegade 37; tel: 33 48 99 00; www.copenhagenstrand.dk, copenhagenstrand@arp-hansen.dk; €€€–€€€€; map p.139 C2
Opened in 2000, this hotel is in a converted warehouse dating from 1869. Situated on a side street just off Nyhavn, its decor is slightly rustic yet modern and calls to mind its maritime position and history.

Hotel d'Angleterre
Kongens Nytorv 34; tel: 33 12 00 95; www.remmen.dk; €€€€; bus: 1a, 15, 19, 26, 999, S-tog: Kongens Nytorv; map p.138 C3
Elegant rooms with a rather formal, old-fashioned ambience, plus a palm court, several banquet rooms, a fabulous spa and fitness centre with a 10x12m heated pool and a restaurant.
SEE ALSO PAMPERING P.110

Below: the wealthy, the important and the beautiful all take refuge behind the grand façade of the Hotel d'Angleterre.

Prices for a standard double room in high season:
€ under 1000DKK
€€ 1000–1400DKK
€€€ 1400–1600DKK
€€€€ over 1600DKK

Some hotels offer very good weekend rates for couples, often including free champagne and tickets to Tivoli or the opera. This especially applies to hotels that are dependent on weekday business travellers, and includes some of the more expensive hotels.

Hotel Opera
Tordenskjoldsgade 15; tel: 33 47 83 00; www.hotelopera.dk, hotelopera@arp-hansen.dk; €€€; map p.139 C2
Located on a side street close to the Royal Theatre on Kongens Nytorv, this charming English-inspired hotel (another in the reputable Arp-Hansen group) dates from 1869. Rooms are comfortable but vary in size – as do the beds. Check the website for more information.

71 Nyhavn Hotel
Nyhavn 71; tel: 33 43 62 00; www.71nyhavnhotelcopenhagen.dk, 71nyhavnhotel@arp-hansen.dk; €€€; map p.139 C3
Delightfully located at the foot of Nyhavn in a well-renovated and carefully restored warehouse, this charming hotel has a rustic atmosphere and great views over the harbour and the Sound, athough the rooms are a bit on the small side.

Amalienborg and Around

Comfort Hotel Esplanaden
Bredgade 78; tel: 33 48 10 00, co.esplanaden@choice.dk; €€€; bus: 1a, 15, 19; map p.135 E2
Located between Amalienborg and the Little Mermaid in the 250-year-old Frederiksstad quarter. A recently renovated hotel, part of the Choice chain, with clean, pleasant, if uninspiring, rooms, all non-smoking.

Copenhagen Admiral Hotel
Tolbodgade 24–8, tel: 33 74 14 14; www.admiralhotel.dk, booking@admiralhotel.dk; €€€–€€€€; map p.139 D3
Standing beside the harbour, equidistant between Nyhavn and the Amalienborg, this hotel was a granary constructed in 1787. Quiet, comfortably converted, with good-sized rooms and a charming, slightly rustic décor. Features its own, very good restaurant, nightclub and sauna.

Front hotel
Skt Annæ Plads 21; tel: 33 13 34 00; www.front.dk, info@front.dk; €€; map p.139 D3

Above: a chic and elegant setting at the Front Hotel.

Another in the sophisticated Remmen chain, this is a stylish, modern boutique hotel in a quiet location a short distance from Nyhavn quay. Kids are welcome and some rooms have a harbour view of the Opera House.

Phoenix Copenhagen
Bredgade 37; tel: 33 95 95 00; www.phoenixcopenhagen.dk, phoenixcopenhagen@arp-hansen.dk; €€€; bus: 1a, 15, 19; map p.139 C4
This is an elegant deluxe hotel in an 18th-century mansion, close to the Royal Palace and Kongens Nytorv. All rooms and suites are air-conditioned and furnished elegantly in the French Louis XVI style.

Rosenborg and Around

Hotel Christian IV
Dronningens Tværgade 45; tel: 33 32 10 44; www.hotelchristianiv.dk, reception@hotelchristianiv.dk; €€; map p.138 B4
A small, pleasant hotel located right beside the lovely King's Garden (Kon-

Below: constructed as a granary in 1787, the Copenhagen Admiral Hotel has retained the 200-year-old Pomeranian pine wooden beams in most rooms.

Prices for a standard double room in high season:
€ under 1000DKK
€€ 1000–1400DKK
€€€ 1400–1600DKK
€€€€ over 1600DKK

gens Have). Rooms are neat and bright, and fitted with modern Danish furniture; some quieter rooms overlook the inner courtyard. All guests are entitled to free entry to the gym round the corner on Adelsgade (www.fitnessdk.dk). There are plans for flatscreen TVs in the bedrooms.

Above: the laid-back breakfast room at the Bertrams Guldsmeden is like waking up in a Danish home.

Vesterbro and Frederiksberg

Axel Guldsmeden
Helgolandsgade 7–11; tel: 33 31 32 66; www.hotelguldsmeden.dk, axel@hotelguldsmeden.dk; €€€€; map p.137 C3
Opened in May 2007, with 40 of the 130 rooms ready, this is the fourth hotel (and first four-star hotel) in the Guldmedsen group. Following in its sister-hotels' footsteps, it offers lovely, individual rooms decorated in French colonial style – think dark wood and Egyptian cotton sheets, as well as all mod-cons and organic bath lovelies.

The group prides itself on its eco-friendly and organic credentials, which you will certainly encounter at their delicious breakfasts. Its advantages over the other hotels in the group include being closer to the centre of town and, when the hotel is complete, having a wellness centre and pool on site.

Bertrams Guldsmeden
Vesterbrogade 107; tel: 33 25 04 05; www.hotelguldsmeden.dk, bertrams@hotelguldsmeden.dk; €€€; bus: 6a, 26; map p.136 A3–B3
SEE CARLTON GULDSMEDEN BELOW

> Early bookings are usually cheaper than the official rack rates; web bookings are often cheaper still. However, it is always worth ringing up to find out if a hotel (even the expensive ones) can give you a better deal – they may be able to if business is slow.

Best Western Hotel Hebron
Helgolandsgade 4; tel: 33 31 69 06; www.bestwestern.dk, info@hebron.dk; €€; map p.137 C3
Close to the Central Station and Tivoli, and convenient for the shops of Strøget.

Cab Inn Copenhagen Express
Danasvej 32–34, Frederiksberg; tel: 33 21 04 00; www.cabinn.dk, express@cabinn.com; €; bus: 29; map p.130 B4

Cab Inn Scandinavia
Vodroffsvej 55, Frederiksberg; tel 35 36 11 11; scandinavia@cabinn.com; €; map p.136 C4
Both of these hotels in the stylish and popular budget chain are close to Peblinge Sø (Lake), about a 12-minute walk from Rådhuspladsen. You can sleep a family of four for under 1,000DKK. *(See also City Cab Inn p.62.)*

Carlton Guldsmeden
Vesterbrogade 66; tel: 33 22 15 00; www.hotelguldsmeden.dk, carlton@hotelguldsmeden.dk; €€; bus: 6a, 26; map p.136 B3
The Carlton and Bertrams Guldsmeden are both charming hotels with lovely décor belonging to the same chain as the new Axel Guldsmeden. They are both further down Vesterbrogade, which is fine to walk but a bus (these appear to be regular) or cab will be very appealing if you have had a long day.

Centrum
Helgolandsgade 14; tel: 33 31 31 11; www.dgi-byen.com/hotel, centrum@dgi-byen.dk; €; map p.137 C3
Formerly rather drab, this hotel has been renovated and is now significantly more light and airy. It is now part of the DGI-Byen group and guests have free entry to the DGI-Byen swimming centre and spa, 300m away and also a discount at the restaurant.
SEE ALSO PAMPERING P.111

Copenhagen Crown
Vesterbrogade 41; tel: 33 21 21 66; www.profilhotels.dk, copenhagencrown@profilhotels.dk; €;

Below: Bertrams' outdoor garden shows *hygge* at its best.

bus: 6a, 26; map p.136 C3
Newly updated and now part of the ProfilHotel group, this is a fresh, modern hotel, in the centre of things, with amenities for business travellers as well as holiday-makers.

Copenhagen Island
Kalvebod Brygghe 53; tel: 33 38 96 00; www.copenhagenisland.com, copenhagenisland@arp-hansen.dk; €€–€€€€; bus: 30; map p.137 D2
Brand new in 2006, and located on an artificial island in Copenhagen Harbour, just east of Vesterbro, this is Arp-Hansen's newest flagship luxury hotel. It offers all-mod cons, including a lovely restaurant, fitness centre with views over the harbour and flat-screen TVs in the rooms. Note, most Arp-Hansen hotels offer some good weekend deals for couples.

First Hotel
Vesterbrogade 23–29; tel: 33 78 80 00; www.firsthotels.dk/vesterbro, vesterbro@firsthotels.dk; €€; bus: 6a, 26; map p.136 C3
Highly recommended within its price range. Centrally placed on Vesterbrogade, it's not far from anywhere, the minimalist decor is attractive and retains a sense of warmth, thanks perhaps to the cherry-wood furniture, and the rooms are all a decent size. All rooms look down onto an internal, airy atrium where you have breakfast. In days of yore, it used to be the local porn cinema. It's now run by the same group as the Sankt Petri hotel *(see p.65)*.

Below: a calm retreat at the Carlton Guldsmeden.

Above: a room with a spectacular view at the Copenhagen Island hotel.

Grand Hotel
Vesterbrogade 9a; tel: 33 27 69 00; www.grandhotel.dk; €€€; bus: 6a, 26; map p.137 C3
An attractive façade, dating from 1890, fronts another tasteful hotel belonging to the Arp-Hansen group. It has been carefully modernised in a manner that preserves much of its original character, including marble bathrooms.

Hotel Cosmopole
Colbjørnsensgade 5–11; tel: 33 21 33 33; cosmopol@pip.dknet.dk; €; map p.137 C3
Noisy nightclubs for neighbours, but as it is situated near the station, the Cosmopole has the best location in this category, with some spacious rooms.

Hotel DGI-Byens
Tietgensgade 65; tel: 33 29 80 50; www.dgi-byen.com, hotel@dgi-byen.dk; €€; bus: 1a, 65e; map p.137 C3
Situated very close to Central Station and Tivoli, this new hotel is comfortable and the décor Danish minimalist. It's very good for families and also conferences. The Vandkulturhuset, the city's state-of-the-art swimming complex and spa is part of the hotel.
SEE ALSO PAMPERING P.111

Marriott Copenhagen
Kalvebod Brygge 5; tel: 88 33 99 00; www.marriott.com/cphdk; €€€; bus: 30; map p.137 D2
A luxury glass and concrete block offers all that you would expect from Marriott hotels. Waterside rooms overlook the inner harbour and are attractive, large and comfortable. Rates are reasonable when you consider that it is a five-star hotel.

If you're staying a week or longer, renting an apartment might be a more economical and practical option. One agency is **Citilet Apartments** (tel: 33 25 21 29; www.citilet.dk, citilet@citilet.dk). They specialise in business travellers. **Hay 4 You** (Vimmelskaftet 49,1st floor; tel: 33 33 08 05; www.hay4you.dk) offers more cosy apartments suited to families.

Above: Kim Utzon's design for the Copenhagen Island hotel is a wonderful combination of light, water and glass.

Mayfair Hotel
Helgolandsgade 3; tel: 70 12 17 00; www.choicehotels.dk/hotels/dk025, mayfair@choice.dk; €€; map p.137 C3
An early 20th-century hotel that has recently been refurbished. It offers a cosy atmosphere with English-style décor and a good standard of service.

Norlandia Star Hotel
Colbjørnsensgade 13; tel: 33 22 11 00; www.norlandiahotels.dk, service@star.norlandiahotels.dk; €; map p.137 C3
Recently acquired and refreshed by the Norlandia group, this is a functional, central and reasonably priced choice (especially for doubles or through web prices), although perhaps lacking in ambience.

Radisson Falconer Hotel
Falkoner Allé 9, Frederiksberg; tel: 38 15 80 01; www.radissonsas.com, reservations.falconer.copenhagen@radissonsas.com; €€€; bus: 18
In a pleasant location near Copenhagen Zoo, just 2km west of the city centre, this is the smallest of the Copenhagen Radisson hotels. There is a tropical atrium lobby, a fitness centre and rooms in either Scandinavian, 'Oriental' or Art Deco styles, most of which have a good view.

Copenhagen's Suburbs

The suburbs in Copenhagen are not very far away; even if you are out at the airport, you are no more than 15 minutes away by train.

Copenhagen Living
Close to Islands Brygge; double cabin €€–€€€€; map p.137 D2
Open in summer 2007, Copenhagen Living is Copenhagen's first floating hotel and a lovely opportunity, short of wheedling your way onto a house boat, of sleeping on the water. The base of the boat is original while everything else is being overhauled and the interior design will be modern, Danish classic, using good materials. Given that it is a real boat, facilities will probably be limited to three stars, but the floating restaurant Viva is moored alongside and will provide room service and restaurant facilties for the twelve cabins.
SEE ALSO RESTAURANTS P.125

Hotel Fy & Bi
Valby Langgade 62, Valby; tel: 36 45 44 00; www.hotelfyogbi.dk
A charming 100-year-old building painted in traditional Danish yellow, offering modern facilities, a good restaurant and an excellent Danish breakfast buffet. The rooms lack character but the buidling and location make up for it. A few minutes' walk from the zoo and just 10 minutes by bus or S-tog from the city centre.

Radisson Scandinavia Hotel
Amager Boulevard 70; tel: 33 96 50 00; www.radissonsas.com, reservations.scandinavia.copenhagen@radissonsas.com; €€€; bus: 5a, 250s
A 25-storey building and the biggest hotel in Denmark, this hotel across the water on Amager dominates the city's skyline. Rooms are furnished in standard, Scandinavian or 'Oriental' decor, most having fine views. It's convenient for the airport and there are four restaurants, including the recommended Blue Elephant.

Prices for a standard double room in high season:
€ under 1000DKK
€€ 1000–1400DKK
€€€ 1400–1600DKK
€€€€ over 1600DKK

Below: even basic rooms in Copenhagen, such as the Centrum pictured here, are well designed.

Language

The old joke says that Danish is not so much a language as a disease of the throat, and so it sometimes seems. To make the language even more difficult, Danish has three extra letters – æ, ø and å – plus sub-glottal stops, and myriad local dialects and accents that confuse matters even more. Although the Danes are generally very good at speaking English – and French and German – and usually very courteous towards foreigners, a knowledge of a few basic pronunciation rules will help to fathom out a notice, road sign or headline. Of course, attempts to speak a little Danish are also much appreciated.

Pronunciation

English is widely spoken and understood. Danish is perhaps the most difficult northern-European language for relating the written word to speech; it's almost impossible to pronounce simply by reading the words, as many syllables are swallowed rather than spoken. Thus the island of Amager becomes Am-air, with the 'g' disappearing, but in a distinctively Danish way difficult for the visitor to imitate. The letter 'd' becomes something like a 'th', but with the tongue placed behind the lower teeth, not the upper. And the letter 'r' is, again, swallowed.

VOWELS

a – aa, as in bar
å – aw, as in paw
æ – as in pear
e – as in bed
i – ee, as in sleep
ø – as in fur

> There are 29 letters in the Danish alphabet including 'æ' (as in egg), 'ø', and 'å' (as in port). They appear after the usual 26 (a point to note when looking up names in phone books and lists).

Despite their differences of grammar, usage and vocabulary, Danes, Norwegians and Swedes are able to understand one another. In a tripartite conversation, each will speak his or her own national language, and on an SAS (Scandinavian Air Services) flight the captain and head steward will make the flight announcements in their native tongue.

Useful Words & Phrases

GENERAL

yes/no *ja/nej*
big/little *stor/lille*
good/bad *god/dårlig*
possible/impossible *muligt/umuligt*
hot/cold *varm/kold*
much/little *meget/lidt*
many/few *mange/få*
and/or *og/eller*
please/thank you *vær så venlig/tak*
I *jeg*
you (formal) *du (de)*
he/she *han/hun*
it *den/det*
we *vi*
you (formal) *I (de)*
they *de*
foreigner *udlænding*
foreign *fremmed*

NUMBERS

1	*en/et*
2	*to*
3	*tre*
4	*fire*
5	*fem*
6	*seks*
7	*syv*
8	*otte*
9	*ni*
10	*ti*
11	*elleve*
12	*tolv*
13	*tretten*
14	*fjorten*
15	*femten*
16	*seksten*
17	*sytten*
18	*atten*
19	*nitten*
20	*tyve*
21	*enogtyve*
30	*tredive*
32	*toogtredive*
40	*fyrre*
43	*treogfyrre*
50	*halvtreds*
54	*fireoghalvtreds*
60	*tres*
65	*femogtres*
70	*halvfjerds*

76	*seksoghalvfjerds*
80	*firs*
90	*halvfems*
100	*hundrede*

FOOD AND DRINK
breakfast *morgenmad*
lunch (break) *frokost (pause)*
dinner *middag*
tea *te*
coffee *kaffe*
beer *fadøl*

GETTING AROUND
left *venstre*
right *højre*
street *(en) gade/vej*
bicycle (path) *(en) cykel (sti)*
car *(en) bil*
bus/coach *(en) bus*
train *(et) tog*
ferry *(en) færge*
bridge *(en) bro*
traffic light *(et) trafiklys*
square (et) *torv*
north *nord*
south *syd*
east *øst*
west *vest*

MONEY
How much is it? *Hvad koster det?*
Can I pay with... *Må jeg betale med...*
travellers' cheques *rejsechecks*
money *penge*
notes/coins *sedler/mønter*
Please may I have the bill? *Må jeg få regningen?*
May I have a receipt? *Må jeg få en kvittering?*
bank *(en) bank*
exchange *veksle*
exchange rate *kurs*
business hours *åbningstider*
open *åben*
closed *lukket*

MEDICAL
pharmacy *(et) apotek*
hospital *(et) hospital*
casualty *(en) skadestue*
doctor *(en) læge*

TIME
What time is it? *Hvad er klokken?*
good morning *godmorgen*
good day/evening *goddag*
goodnight *godaften/godnat*

Left: Nikolaj Contemporary Art Centre.

today *i dag*
tomorrow *i morgen*
yesterday *i går*
morning (9–12) *formiddag*
noon *middag*
afternoon *eftermiddag*
evening *aften*
night *nat*
It's five *Den er fem*

PLACES
Copenhagen *København*
Elsinore *Helsingør*
Zealand *Sjælland*
Funen *Fyn*
Jutland *Jylland*

CALENDAR
Weekday names are from Nordic mythology (reflected in the English):
Monday *mandag* (moon day)
Tuesday *tirsdag* (from the Latin *dies Martis*)
Wednesday *onsdag* (Odin's day)
Thursday *torsdag* (Thor's day)
Friday *fredag* (Freja's day)
Saturday *lørdag* (from the Old Norse *laugardagr*, 'washing day')
Sunday *søndag* (from the Latin, *dies solis*, the day of the sun).

January	*januar*
February	*februar*
March	*marts*
April	*april*
May	*maj*
June	*juni*
July	*juli*
August	*august*
September	*september*
October	*oktober*
November	*november*
December	*december*

ABBREVIATIONS
DKK **Danish Kroner**
DSB **Danish State Railways**
HT **Copenhagen Transit**
Kbh. **Copenhagen**
km/t. **kilometres per hour**
MOMS **value added tax**

Literature and Theatre

Denmark's strongest artistic tradition is literary. Though it may have been a while since it last happened, Danish authors have still won more Nobel Prizes *per capita* than any other country. Henrik Pontoppidan (1857–1943) and Karl Gjellerup (1857–1919) shared one in 1917, and Johannes V. Jensen (1873–1950) repeated the feat in 1944. Many of the best writers have close links with the Danish Royal Theatre, providing the first Danish plays for it to perform.

From Sagas and Songs

Danish literary tradition reaches back from the sagas and folk songs of medieval times, to Ludvig Holberg in the Age of Enlightenment, to the Romantic poet Adam Oehlenschläger (1779–1850), to Hans Christian Andersen and Søren Kierkegaard in the 19th century. Georg Brandes (1842–1927), the most influential personality in Danish letters from 1871 to World War I, wrote Denmark into the modern century. In the 1920s and 1930s there was a strong realistic movement in Danish literature, with writers such as Martin Andersen Nexø, Hans Kirk and H.C. Branner leading the way.

Today, more than 20 per cent of public funds for culture go to the public libraries. As many as 65 per cent of adults and nearly 80 per cent of young people use libraries. Authors receive remuneration not for their lending rates but according to the number of volumes on the shelves. In most cases, the 'library money' is what keeps them afloat.

Hans Christian Andersen

Still one of the world's favourite fairytale writers, Hans Christian Andersen (1805–75) gave folk tales a new, humorous twist. During 1835–75, he published no fewer than 150 fairytales, with *Tin Soldier*, *The Ugly Duckling*, and *The Emperor's New Clothes* among the best

Above: a statue of the man himself on H.C. Andersen Boulevard.

known. His story, the *Little Mermaid*, has also given the city its famous symbol. Andersen came from a poor background and had to wait some time for recognition. He initially hoped for a career on the stage and only later did he discover his talent for writing. Andersen stayed at an inn at no. 18 Vestergade when, as a young man, he first arrived in Copenhagen from Odense in 1819.

His own life story, *The Fairy Tale of My Life*, written in

Quite apart from his skill as a writer, H.C. Andersen had a good singing voice and was a talented artist. At the age of 14, he set off to Copenhagen to attend the Royal Theatre School with the intention of 'becoming famous'. Though his only success there was a walk-on part as a troll, the theatre board was perceptive enough to realise his gifts, and found him a place at a grammar school in Helsingør. His travels began early with a visit to Germany, and ranged widely. Later, he stayed in the castles and manor houses of his patrons, but Copenhagen remained his permanent home.

Left: the grand interior of the Royal Theatre is a sight to see in itself.

1855, is as fascinating as any of his well-loved tales. The son of a poor shoemaker's son, he achieved national acclaim during his lifetime, travelled the world and was a guest of the rich and famous.

Further Reading

Complete Hans Christian Andersen Fairy Tales (Gramercy Books).

The Fairy Tale of My Life (Cooper Square Press)

SEE ALSO CHILDREN P.35

Karen Blixen

The greatest female writer in Danish literary history, Karen (Tania) Blixen (1885–1962) was the sort of person who courted controversy. In her work she was not concerned with social or psychological realism. For her, the questions that mattered were, 'Why are we on earth?' or 'What does God want from us?' Although Blixen's stylised language is not easy to penetrate, the success of her books demonstrates that she struck a chord with her readers. But many Danes disdained the baroness's superior attitude. Blixen insisted on being addressed by her title, she always dressed elegantly and spoke in a strictly correct, rather old-fashioned style. It is often forgotten, however, that she was one of the first Danes to take on the issue of women's rights.

From 1914–31 Blixen lived as a coffee grower in East Africa, where she wrote her most successful novels including her 1938 novel *Out of Africa*, which provided the inspiration for the 1985 film of the same name starring Meryl Streep and Robert Redford.

After returning to Denmark, she wrote *Seven Gothic Tales* (1934), which brought her international acclaim. This was followed by *Winter's Tales* (1942), *The Angelic Avengers* (1946), *Last Tales* (1957) and *Anecdotes of Destiny* (1958).

When she returned to Denmark, she settled at her

Right: though no one denies her literary importance, Karen Blixen evokes a mixed response from Danes.

Denmark's first internationally-recognised literary figure, Ludvig Holberg (1684–1754) produced a wealth of comedies, albeit with a serious message. He enjoyed great success with his Utopian story *Niels Klim's Underground Journey* (1741), in which he appointed himself as a spokesman for religious tolerance. Holberg wrote the novel in Latin so that he could maximise his readership, but it was soon translated into German, Dutch, French, English, Danish and Swedish, and later into Russian and Hungarian. The book is still very popular and widely available today. He remains the most popular Danish playwright. A child of the Enlightenment, his plays are in the comedic tradition of Molière. Holberg is always playing somewhere in Denmark.

Above: an illustration from Holberg's *Niels Kim* showing the death of the King.

parents' home in Rungstedlund, north of Copenhagen, where she is now buried. In 1991 the house was converted into a museum.

Further Reading

Out of Africa (Penguin Modern Classics).

Seven Gothic Tales (Penguin Modern Classics)

Below: a snow-covered statue of the philosopher Søren Kierkegaard at the Royal Library Gardens.

Winter's Tales (Penguin Modern Classics).

Anecdotes of Destiny (Penguin Modern Classics)

Karen Blixen Museet

This museum sheds light on the intriguing personality of Denmark's most celebrated female literary figure.

SEE ALSO MUSEUMS AND GALLERIES P.88–9

Peter Hoeg

Denmark's most famous modern author, Peter Høeg (born 1957) achieved international success in 1991 with *Miss Smilla's Feeling for Snow*, which made it to the top of the best-seller lists in London and New York. Danish director Bille August turned the novel into a Hollywood film.

The murder mystery examines the touchy relationship between Denmark and the Inuit people of its former colony, Greenland. Høeg's characters are often misfits, on the fringes of normality. Other titles include *A History of Danish Dreams* (1988) and *The Borderliners* (1994).

From the mid-1990s Høeg was a virtual recluse and all but disappeared from the Danish cultural radar until he released *The Quiet Girl* in 2006.

Further Reading

Miss Smilla's Feeling for Snow (Harvill Press)

Søren Kierkegaard

The philosopher Søren Kierkegaard (1813–55) lived most of his life in Copenhagen. His literary works were unique, and he cannot be categorised under the usual aesthetic criteria as his writings consist of essays, philosophical analyses, polemics, literary criticism, psychological dissertations and religious theses.

Kierkegaard is noted for his remarkable command of language, and also the complex structure of his works. A small exhibition in Københavns Bymuseum celebrates the intellectual contributions of the philosopher.

Further Reading

Papers and Journals: a Selection (Penguin Classics). some of Kierkegaard's personal writings that trace the development of his own thought and personality.

Either/Or (Penguin Classics) Kierkegaard's masterpiece of duality.

Other fiction

Martin Andersen Nexø

Born in poverty in Copenhagen's poorest neighbourhood, Nexø (1869–1954) was the first Danish novelist to champion the underclass of society and devoted his work to social criticism. His book *Pelle the Conqueror* (1906–10; 4 parts; reprinted 2006 by Mondial) describes poverty and exploitation among Danish peasants in the late 19th century. With its first-hand description of poverty as well as the growth of the labour movement, it was regarded by socialists as a heroic epic (in 1987, it was made into an award-winning film, directed by Bille August). For a long time, however, Nexø was denied recognition in Danish literary circles.

Klaus Rifbjerg

Born in 1931, and based mostly in Spain, Rifbjerg has more than 100 titles to his name, starting with his then scandalous novel *Den kroniske Uskyld* (*Chronic Innocence)* in 1958, now the most widely read and most frequently reprinted book in Danish literary history, though unavailable in English.

Having survived the radical movement of the 1960s and early 1970s, Rifbjerg still turns out a novel or two a year. He has also written revues, television shows, plays, film scripts and newspaper articles, but considers himself a poet at heart, and is most at home when writing verse. His most recent book to be translated into English was *Krigen* (War, 1995).

Poetry

Inger Christensen

Born in Jutland in 1935, Christensen is one of Denmark's leading poets. Her works often use strict mathmatical systems to develop her poetry. Her collection *it* (reprinted in English by New Directions Publishing) is a landmark of Danish poetry. *Alphabet* (Bloodaxe Books) is also available in English.

Pia Tafdrup

Her early volumes focus on desire and sex and make for sensual reading. She has since moved outwards, writing about nature, the city, and 'the Other'. Her only collection available in English is *Queen's Gate* (Bloodaxe Books).

Above: an illustration for an edition of Hans Christian Andersen's fairy tale *The Emperor's New Clothes*.

Below: leading the way amongst contemporary Danish writers is the reclusive Peter Høeg, whose latest novel, *The Quiet Girl,* was released in 2006.

Reading List

HISTORY

An Account of Denmark as it was in the Year 1692, by Robert Molesworth (Wormanium Publishers, Århus, Denmark).

A Conspiracy of Decency, by Emmy Werner (Basic Books, US). The story of how most of Denmark's Jews were saved from the Nazis, based partly on eyewitness accounts.

The Bog People: Iron Age Man Preserved, by P. V. Glob (New York Review of Books).

Dan Turèll was a highly prolific and beloved author from the 1970s until his death in 1993. This beat poet and 'Karma Cowboy' was known for his musical recitals and rapid-fire delivery. A Copenhagen landmark – a café is named after him *(see page 29)* – 'Uncle Danny' also found time to write more than 40 mystery novels, and perform with his jazz band The Silverstars.

A fascinating account of both Iron Age civilisation and early religious practices by studying the remains of victims of ritual sacrifices preserved by the bogs they were buried in.
Defying Napoleon: How Britain bombarded Copenhagen and seized the Danish Fleet in 1807, by Thomas Munch-Petersen (Sutton Publishing). A modern look at one of Nelson's greatest accomplishments and one of Denmark's darkest days. Munch-Petersen pays special attention to the personalities of the day and the fact that it was the first ever use of terror bombardment used against a European city. He also draws parallels with the 2003 invasion of Iraq, as this pre-emptive

Right: a statue of Holberg stands outside the Royal Theatre to commemorate his contribution to Danish drama.

strike was based on largely inaccurate intellegence reports.
A History of Denmark, by Knud J.V. Jespersen (Palgrave, Macmillan). A short but authoritative account of the last 500 years of Danish history by the royal historiographer to H.M. the Queen of Denmark.
Roar's Circle: A Viking Ship Returns to the Sea, by Henrik Juel (Lutterworth Press). An account of the Vikingskibsmuseet's attempt to recreate a Viking ship using only traditional tools and techniques and then to set sail on the open seas.

CINEMA

The Name of This Book Is Dogme 95, by Richard Kelly (Faber). Was Denmark's most famous cinematic innovation a genuine breakthrough or just a clever marketing ploy? Includes interviews with all the key figures, including Lars von Trier.

OTHER FICTION

The Royal Physician's Visit, by Per Olov Enquist (Simon and Schuster). A tense historical novel based upon the love triangle involving Princess Caroline Mathilde of England, her mad husband King Christian VII and her lover, his physician Johann Streunse.
The Torso, Helene Tursten (Soho Press). Swedish crime writer Tursten allows her serialised Inspector Huss across the Øresund for a grisly mystery involving dismembered bodies in Copenhagen.

Book Shops

Around Filstræde, which branches off Strøget near the Vimmelskaftet, is the university quarter, with a number of antiquarian book shops. Other bookshops of interest are listed below.

Arnold Busck
Købmagergade 49, tel: 33 73 35 00; www.arnoldbusck.dk; Mon 10am–6pm, Tue–Thur 9.30am–6pm, Fri 9.30am–7pm, Sat 10am–4pm; map p.138 B3

Arnold Busck Antikvariat
Fiolstræde 24; tel: 33 73 35 45; Mon–Thur 9am–5.30pm, Fri 9am–6pm, Sat 10am–2pm; map p.138 A3

One of Denmark's largest booksellers, with over 20 branches throughout the city. A devoted children's book store is next door to the Købmagergade shop and the

Below: antiquarian book shops can be found in Copenhagen's university quarter. English language books are also easy to find.

antiquarian branch is on nearby Fiolstræde.

GAD

Fiolstræde 31–3; tel: 33 12 91 48; www.gad.dk; Mon–Thur 8am–6pm, Fri 9.30am–7pm, Sat 10am–3pm; map p.138 A3

A large selection of books in English, German and French. Over a dozen branches in the city, including another one at the Central Station.

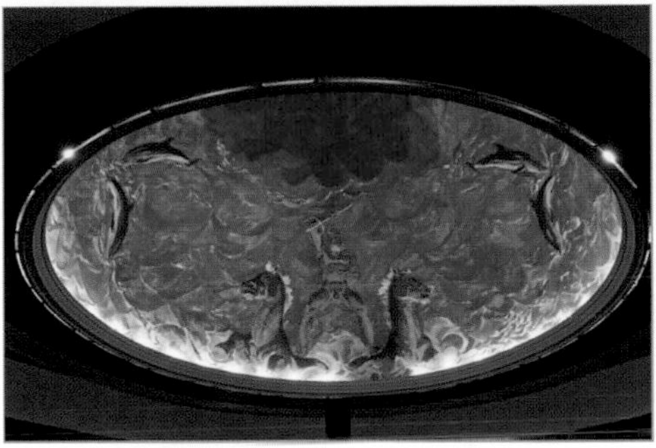

Above: a mural depicting Neptune at the Royal Theatre.

Det Kongelige Bibliotek

The Kongelige Bibliotek dates back to 1482 and is the largest library in Scandinavia, with more than 2.5 million volumes, 4 million charts and pictures, and more than 55,000 manuscripts, including some by famous Danes such as Hans Christian Andersen, Søren Kierkegaard and Karen Blixen.

SEE ALSO SLOTSHOLMEN P.11; ARCHITECTURE P.26

Det Kongelige Teater

Danish Royal Theatre, Kongens Nytorv; tel: 33 69 69 69; www.kgl-teatr.dk; bus: 1a, 15, 19, 26, S-tog: Kongens Nytorv; map p.138 C3

Danish drama began with the formation of the Royal Danish Theatre in 1748 to perform popular plays from abroad. Native theatre came into its own between 1800–50, the Golden Age of fine arts in Denmark. The tragedies of Adam Oehlenschläger, comedies of Johan Ludvig Holberg (both commemorated with statues outside the main entrance, *see picture left*) and Henrik Hertz helped put the theatre on the international map. This allowed its Old Stage the privilege of being the first theatre in the world to stage Henrik Ibsen's *A Doll's House* in 1879.

Today it still invests in Danish talent, but also stages major international classics. More than one-third of the state funds allocated to theatre go towards financing the National Theatre. A quarter of the public funds go to 20 smaller Copenhagen theatres, such as **Aveny-t** and **Det Ny Teater**, where much good innovative work is shown.

Aveny-T

Frederiksberg Allé 102, Frederiksberg; tel: 33 23 31 00, 70 20 10 31; www.aveny-t.dk; bus: 26; map p.136 A3

Det Ny Teater

Gammel Kongevej 29, Vesterbro; tel: 33 25 50 75; www.detnyteater.dk; bus: 6a, 14, 15, 26; map p.136 C3

Below: a collection of dresses from the Teatermuseet, *see p.98.*

Children's Theatre

Some 100 touring children's theatre companies, as well as a handful of permanent theatres, such as **Det Lille Teater** (The Little Theatre), in Copenhagen, cater for the youngest audiences. Only a select few receive state support. Others make do on their own, like the popular Batida musical theatre company, which since the mid-1980s has delighted children all over Denmark .

Det Lille Teater

Lavendelstræde 5–7; tel: 33 12 27 13; www.detlilleteater; map p.138 A2

Grønnegårdens Teater regularly performs outdoors in the courtyard of the Kunstindustrie Museet. They stage a Holberg play at least every other summer, often using extravagant costumes.

Monuments and Fountains

Most of Copenhagen's historic monuments and fountains can be found in and around Slotsholmen, where Bishop Absalon built the city's first castle. A walking tour of the old city, Strøget and Rådhuspladsen is a good way to explore these monuments to Danish history and get a feel of how the city developed. More contemporary statues, such as the city's Little Mermaid, are clustered at Langelinie near Kastellet north of the city centre. A water taxi from Nyhavn is the best way to approach them.

Bishop Absalon

Højbro Plads; map p.138 B2

This statue *(right)* of Bishop Absalon (1128–1201), the founder of Copenhagen, points towards Slotsholmen where he built a fortified castle to defend the young village from attacking German tribes. The statue is the work of Vilhelm Bissen (1836–1913), who also worked with his father Herman Wilhelm Bissen on the equestrian figure of Frederik VII *(see page 80)* nearby. It was put up in 1902.

SEE ALSO SLOTSHOLMEN P.10

Caritas Fountain

Gammeltorv; bus: 6a; map p.138 A2

Dating from 1608, this gilded statue of a woman holding two children represents Charity. It is one of the oldest statues in Copenhagen.

SEE ALSO STRØGET AND AROUND P.8

Below: reerected in the 19th century, the Caritas Fountain is one of the oldest monumental fountains in the world.

Below: in the centre of Kongens Nytorv stands the statue of Christian V, the founder of Danish Law.

Carlsberg Elephants

Gamle Carlsberg Vej 11; map p.136 A2

These elephants are part of the second brewery built in 1889 by Jacobsen's son Carl. They date from 1901 and are partly drawn from the elephants holding up the organ in Vor Frelsers Kirke *(see page 39)*. The elephant is also an important early royal emblem, as shown by the name of the highest accolade in the realm: the Order of the Elephant, founded by Christian I around 1450.

SEE PICTURE IN MUSEUMS AND GALLERIES P.84

Christian V

Kongens Nytorv; bus: 1a, 15, 19, 26, 999, S-tog: Kongens Nytorv; map p.138 C3

This statue of Christian V (reign 1670–99) dates from 1687 and was the first equestrian statue to be erected in Scandinavia. It shows the king, who established Danish Law in 1683 (much of which still governs the country today), dressed as a Roman emperor and rid-

Left: Bishop Absalon, the city's founder, surveys Højbro Plads from his horse.

> Danish Law from 1687 stated that any promise intended to create obligations should be considered binding, regardless of the form of the promise. Even a verbal promise to give a present or to sell a property was considered as binding as if it had been in writing. This is still the norm in Denmark today, and even expected of politicians who betray this consensus at their own risk.

ing over Envy, who lies prostrate beneath the horse's hooves; a fitting symbol for a king whose motto was 'Fear of God and justice'.

The figures at the four corners are Queen Artemisia, Alexander the Great, the goddess Pallas Athene and Hercules. It was sculpted by the Frenchman Abraham César Lamoureux. Originally made of gilded lead because such big bronze castings were not then possible, it has been repaired many times and was recast in bronze in 1946.

SEE ALSO KONGENS NYTORV P.12, 13

Den Lille Havfrue (The Little Mermaid)

Langelinie; map p.135 E3

Copenhagen's most famous monument is very small (and usually being crawled over by tourists). It is based on Hans Christian Andersen's tale about a little mermaid who falls in love with a prince and sacrifices her beautiful voice and loving family to leave the ocean to try and gain his love for him only to reject her.

The statue was commissioned by Carl Jacobsen, of Carlsberg Brewery fame, who also chose the site. The artist, Edvard Eriksen modelled her on his wife Eline.

The Little Mermaid has been staring out to sea since 1913. Unfortunately, she has been vandalised on several occasions and she may be moved further into the channel to improve her security.

SEE ALSO AMALIENBORG P.17; LITERATURE P.72

Dragon's Leap Fountain

Rådhuspladsen; bus: all Rådhuspladsen buses; map p.138 B2

The centrepiece of Rådhuspladsen, this impressive fountain was designed by Joachim Skovgård and is all that is left to see on Rådhuspladsen once the winter scares away the cafés.

Fiskerkone (Fishwife)

Gammel Strand; map p.138 B2

This statue, dating from 1940, was put up as a reminder that this beach was where fishwives sold the herring caught by their husbands at sea in medieval times. Herring was the original source of wealth to Copenhagen and buoyed the economy for centuries.

Below: the Dragon's Leap Fountain on Rådhuspladsen.

Frederick V

Amalienborg Plads; map p.139 D4
Standing proudly in the centre of the Amalienborg surveying the district that he founded, this statue of Frederik V took 20 years to complete because the Frenchman who made it, Jacques Saly, was enjoying his life in Copenhagen a bit too much to work on it steadily.

Besides founding Amalienborg, Frederik V, whose motto was 'With care and constancy' had a rather unremarkable reign, but was seen as a transitional figure moving away from absolutist monarchs towards enlightened despotism. When this statue was unveiled in 1771, a 27-gun salute was sounded in its honour.
SEE ALSO AMALIENBORG P.16

Frederik VII

Slotsholmen; map p.138 B2
In the forecourt of Slotsholmen on the Øresund side, the equestrian statue by the Neoclassical sculptor Vilhelm Bissen is of Frederik VII who reigned between 1848 and 1863. He is well esteemed for ending royal absolutism on his accession, but he failed to provide a direct heir and the house of Oldenborg came to an end with his reign. He was succeeded by his cousin Christian IX, of the house of Schleswig-Holstein-Sonderburg-Glücksburg who is represented in a pendant statue by Anne Marie Carl Nielsen, wife of the famous composer Carl Nielsen, in the riding ground.

Frihedstøtten (Freedom Monument)

Vesterbrogade, opposite Reventlowsgade; map p.137 C3
Until the late 18th century men born on farmland were obliged to work for the landowner, but agricultural reform allowed them to leave the land, thus freeing them from this serf-like requirement. Unsurprisingly many of them headed to Copenhagen in search of better pay. This pillar was erected to recognise their new independence.
SEE ALSO VESTERBRO AND FREDERIKSBERG P.18

Gefionspringvand (Gefion Fountain)

Nordre Toldbod; map p.135 E2
Near Kastellet, with her back to the harbour, the goddess Gefion drives her ox-drawn plough. The sculptor Anders Bundgaard took 11 years to complete this colossal masterpiece.

Legend has it that the king of Sweden, thinking her a poor old woman, promised Gefion that she could have as much land as she could plough up in one night. She turned her sons into oxen and ploughed up the land that is now known as the island of Sjælland. The statue was commissioned by Carl Jacobsen in 1909.
SEE ALSO AMALIENBORG P.17

Hans Christian Andersen Statues

Kongens Have; bus: 350s; map p.138 B4; **H.C. Andersen Boulevard**; bus: 33; map p.138 A2; **Kongens Nytorv**; bus: 1a, 15, 19, 26, 999, S-tog: Kongens Nytorv; map p.138 C3
There are three statues of Denmark's most celebrated author in the city. The one in Kongens Have was modelled from life by artist August Saaybe and was unveiled after the writer's death in 1875. The one opposite Tivoli on H.C. Andersen Boulevard is by Henry Lukow-Nielsen and was unveiled in 1961. There is another statue in the foyer of the Kongelige Teater on Kongens Nytorv; young Andersen's aspirations lay in becoming a great actor when he arrived in Copenhagen.
SEE ALSO LITERATURE AND THEATRE P.72–3

According to legend, the good burghers of Copenhagen will hear the horn blasts of the Viking Lurblœserne *(left)* when a virgin passes by. They are still waiting...

H.C. Andersen was born into a humble home in Odense, the son of a cobbler. The people of Odense commemorate his life with two museums, but he seemed less proud of his rural roots. He once said 'being born in a duck yard does not matter, if only you are hatched from a swan's egg'.

Above: the Royal Tombs of Roskilde Cathedral mark out Danish history through the graves of generations of monarchs.

Lurblœserne (The Hornblowers)

Rådhuspladsen; bus: all Rådhuspladsen buses; map p.138 A2

These traditional figures recall Denmark's Viking past. Standing on the top of a tall column to the left of the Rådhus, they are blowing traditional Viking instruments such as can be seen in the National Museum.

Paradise Genetically Altered

Langelinie; map p.135 A3

Copenhagen's newest sculpture is bound to cause controversy. Designed by Bjørn Nørgaard, the sculpture is a triumphal arch, on top of which stands a 9-m genetically altered Madonna, surrounded by Adam, Eve, Christ, Mary Magdalene, The Tripartite Capital and The Pregnant Man.

The genetically altered Mermaid is also a part of the group, although she is closer to the Lille Havfrue. The new sculpture is said to be a 'a provocative and humoristic comment on post-modern society ... [a] 3-D statement about human beings, genetic technology, the future and a prophecy about human appearance in 100–200 years.'

Royal Tombs

Roskilde Cathedral, Roskilde; Apr–Sept: Mon–Fri 9am–4.45pm, Sat 9am–noon, Sun 12.30–4.45pm, Oct–Mar: Tue–Sat 10am–3.45pm, Sun 12.30–3.45pm

Roskilde's Domkirke is the burial place of generations of Danish monarchs. Their elaborate tombs lie inside chapels to the main cathedral. The most impressive chapels are those of King Christian IV, built in 1641 in Dutch Renaissance style with magnificent murals, and the chapel of King Frederik V from 1770, the masterwork of the architect Harsdorff.

SEE ALSO SJÆLLAND P.24

Below: the Stork Fountain on Strøget is often used as a meeting point, or just a place to rest weary legs.

Stork Fountain

Højbro Plads, Strøget; map p.138 B3

Erected in 1864, the Stork Fountain (featuring herons, not storks) was a congregation point for hippies in the 1960s. It even had a popular protest song written in its honour: The Big, Bad Stork Fountain. Now it serves as an elegant meeting point for tamer rendezvous.

Tombs of Famous Danes

Assistens Kirkegård, Nørrebro; bus: 5a, 18, 350s

Many notable Danes are buried here, including writer Hans Christian Andersen, philosopher Søren Kirkegaard, choreographer August Bournonville, physicist Niels Bohr and artist Henry Heerup.

Even if you're not on a pilgrimage, the cemetery makes for a pleasant summer stroll before a drink in one of Nørrebro's many trendy cafés.

SEE ALSO NØRREBRO P.22; PARKS, GARDENS AND BEACHES P.112

Museums and Galleries

Copenhagen has enough excellent museums for a city twice the size; from the grand national collections of historic artefacts and art to hands-on, hi-tech places like the Experimentarium, and specialist exhibitions, such as the Arbejdermuseet (the Workers' Museum). Most are in the city centre, within walking distance of each other. Although the majority charge an entrance fee, many museums are free at least one day a week; plus there is the good-value Copenhagen Card.

Amagermuseet

Hovedgaden 4 and 12, Store Magleby, Dragør; tel: 32 53 02 50; www.amagermuseet.dk; May–Sept: Tue–Sun noon–4pm; entrance charge

This tiny museum recreates life on a farm at the beginning of the 20th century. Children get a chance to pet the pigs and other animals, staff dress up in period costume and there is a collection of work by Danish artists such as portrait painter Jens Juel, National Romantic painter Julius Exner and Julius Friedlænder.

Amalienborg Museum

Christian VIII's Palace, Amalienborg Plads; tel: 33 12 21 86; www.amalienborgmuseet.dk; Nov–Dec 18, Jan–Apr: Tues–Sun 11am–4pm, May– Oct: daily 10am–4pm, Bel-étage tour every second week, Wed, Sun 11.30am, 1pm, 2.30pm; map p.139 C4

Housed in the northern building of Amalienborg Palace is the small Palace Museum of Christian VIII. This lovely, intimate collection is set in some of the private rooms of kings Christian IX (1863–1906), Frederik VIII (1906–12), Christian X (1912–47) and Frederik IX (1947–72). It is interesting to see different period styles as well as how the personalities of the different monarchs are represented.

There's some rather dodgy art here produced by earlier royals, though the current monarch is obviously more gifted. Look out too, for Frederik IX's pipe collection – he was clearly an avid smoker. The royals have obviously been very family-orientated, as there are photographs everywhere. Go on the Bel-étage tour if you can, to get a less museum-like impression of the palace.

SEE ALSO AMALIENBORG P.16

Below: Dutch settlers founded the village of Store Magleby in the 16th century and their farming techniques and way of life are remembered at the Amagermuseet.

Arbejdermuseet

22 Rømersgade; tel: 33 93 25 75; www.arbejdermuseet.dk; daily 10am–4pm; entrance charge; S-tog: Nørreport; map p.138 A4

Historical museums usually focus on the great and the

Left: mother and child at the Glyptotek's Winter Garden.

Most museums charge entry, but some are free for kids. Many are free on Wednesdays, which is also often the day for late opening. Free museums include Arken, the Georg Jensen Museum, the Music History Museum and Royal Cast Collection.

good, if not the rich and the powerful. The Workers' Museum tells a different story, and in a livelier and more informative way than is normal, though may only be of interest for those of a political persuasion. Many socialist heroes, such as Wilhelm Liebknecht, August Bebel, Rosa Luxembourg and Clara Zetkin, spoke at public meetings in the large room at the back of this building. It was, therefore, the ideal place for a museum dedicated to the class struggle.

The exhibitions begin in 1870 at a time when many employees were being exploited by industrialisation, when workers' leaders found themselves in prison and the police spied on meetings. Life was harsh and conditions in the factories bleak. One of the most impressive displays traces the Sørensen family through three generations, mainly in the years before World War II. It shows how impoverished farmers arrived in the towns full of hope, how the world economic crisis affected everyday life, how working conditions changed in the various professions, and the improvements that had to be fought for.

SEE ALSO CAFÉS AND BARS P.29

Arken

Skovej 100, Ishøj ; tel: 43 54 02 22, tours tel: 43 57 34 55; www.arken.dk; Thur–Tue 10am–5pm, Wed 10am–9pm; free; S-tog: Ishøj then bus 128 or signposted 30–40-minute walk

The Arken Museum for Modern Art was set up in 1996 in an effort to boost the culturally barren southern environs of Copenhagen, by the Baltic coast.

Nicknamed the 'Ark', this museum's bold concrete design in the shape of a ship's hull, merges well with the surrounding countryside. The main art axis, which extends for the full length of the 'Ark', serves as the hub for all the other rooms. Concrete walls, some 12m high, and huge, riveted steel plates lend a harsh, uncompromising feel to the gallery, while the side rooms at various levels create a playful effect.

The bold and unusual design of the interior provides an ideal setting for the *avant-garde* works of art displayed here. As the

Below: the old-fashioned furnishings at the Amagermuseet were donated by local residents – decendants of the original Dutch settlers.

Above: it's not just lager that is produced in Carlsberg's brewery. Dozens of other varieties, such as dark ale, porter and wheat beer, are for sale at the museum and in shops around Copenhagen.

museum's own collection is currently rather modest, special exhibitions are usually the main focal point of a visit.

There is a very good shop and a nice café with sea views. An extension is being built until 2008 but there will continue to be special exhibitions and the shop and café will remain open.

SEE ALSO SJÆLLAND P.25

Bakkehusmuseet

Rahbeks Allé 23, Vesterbro; tel: 33 31 43 62; www.bakkehusmuseet.dk; Wed–Thur, Fri–Sat 11am–3pm; entrance charge; bus: 6a, 18, 26, 832, S-tog: Valby; map p.136 A2

This old house, formerly the home of Kamma and Lyhne Rahbek – literary personalities of the 19th-century Golden Age, is now a cultural museum.

Four rooms are furnished in the original style of 1802–30, when the couple lived here, and two are dedicated to the Danish poets Johannes Ewald and Adam Oehlenschläger. For buffs of Hans Christian Andersen, this was a regular meeting place in his youth and there is also some memorabilia that relates to him on show.

> Check these websites for news of upcoming special exhibitions and other cultural events:
> www.kulturnet.dk
> www.aok.dk
> www.cphpost.dk
> www.woco.dk

Carlsberg Visitors Centre and the Jacobsen Brewery

Gamle Carlsberg Vej 11, Vesterbro; tel: 33 27 13 14, 12 82; www.visitcarlsberg.dk; Tue–Sun 10am–4pm; entrance charge; bus: 18, 26, S-tog: Enghave; map p.136 A2

Learn all about the history of the brewing industry in the historic premises fronted by the Elephant Gate: four 5m high Indian elephants, sculpted in 1901 by Vilhelm Dahlerup, one of Copenhagen's most celebrated architects.

Inside, you can view the production process and a collection of 13,000 of its 16,000 Carlsberg label and bottle designs, see the dray horses in their stables and, of course, sample probably the world's best-known lager in an airy, attractive bar.

SEE ALSO MONUMENTS AND FOUNTAINS P.78

Charlottenborg Slot

Kongens Nytorv; tel: 33 13 40 22; www.charlottenborg-art.dk; Thur–Tue 10am–5pm, Wed 10am–7pm; entrance charge; bus: 1a, 15, 19, 26, 999, S-tog: Kongens Nytorv; map p.139 C3

This former palace dates from the end of the 17th century. Since 1754 it has housed the Royal Academy of Fine Arts, where painters,

Below: the famous elephants mark the entrance to the old brewery.

sculptors and architects receive their formal training.

The gallery (Charlottenborg Udstillingsbygning) is the venue for changing exhibitions of contemporary Danish and international art. Enter the courtyard through the palace front gate on Kongens Nytorv to find the exhibition area.

SEE ALSO KONGENS NYTORV P.13

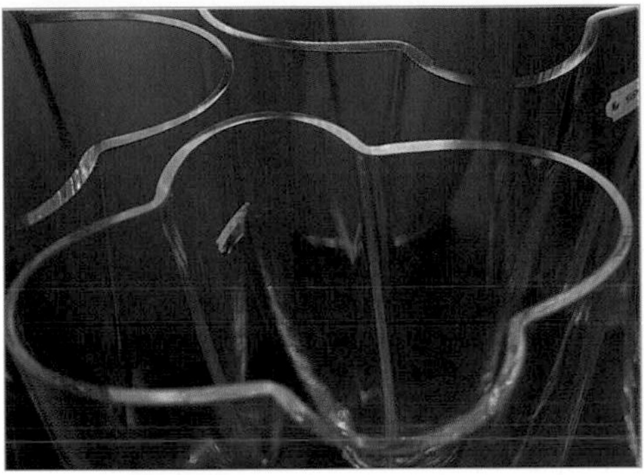

Above: exhibitions at the Dansk Design Centre change regularly; they have included housewares, automobiles and glasswork.

Cisternerne – Museet fro Moderne Glaskunst

Søndermarken, Roskildevej 25, opposite Frederiksberg Slot; tel: 33 21 93 10; www.cisternerne.dk; Thur–Fri 2–6pm, Sat–Sun 11am–5pm; entrance charge

Deep beneath the grassy lawns of Frederiksberg Have, just opposite the castle and the zoo, lies this atmospheric glass museum.

This is home to an impressive collection of stained glass and statuary by artists such as Per Kirkeby, Carl Henning Pedersen and Robert Jacobsen. The exhibits glow in the candlelit gloom of their cavernous home like stalagtites growing from the ceiling dripping onto the floor below.

Contemporary Art Centre Nikolaj, KBJ

Nicolaj Plads 10; tel: 33 18 17 80; www.kunsthallennikolaj.dk; daily noon–5pm; entrance charge, under-15s free, Wed free; map p.138 B3

Copenhagen's third oldest church building originally dating from the 13th century, Nicolaj Kirke suffered in the fire of 1795 and ceased to function as a church in 1805. It stands just off Strøget, not far from Kongens Nytorv and is now a space for changing contemporary art exhibitions. Seven to nine are held every year, one is always a children's exhibition and another a major presentation of an older artist whose work has had a pioneering impact on art today. The café also comes highly recommended.

SEE ALSO CAFÉS AND BARS P.30

Below: the old Nikolaj Church has provided a prime, city-centre location for contemporary art since 1957.

Dansk Arkitektur Centre

Strandgade 27B; tel: 32 57 19 30; daily 10am–5pm; entrance charge; map p.139 C2

Housed in a restored 19th-century warehouse, the Dansk Arkitektur Center is used as a venue for exhibitions. With its bright rooms, exposed beams and newly laid wooden floors, there could be no better example of how to renovate an old building. And once you've soaked up all the art and ambience, treat yourself in the excellent cafeteria overlooking the water.

Dansk Design Centre

H.C. Andersens Boulelvard 27; tel: 33 69 33 69; www.ddc.dk; Mon–Fri 10am–5pm, Wed 10am–9pm, Sat–Sun 11am–4pm; entrance charge; bus 33; map p.138 A2

Opposite Tivoli, the Danish Design Center is housed in an impressive modern build-

ing that suitably reflects the country's taste for cool, clean, elegant lines, for which it has earned an international reputation. Their semi-permanent and changing schedule of exhibitions on design, past and present, are worth checking out. There's also a café and a small shop.
SEE ALSO DANISH DESIGN P.40

Davids Samling Museum

Kronprinsessegade 30–2; tel: 33 73 49 49; www.davidmus.dk; closed for renovation until Aug 2008, usually daily 10am–4pm; map p.138 B4

On the edge of Kongens Have stands this lovely museum, housed in a 19th-century town house, with lovely interior staircases.

It was originally a private collection built up by a Danish barrister, one Christian Ludwig David (1878–1960), who clearly had a great love and knowledge of European applied arts from the 18th to the 20th centur. It includes paintings, silverware, ceramics and furniture, as well as Islamic art spanning the 7th to the 19th centuries and a geographical scope reaching from Spain in the west to India in the east.

Until it opens its doors again in 2008, much of its collection can be seen in touring exhibitions.

Den Hirschsprungske Samling

Stockholmsgade 20; tel: 35 42 03 36; www.hirschsprung.dk; Wed–Mon 11am–4pm; entrance charge, under-18s free, Wed free; map p.135 D2

Just behind the Statens Museum for Kunst is another, delightful temple of art, Den Hirschsprungske Samling, which focuses on Danish art with a preference for 19th-century art of the Golden Age and early 20th-century painting. The latter includes works by the Skagen painters such as Michael and Anna Ancher and P.S. Krøyer, Denmark's answer to the French Impressionists – interested in painting 'real' life in a natural light and setting. This is the best collection outside of the Skagen Museum itself in northern Jutland.

There are also memorable paintings by important Danish artists such as CW Eckerberg, Fritz Synen, Vilham Hammershøi and Harold Slot Møller. The collection owes its survival to the tobacco magnate, Heinrich Hirschsprung (1836–1908), who donated it to the state in 1902.

Below: the David collection has continued to expand after the death of its founder, and now features a larger collection of Islamic art and Persian carpets.

At *Kulturnatten* – 'Night of Culture' (mid-October, 6pm–midnight) – all of Copenhagen's 300 museums, galleries and other public buildings and palaces are open with free admission. See www.kulturnatten.dk for more information.

Den Kongelige Afstøbningssamlingen

Vestindisk Pakhus, Toldbodgade 40; tel: 33 74 85 85; www.smk.dk; Wed 10am–8pm; free; map p.139 D4

This former shipping warehouse houses the Royal Cast Collection of over 2,000 casts of works dating back as far as ancient Egypt and antiquity. It is one of the largest cast collections in the world and a visit will ensure that you have seen the world's best sculpture – even if you haven't seen it all in the flesh. You can't miss it as you walk along the waterside – Michelangelo's David looms large just outside.

Experimentarium

Tuborg Havnevej 7, Hellerup; tel: 39 27 33 33; www. experimentarium.dk; Mon, Wed–Fri 9.30am–5pm, Tue 9.30am–9pm, Sat–Sun 11am–5pm; entrance charge, under 2s free; bus: 1a, S-tog: Hellerup

This imaginative and fun science museum is situated in the northern district of Hellerup in a wing of Copenhagen's last Tuborg brewery. It sets out to explain a variety

Left: the battered armoured car at the Frihedsmuseet illustrates the military disadvantage faced by the Danes in World War II.

of scientific principles, frequently using hands-on techniques and visitors of all ages are positively encouraged to tinker around with exhibits.

The enormous 4,000sq. m hall contains some 300 working exhibits sponsored by private companies.

'Learn by doing' is the message for everyone; you can test the capacity of your lungs, devise a calorie plan to suit your body, establish the radioactivity of naturally occurring substances, or look at various ways of saving energy.

Cell research, communication and data transfer, air and water, energy and environmental protection, nutrition and the workings of various human organs are just some of the topics which the inquisitive visitor can explore.

Special educational programmes have been devised, so school parties make up most of the visitors on weekdays. Temporary exhibitions, with experimentation as the main theme, are also held during the year.

It may sound serious, but it's actually great fun and there is a soft play area for very small kids.

Frihedsmuseet

Churchillparken 7; tel: 33 13 77 14; www.natmus.dk; May–Sept: Tue–Sat 10am–4pm, Sun 10am–5pm, Oct–Apr: Tues–Sat 10am–3pm, Sun 10am–4pm; entrance charge, under-16s free, Wed free; map p.135 E2

This museum documents the activities of the Danish Resistance Movement during the German occupation (1940–45). Displays illustrate the daring exploits of the Danish activists, who spirited Jews across the Sound to Sweden, manned radio stations and operated printing presses. Others made weapons, committed acts of sabotage or fought alongside Allied Forces. Period documents and newspaper cuttings show how the occupying forces reacted to the resistance movement. It makes for a fascinating and moving exhibition.

Geologisk Museum

Øster Voldgade 5–7; tel: 35 32 23 45; www.geological-museum.dk; Tue–Sun 1–4pm; entrance charge, under-6s free, Wed free; bus: 26; map p.138 B4

A Renaissance building in the Botanical Gardens houses the Geologisk Museum, a mine of marvels, which will be of interest to all, particularly some of the more outlandish items: the imprint of a 150-million year old jellyfish, fossilised dinosaur remains, and a 20 tonne meteorite.

The meticulously arranged mineral collection, the meteorites and the Greenland exhibition are the main focal points.

There are also activities on Sundays between 2 and 3pm and also in the holidays.

The entrance to the museum is on Øster Voldgade 5–7 (you can't enter the museum directly from the Botanical Gardens).

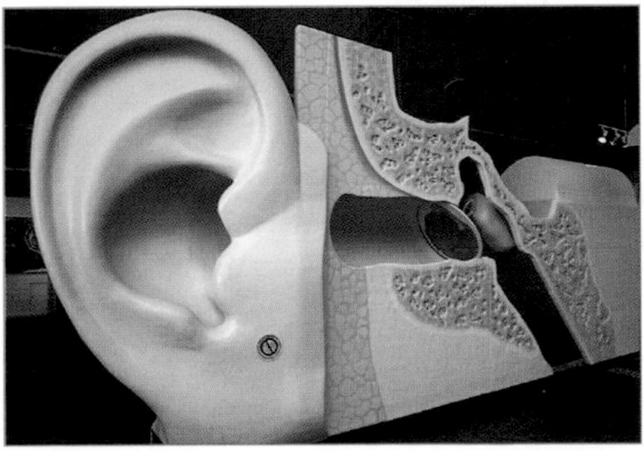

Right: exhibit at the Experimentarium showing the smallest bones in the human body (the ear ossicles).

Above: fine silver bowls on display at the Georg Jensen Museum. His elegant designs have become classics and contemporary versions are sold in the flagship store.

Georg Jensen Museum

Amager Torv 4; tel: 33 14 02 29; Mon–Thur 10am–6pm, Fri 10am–7pm; free; map p.138 B3

If you are interested in early 20th-century silver jewellery and homeware, this is a lovely little museum in the basement of the Georg Jensen shop on Strøget, which displays some of the designer's key pieces. You can also see some of his correspondance.

SEE ALSO DANISH DESIGN P.43

Guinness World of Records Museum

Østergade 16; tel: 33 32 31 31; www.guinness.dk; Jan–June: daily 10am–6pm, June–Aug: daily 10am–10pm, Sept–Dec: Sun–Thur 10am–6pm, Fri–Sat 10am–8pm; entrance charge, under-4s free, combination ticket available with Ripley's Believe it or Not, Wonderful World of Hans Christian Andersen and Exploratorium; map p.138 C3

This attraction charts the world as well as human endeavour from the bizarre, such as bicycle-eating men and enormous food, to international records in sport and science. You can find out for instance, how 1.3 million dominoes tumble and what it feels like to drive at 550km/h.

Copenhagen's art scene is concentrated in the streets around Kongens Nytorv, where the Royal Academy of Fine Arts is located. Galleri Susanne Ottesen at Gothersgade 49 is one of the most prominent. Nearby Bredgade is especially well known for its designer goods and antique shops.

Jewish Museum

Royal Library, Slotsholmen; tel: 33 11 22 18; www.jewmus.dk; Sept–May: Tue–Fri 1–4pm, Sat–Sun 10am–5pm, June–Aug: Tue–Sun 10am–5pm; entrance charge, children free; map p.138 C2

One of Copenhagen's newest museums, this impressive little museum is housed next to the old bibliothèque nationale on Slotsholmen and fronted by a pretty little enclosed garden.

The historic nature of the fabric of the building is sharply in contrast with the new interior, designed by Daniel Libeskind to complement the exhibition inside, which charts the life of the Jewish community in Copenhagen from the 17th century, when immigrants were rather aristocratic to the mid 20th century, just before the World War II, when lower class sections of society began to arrive to escape the hardships of eastern Europe.

The interior, made up of interlocking sections, often tilting to one side, is highly effective and is intended to reflect the amicable history of the Jewish community with its Danish neighbours. The exhibition does not cover the Holocaust or World War II. If you want to know about these, visit the Frihedsmuseet *(see page 87)*.

Karen Blixen Museet

Rungstedlund, Rungsted Strandvej 111, Rungsted Kyst; tel: 45 57 10 57; www.karen-blixen.dk;

Below: Blixen is most famous for her book written while in East Africa.

May–Sept: Tue–Sun 10am–5pm, Oct–Apr: Wed–Fri 1–4pm, Sat–Sun 11am–4pm; entrance charge; S-tog: Lyngby then bus 388
From 1914–1931, the author Karen Blixen (Isak Dinesen) lived as a coffee grower in East Africa, where she wrote her most successful novels, including the famous *Out of Africa* (1985 movie, starring Meryl Streep and Robert Redford).

When Blixen returned to Denmark after her divorce and the death of her lover in 1931, she settled at her parents' home in Rungstedlund, north of Copenhagen, where she had been born in 1885. In 1991 the house was converted into the Karen Blixen Museum, which sheds light on the intriguing personality of Denmark's most celebrated female literary figure.

Nothing has changed since she lived here and you can see her paintings, letters, drawings and poems, as well as her grave, which is beneath a tree at the foot of 'Ewals' Hill' in her lovely garden.
SEE ALSO LITERATURE AND THEATRE P.73–4

Københavns Bymuseet

Vesterbrogade 59; tel: 33 21 07 72; www.kbhbymuseum.dk; Thurs–Mon 10am–4pm, Wed 10am–9pm; entrance charge, under-17s free, Fri free; bus: 6a, 26; map p.136 B3
The City Museum occupies the former premises of the Royal Shooting Club (1786) on Vesterbrogade.

Its exhibits are particularly impressive for their originality and credibility as they focus not only on the glorious days of the city's past, but also on the difficult periods in its development. It looks closely, for example, at Copenhagen around the middle of the 18th century, when, within the space of only a few decades, the population doubled. A smaller section is devoted to Søren Kierkegaard, the father of existentialism.

A clay model outside the museum shows what the city would have looked like around 1530, and the nearby cobbled Absalonsgade has been turned into a museum street, where lanterns, fire hydrants and an art nouveau telephone kiosk covered with original advertising posters revive the atmosphere of the early 20th century.
SEE ALSO LITERATURE AND THEATRE P.74–5

Above: the temporary exhibition hall at the Kunstindustrie Museet explores different themes in Danish and international design.

Below: the nearly 6ha of land around the Blixen home, comprising a maintained garden and a wild grove, is maintained as a bird sanctuary.

Kunstindustrie Museet

Bredgade 68; tel: 33 18 56 56; www.kunstindustrimuseet.dk; Tue–Sun noon–4pm, Wed noon–6pm; entrance charge, under-18s free; bus: 1a, 15, 19; map p.139 D4
This grand old Rococo building (1754) was a hospital until 1910 and in 1919 it became the Museum of Decorative and Applied Arts. The principal attractions here are the collection of *objets d'art*, some fine French Rococo furniture and various cutting-edge works by Danish designers, ranging from shiny kitchenware to motorbikes and cardboard furniture.

Above: the reclining figures of Henry Moore look over the Øresund, and are just one of the masterpieces in the Lousiana's gardens.

There are also Oriental handicrafts dating from the Middle Ages to the present, a poster and print collection and lovely dress and textiles on display.

Its library contains around 6,500 books and periodicals on art, costume and industrial design. Its pretty garden is an inviting place to stop for a rest and, in the summer you can see Shakespeare performances (in Danish).

SEE ALSO DANISH DESIGN P.41

Left: there is a fine collection of vintage instruments, such as this harpsichord, on display at the Musik Historisk Museet.

Little Mill

Christianshavns Voldgade 54; tel: 33 13 44 11; June–Sept: tours in Danish Tue–Sun 1pm, 2pm, 3pm; entrance charge, children free; map p.139 D1

Part of the National Museum, this is one of the last mills on the Christianshavn ramparts. The house is five storeys high and charmingly furnished exactly as it was when the couple to whom it belonged last lived here in the early 20th century.

Louisiana Museum for Moderne Kunst

Gammel Strandvej 13, Humlebæk; tel: 49 19 07 91; www.louisiana.dk; Thur–Tue 10am–5pm, Wed 10am–10pm, café Thur–Tue 10am–4.30pm, Wed 10am–9.30pm; entrance charge, under-18s free; train then walk or bus 388

The Louisiana Modern Art Museum at Humlebæk is a gallery with a difference. Housed in a 19th-century mansion set in beautiful gardens on the water's edge with a view across the Øresund to Sweden, it is easy to while away most of a day here soaking up the art and the atmosphere.

Airy white-washed galleries form the backdrop to an extensive collection, including works by Picasso, Warhol and Rauschenberg, CoBrA artists such as Asger Jorn, and more recently, Per Kirkeby. A glazed corridor

Since the mid-1950s, the Louisiana Museum has gradually expanded from its original 19th-century villa to a modern exhibition space. It was Jørgen Bo and Vilhelm Wohlert's first commission to transform the villa to a museum, and they are still in charge of the museum's architectural growth some 50 years later.

leads past a group of Giacometti figures to a terrace featuring metal mobiles by Alexander Calder.

The café offers delicious Danish food, the shop has a wide selection of books, posters and designer items, and the children's wing runs a variety of inspired activities.

Look out for their special exhibitions. Each year the Louisiana Museum holds a half dozen or so major exhibitions on modern and contemporary art from modern masters to up-and-coming international artists.

Medicinsk Museum

Bredgade 62; tel: 35 32 38 00; www.mhm.ku.dk; tour only Sept–June: Wed–Fri 11am, 1pm, Sun 1pm, July–Aug: Wed–Fri, Sun 1pm; bus: 1a, 15, 19; map p.139 C4

Not for the faint-hearted (but for the unsquemish, it is very interesting). This museum covers the history of health and disease from the 18th century onwards, with plenty of scary-looking hardware to boost the imagination.

Museum Erotica

Købmagergade 24; tel: 33 12 03 11; www.museumerotica.dk; May–Sep: daily 10am–11pm, Oct–Apr: Sun–Thur 11am–8pm, Fri–Sat 10am–10pm; entrance charge; map p.138 B3

Copenhagen, with its liberally-minded citizens, is one of the few places in Europe that would tolerate a Museum of Erotica.

This place is not simply a display of naked bodies. It attempts to discriminate between love, sex and pornography. So, if you're curious to discover if they've got the balance right, you'll probably enjoy seeing how eroticism and sexuality have been expressed since the time of the ancient Greeks.

Beware: the further into the museum you go the more explicit the exhibits become. When you reach the fourth floor, a dozen screens are showing erotic films, from 1920s black-and-white to today's full-colour hardcore.

Be warned, you may wish you had not seen some of the exhibits on display, of course others will wish they had seen them sooner.

Musik Historisk Museet

Abenrå 30; tel: 33 11 27 26; www.musikhistoriskmuseum.dk; Oct–Apr: Tue–Wed, Sat–Sun 1–3.50pm, May–Sept: Thur–Sun 1–3.50pm; free; map p.138 B4

Close to the gardens of Rosenborg Slot, situated in narrow Åbenrå, the Musikhistorisk Museet is a source of fascination to anyone who loves music, charting as it does the history of European musical instruments over the last 1,000 years, with a special emphasis on the period from the Renaissance to the early 20th century.

Amid its marvellous collection of instruments, you can see such curiosities as the amoeba-shaped violin and the giraffe-piano. There is also a 'play-with-sound' room for kids to experiment with percussion instruments.

Occasionally, the museum stages classical music concerts. These often use some of the ancient, and rather fragile, instruments normally kept on display. Ask at the information desk for details.

Below: the classic phallic sculpture in the Museum Erotica, one of the more impressive exhibits about human sexuality.

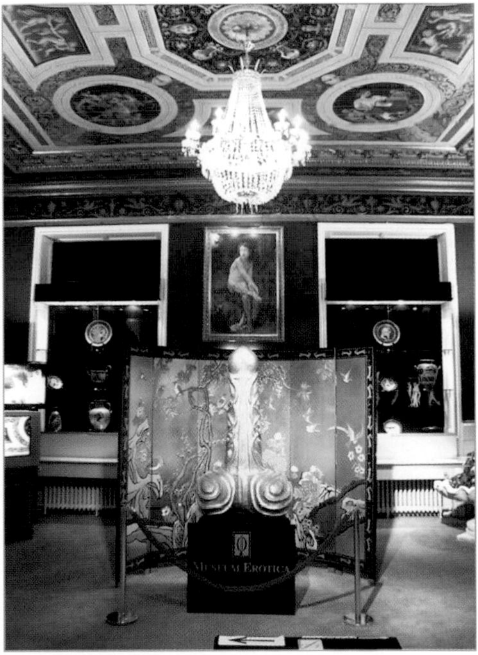

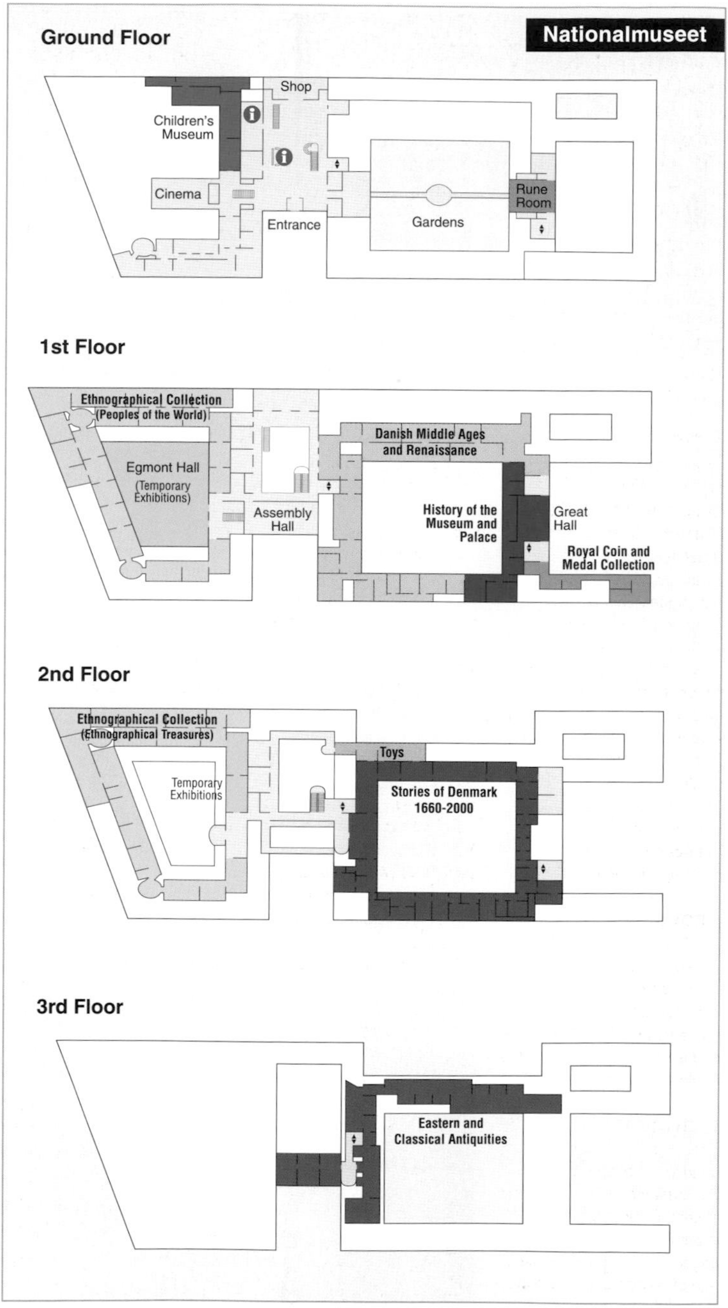
Nationalmuseet
Ground Floor
Shop
Children's Museum
Cinema
Entrance
Gardens
Rune Room
1st Floor
Ethnographical Collection (Peoples of the World)
Egmont Hall (Temporary Exhibitions)
Assembly Hall
Danish Middle Ages and Renaissance
History of the Museum and Palace
Great Hall
Royal Coin and Medal Collection
2nd Floor
Ethnographical Collection (Ethnographical Treasures)
Temporary Exhibitions
Toys
Stories of Denmark 1660-2000
3rd Floor
Eastern and Classical Antiquities

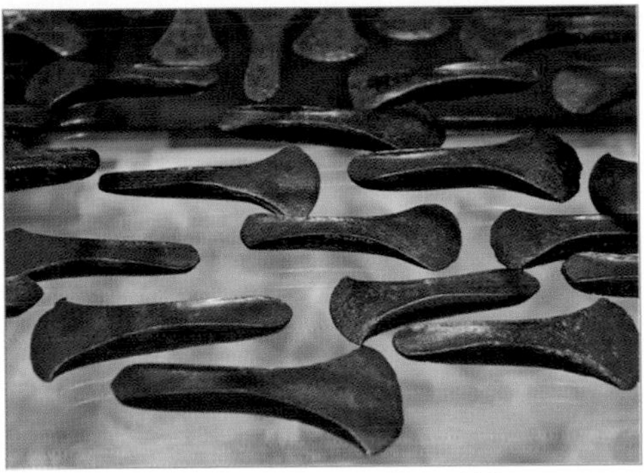

Above: the Bronze Age exhibits at the National Museum are some of the finest in all of Europe.

Nationalmuseet

Ny Vestergade 1; tel: 33 13 44 11; www.natmus.dk; Tue–Sun 10am–5pm; entrance charge, Wed free; prehistoric collection closed until May 2008; bus: 6a, 12, 26, 29, 33; map p.138 B2

The biggest museum in Scandinavia with over 10,000sq. m of exhibition space, it focuses on Danish history from the Stone Age to modern times, but houses an astonishing collection of artefacts ranging from Stone Age Danish rock carvings, Mongolian horse-riding equipment and tents, to 17th-century royal interiors and Imperial dragon robes.

A ROYAL RESIDENCE

The Prince's Palace which houses the museum was once home to royalty in the 18th century. Its great hall preserves the look of the era and is still decorated with the original Flemish tapestries.

PREHISTORIC TREASURES

Though the surroundings may sparkle the main attraction at the museum is it's prehistoric collection that traces 14,000 years of Danish prehistory, especially rich is their collection of bronze age artefacts. One of the most striking exhibits is the Trundholm Sun Chariot (1200 BC), dating from a period when the Danes worshipped the sun, imagining it as a disc of gold riding through the sky in a chariot behind a celestial horse. Unfortunately, at time of press, much of the pre-history exhibitions are not on display. The new prehistory exhibition is scheduled to open in May 2008.

FROM GOLDEN ALTARS TO DEADLY AXES

The museum has several elaborate golden altars preserved from churches built during Denmark's Middle Ages.

A more gruesome exhibit is the executioner's axe 'probably' used to cut off the head of Johann Friedrich Struensee, a moderniser who effectively ruled the country as he was physician to the mentally ill King Christian VII until his death in 1772 *(see the Reading list on page 76)*.

Other sections of the museum contain ethnographic exhibits from around the world, including a reconstructed Inuit camp from Greenland, classical antiquities and the Royal Coin and Medal Collection. There are also several oak burial coffins dating from 1400 BC and the well-known silver Gundestrop cauldron, an iron-age vessel found in a peat bog.

CHILDREN'S MUSEUM

A hands-on Children's Museum provides an interesting diversion for youngsters, including theatrical performances, copies of Viking ships and concerts.
SEE ALSO CHILDREN P.35

The National Museum has created several self-guided tours, such as *The History of Denmark in 60 Minutes*, in English and other languages that allow you to explore your own interests in your own time.

Below: the Trundholm Sun Chariot is over 3,000 years old.

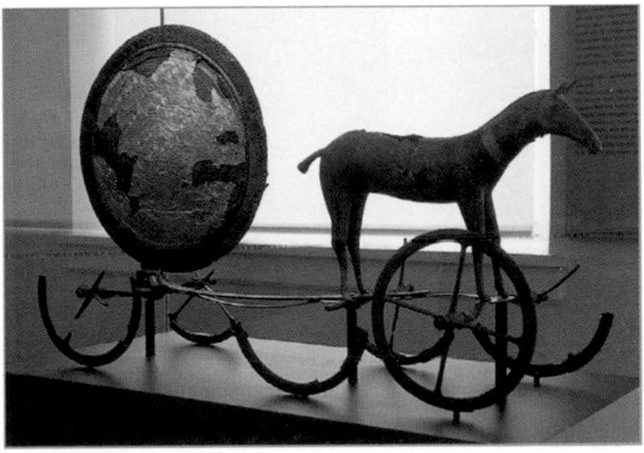

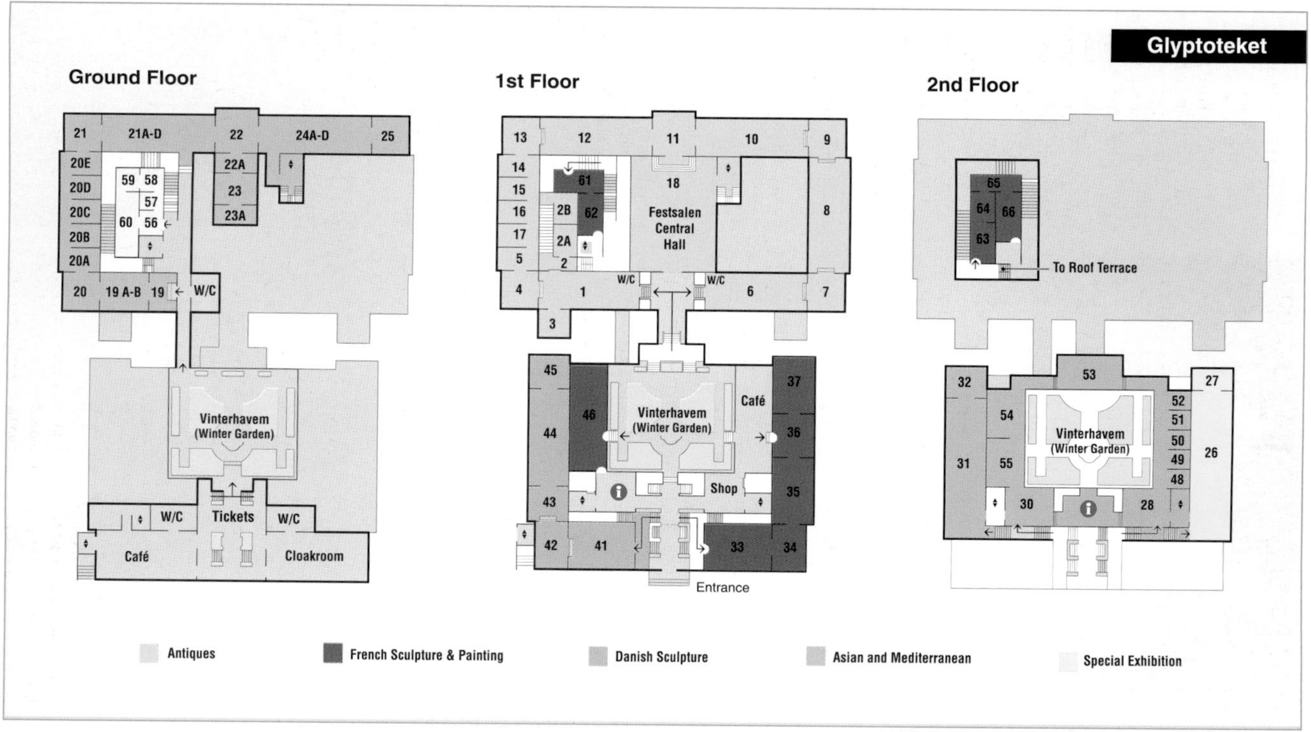
Glyptoteket
Ground Floor
21
21A-D
22
24A-D
25
20E
20D
20C
20B
20A
20
19 A-B
19
W/C
59
58
57
60
56
22A
23
23A
Vinterhavem
(Winter Garden)
W/C
Tickets
W/C
Café
Cloakroom
1st Floor
13
12
11
10
9
14
15
16
17
5
4
3
2B
2A
2
61
62
18
Festsalen
Central
Hall
8
W/C
W/C
1
6
7
45
46
44
43
42
41
Vinterhavem
(Winter Garden)
Café
Shop
37
36
35
33
34
Entrance
2nd Floor
65
64
66
63
To Roof Terrace
32
53
27
54
31
55
Vinterhavem
(Winter Garden)
52
51
50
49
48
26
30
28
Antiques
French Sculpture & Painting
Danish Sculpture
Asian and Mediterranean
Special Exhibition

Left: this Egyptian cosmetic spoon portrays a young woman in a papyrus thicket and dates from the 14th century BC.

Ny Carlsberg Glyptotek

Dantes Plads 7; tel: 33 41 81 41; www.glyptoteket.dk; Tue–Sun 10am–4pm, tour: June–Sept Wed 2pm; entrance charge, under-18s free, Wed, Sun free; bus: 33; map p.138 A1

Opposite Tivoli, with the entrance on H.C. Andersen Boulevard, this distinctive Classical building with a columned portal and domed roof houses Ny Carlsberg Glyptotek, an art museum financed by the founder of the Carlsberg brewery.

The Glyptotek was founded on the classical art and statuary collection of Carl Jacobsen (1842–1914), a Danish brewer and art connoisseur. Under its elaborate roof lies one of the world's foremost displays of Egyptian, Greek, Roman and Etruscan art.

The sub-tropical Winter Garden in the central hall, complete with goldfish pond, appears to have been transplanted directly from ancient Rome. It was the fashion at the time for all rich men to possess a garden. The Glyptotek was designed for this to be the centre with all exhibition halls leading to it.

In contrast, the French collection – works by Gauguin, van Gogh and Monet, Rodin sculptures and a complete set of Degas bronzes – is housed in a glorious spacious new wing, which has great views of Tivoli from the roof.

The museum also hosts regular concerts, and the café set in the Winter Garden is worth the admission charge alone.

SEE ALSO CAFÉS AND BARS P.28

> Despite its wonderful collection of art and calm gardens, the Glyptotek is behind the times in terms of accessibility, partly due to its status as a preserved building. Prams and pushchairs must be left outside and the wheelchair entrance is tucked around the back and requires assistance to be used; several of the exhibition halls are only accessible via stairs.

Øksnehallen

Halmtørvet 11; tel: 33 86 04 00; www.dgi-byen.com/oeksnehallen; check website for details; map p.137 C3

Located in an abandoned industrial area behind Central Station (Hovedbanegårde) is this innovative exhibition centre housed in a huge former abattoir.

Øksnehallen serves as a symbol for the reviving of Vesterbro. Using reclaimed building materials, the old slaughter house has been turned into an ingenious new 4,000sq. m exhibition hall for the arts, business and culture, while retaining some of the less gruesome details of the original building. As well as hosting temporary displays, a permanent exhibition in the building will describe Vesterbro's ongoing renewal.

SEE ALSO VESTERBRO AND FREDERIKSBERG P.19

Ørdrupsgaard

Vilvordevej 110, Charlottenlund; tel: 39 64 11 83; www. ordrupgaard.dk; Tue, Thur– Fri 1–5pm, Wed 10am–6pm, Sat–Sun 11am–5pm; entrance charge, under-18s free; S-tog: Klampenborg then bus, 2 per hour, or turn left out of station, not on

Below: one of the finest attractions of the Glyptotek is its Winter Garden, which is located under the building's central arch and is full of tropical flora.

Above: reading a telegraph at the Post and Tele Museum.

the beach side, turn right at Dyrehavnbakket then turn left at sign to Lyngby 4
Two kilometres from Klampenborg, this lovely art collection of Impressionist paintings is housed in a 19th-century villa with a pretty garden. There is a modern, recent extension and a nice café serving food by Tivoli's The Paul. The collection boasts lots of big names and also has an interesting collection of art by Danish artists such as Willem Hammershøi – some of his work bears a resemblance to the English artist Whistler. Its new wing, which opened in 2005, was designed by the Iraqi-born architect Zaha Hadid.

Orlogsmuseet

Overgaden 58–64; tel: 33 11 60 37; www.orlogsmuseet.dk; Tue–Sun noon–4pm; entrance charge, under-15s free, Wed free; map p.139 D2
The Royal Danish Naval Museum is housed in a long Rococo building, formerly used as a school, a prison, a hospital and then a rehabilitation centre for wounded naval personnel. Today, it houses a beautiful collection of model ships from the 17th century, uniforms, nautical instruments and weapons.

Politihistorisk Museum

Fælledvej 20, Nørrebro; tel: 35 36 88 88; www.politimuseum.dk; Tue, Thur, Sun 11am–4pm; map p.134 B2
Although information in English is sparse, the exhibits in the Police Museum – housed in the city's oldest police station, which dates from 1884 – tell their own story.

From early photographs of murder scenes and illegal pornography, to the workings of the criminal mind and the tools of the job – including motorbikes, weapons and uniforms – the Police Museum sets out the history of the police in Copenhagen from the 17th century to the present.

Post and Tele Museum

Købmagergade 37; tel: 33 41 09 00; www.ptt-museum.dk; Tue, Thur–Sat 10am–5pm, Wed 10am–8pm, Sun noon–4pm, tour Sun 2pm; free; map p.138 B3
Not far from the Rundetårn, inside Copenhagen's main post office, you'll find a nicely laid out museum charting the history of modern communication from the 17th century to today, via ice boats, motorbikes and huge, early mobile phones.

English labelling is virtually non-existent but the exhibits are interesting nonetheless and the top-floor café has great views.
SEE ALSO CAFÉS AND BARS P.29

Ripleys Believe it or Not! Museum

Rådhuspladsen 57; tel: 33 32 31 31; www.ripleys.dk; Sept–Dec, Jan–mid-Jun: Sun–Thur 10am– 6pm, Fri–Sat 10am–8pm, mid-Jun–Aug: daily 10am–10pm; entrance charge; bus: all Rådhuspladsen buses; map p.138 A2
This US-style museum of 'bizarre but true' curiosities (which is a bit tired, if we are going to be honest) is based on a venerable American newspaper strip.

If you are keen to learn more about the demise of aviation pioneers, or you are interested in how you can smoke with your eyes, Ripleys has all this and more wacky wonders; it is particularly appealing to older kids. You can even try the chilling equilibrium tunnel.

Royal Porcelain Museum

2nd floor, Amagertorv 6; tel: 38 14 92 97; free, porcelain painting, 1 hour, 250DKK + shipping, glass painting, 1 hour, 250DKK + shipping, telephone to arrange in advance; map p.138 B3
This museum, formerly out in Vesterbro, has very recently been brought into the centre as part of Royal Copenhagen's makeover of its hisotoric shop on Strøget, which has been home to Royal Copenhagen since 1911.

Alongside films and informative displays, visitors will be able to follow the various stages of production and have the opportunity to hand-paint the famous patterns on glass and porcelain.
SEE ALSO DANISH DESIGN P.41

Slotsholmen Ruins

Christiansborg Palace; May–Sept: daily 10am–4pm, Oct–Apr: Tue–Sun 10am–4pm; entrance charge; map p.138 B2
The ruins beneath Chris-

The Statens Museum for Kunst is home to plenty of innovative art, including Matisse's portrait of his wife (1905), also known as 'the Green Stripe', which influenced to the 'Fauve' or 'wild beast' school of painting and had great implications for the development of modern art.

tiansborg Palace on Slotsholmen are an atmospheric and fascinating view into Copenhagen's past, revealing parts of Absalon's ancient castle dating from 1167 as well as later structures. Well worth a visit.
SEE ALSO SLOTSHOLMEN P.10

Above: the Stables Museum at Christiansborg showcases the elegant carriages used by past kings and queens.

Stables Museum

Christiansborg Ridebane; tel 33 40 26 77; Oct–Apr: Sat–Sun 2–4pm, May–Sept: Fri–Sun 2–4pm; free; map p.130 D2

A small museum on Slotsholmen, this is an intriguing view in to 17th-century royal life, where even the horses lived in palatial splendour.

Statens Museum for Kunst

48–50 Sølvegade; tel: 33 74 84 94; www.smk.dk; Tue–Sun 10am–5pm, Wed 10am–8pm; entrance charge, under-18s free; bus: 6a, 26, 184, 185, 150; map p.135 D2

The National Gallery of Art is housed in a grand building dating from 1896, and is well worth a visit for probably the best all-round collection of art in the country. Any resemblance of the building to the Ny Carlsberg Glyptotek *(see page 95)* is not a coincidence – both were designed by Vilhelm Dahlerup.

Inside, the fine collection of European art dates from around 1530, including work by Fra Filippo Lippi, Albrecht Dürer, Rubens, Mantegna and Titian. The main themes are Danish painting and French 19th-century painting.

A gleaming new four-storey building extending towards the park has been built to house the gallery's collection of modern art – an attraction in itself. Exhibitions are held here, too. A collection of copperplate engravings and drawings, as well as montages by children, are of particular interest. There is also a very good set of children's activities.
SEE ALSO CAFÉS AND BARS P.32

Below: the interior of the Statens Museum for Kunst has been redeveloped recently to allow for more of their collection to be displayed with better lighting and space.

Storm P Museum

Frederiksberg Runddel, Frederiksberg; tel: 38 86 05 23; daily 10am–4pm; entrance charge, children free; bus: 18, 26; map p.136 A3

On the corner of the street with the entrance to Frederiksberg Have, this is a small and delightful museum dedicated to the humour and wit of Storm P, a Danish cartoonist who seems to combine the social realism of the late 19th and early 20th centuries with the ludicrous invention of Heath Robinson and some of the cartoon qualities of Mr McGoo. Marvellous if you understand Danish but still worth popping in for the visual style and humour, even if you don't.

Teatermuseet

Christiansborg Ridebane 18; tel: 33 11 51 76; www.teatermuseet.dk; Tue, Thur 11am–3pm, Wed 11am–5pm, Sat–Sun 1–4pm; entrance charge, under-16s free; map p.138 B2

This is one of the oldest court theatres in the world, designed by the French architect Nicolas-Henri Jardin. From 1767–1881 it was a stage for opera and drama. Now visitors can visit the auditorium, wandering through the boxes, onto the stage, surrounded by props and other memorabilia. Unlike the rest of the palace, it survived the fire of 1794 along with the Stables Museum.

SEE PICTURE, LITERATURE AND THEATRE P.77

Thorvaldsens Museum

Bertel Thorvaldsens Plads 2; tel: 33 32 15 32; www.thorvaldsensmuseum.dk; Tue–Sun 10am–5pm; entrance charge, Wed free; map p.138 B2

This gallery in Slotsholmen is dedicated to the works of Denmark's great sculptor, Bertel Thorvaldsen (1770–1844), who lived and worked in Rome for 40 years.

He bequeathed his works, his own collection and his estate to the nation on the condition that a museum was built for the artistic treasures.

His plans, castings, originals and replicas, plus his antiques – including examples of Egyptian, Greek, Etruscan and Roman works – and his collection of paintings – are all on display here. Thorvaldsen also lies buried at the centre of the museum, which opened in 1848. On the outside walls a coloured frieze with life-size figures depicts Thorvaldsen's triumphant homecoming from Italy in 1838.

The CPH Card, available from the Tourist Information Office, lasts for 1–3 days and gives free or reduced admission to more than 60 popular museums and sights in the city. Two children under 10 may accompany each card-carrying adult free of charge.

Tøjhusmuseet

Tøjhusgade 3, Frederiksholmskanal; tel: 33 11 60 37; www.thm.dk; Tue–Sun noon–4pm; entrance charge, under-17s free; map p.138 B2

This 400 year old, 163m-long brick building houses the Arsenal Museum: an awesome collection of weaponry ranging from daggers and cannons to Hawk missiles and exquisitely inlaid duelling pistols; considered one of the finest museums of its kind in the world. The huge number of weapons are displayed in a vaulted Renaissance cannon hall, reputedly the longest in Europe.

Tycho Brahe Planetarium

Gammel Kongevej 10; tel: 33 12 12 24; www.tycho.dk; Tue–Thur 9.30am–9pm, Fri–Mon 10.30am–9pm; entrance charge; bus: 14, 15; map p.136 C3

Left: almost all of Thorvaldsens' works are represented in his museum, though many are only plaster casts of the original artwork; these too were created and preserved by Thorvaldsens.

Right: the Tycho Brahe Planetarium cuts a striking figure beside the city's reservoirs.

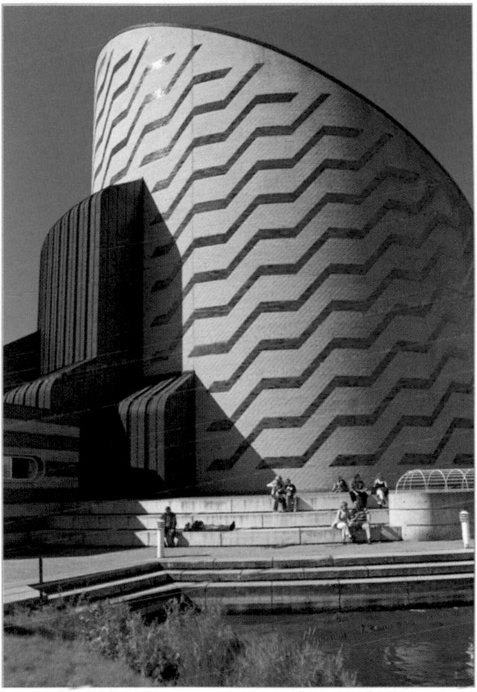

You can't miss this superb planetarium, for its eye-catching architecture alone, with its 36m-high, decorated, cylindrical tower and diagonal roof. For the best view of this striking building, cross to the other side of the lake and take a walk along the promenade.

Inside the planetarium is a small exhibition on astronomy and space travel. The main draw is the film auditorium, with its 23m wide dome-shaped screen. Its *stjerneforestillinger* or 'star shows' are definitely worth sampling.

Thanks to the latest computer technology, visitors can undertake a fascinating journey through space, encountering such phenomena as the Northern Lights, comets and supernovas.

The advertising for the IMAX (huge screen) film performances takes up the same theme: higher, faster, wider, further. What is on offer are clips of free-climbers, rock stars and other vertigo inducing stories.

Victorian House

Ny Vestergade 10; tel: 33 13 44 11; tours July–Sept: Sun 11am, sign up 1 hour before, tour starts at the information desk in the entrance hall of the National Museum; entrance charge, under-18s free; map p.138 B2

Like the Little Mill *(see page 90)*, this belongs to the National Museum and is an excellent opportunity to see a charming old interior; this museum preserves a smart Copenhagen home dating from between 1890 and 1914.

Vikingskibsmuseet

Vindeboder 12, Roskilde; tel: 46 30 02 00; www.vikingskibsmuseet.dk; daily 10am–5pm; entrance charge; train then bus 607, 216, or 20-min walk

In 1962 some extraordinary excavation work started in the Roskildefjord after archaeologists discovered the remains of several Viking ships.

The ships were probably scuttled in the fjord between 1000 and 1050 to block the fjord against raiders. It took a great deal of meticulous work first to remove the fragments from the mud and stones and then to conserve them.

The results of the laborious treatment can be seen in the Vikingskibsmuseet. There are five ships here altogether, including an ocean-going merchant ship, a warship and an inshore boat, which probably served as a ferry.

From the glass façade of the Viking Ship Museum you can look out over the fjord, where reconstructions of Viking ships are moored. During the summer they are used to take visitors for a trip on the fjord. Living workshops, models, videos, special exhibitions, and a film showing how the boats were salvaged, form part of the museum. A must-visit to understand the early history of Northern Europe.

SEE ALSO SJÆLLAND P.24

Wonderful World of Hans Christian Andersen

Rådhuspladsen 57; map p.138 A2

SEE ALSO CHILDREN P.35; LITERATURE AND THEATRE P.72

Music and Dance

International acclaim for the Danish National Symphony, Royal Ballet and Royal Opera grows louder each year. Their accomplishments are even more impressive as they draw on a smaller population than their European rivals based in much larger cities. Maintaining the Danes' historic choral tradition is the main function of the city's churches, which hold numerous concerts throughout the year. A thriving jazz scene culminates each year with the Copenhagen Jazz Festival in July, while the Roskilde Festival and the university keep the city firmly planted at the heart of Europe's rock and pop music scene.

Classical Music

COMPANIES

Concerto Copenhagen
Sankt Peders Stræde 39; tel: 33 91 73 00; www.coco.dk
Denmark's leading period instrument ensemble, known as 'Coco' for short, often performs alongside the Royal Opera and gives independent performances at the Royal Theatre and various churches.

Danish National Symphony Orchestra (DNSO)
www.dr.dk
Though it is seen as one of the best symphony orchestras in Scandinavia, the DNSO began as only a radio orchestra with 11 musicians in 1928.

Since then it has grown immensely and its focus has shifted away from radio programmes, though they still give weekly concerts at the Radiohusets Koncertsal.

Their principal guest conductor is the charismatic Yuri Temirkanov. Currently performing at the Royal Theatre and the Radiohusets Koncertsal, a new concert hall designed by French architect Jean Nouvel, which will be inaugurated in August 2008.

Much like H.C. Andersen, Carl Nielsen *(right)* began life in a poor family but came to represent Danish art on the global stage. It was his penultimate symphony, No. 5, that first extended his name beyond Scandinavia when it was performed at the Edinburgh International Festival in 1950. Nielsen also wrote two books, *My Childhood on Funen* and *Living Music.*

VENUES

Black Diamond
Soren Kirkegaards Plads 1; tel: 33 47 47 47; www.kb.dk; bus: 47, 66; map p.138 B1/C1
In addition to maintaining their own group, the Diamant Ensemble, the library hosts classical, world music and jazz concerts throughout the year. See their website for more information.

Radiohusets Koncertsal
Julius Thomsensgade 1, Frederiksburg; tel: 35 20 62 62; train: Forum, bus: 2A; map p.134 B1
This Functionalist building designed by Vilhelm Lauritzen opened in 1945. The interiors and original furnishings make it a museum to the Functionalist style. It hosts regular Thursday concerts by the Danish National Symphony Orchestra.

Tivoli Koncertsalen
Tietgensgade 20; tel: 33 15 10 12; www.tivoli.dk; open in summer only; train: Københavns, bus: 1A, 2A 15, 65E; map p.138 A1
The Concert Hall in the famous pleasure gardens is home to the Tivoli Symphony Orchestra, which

Left: the Opera House is a masterpiece of acoustic design, with a gold-leaf ceiling made up of over 100,000 pieces of gold.

accompanies singers, guest musicians and conductors. Foreign orchestras also perform here. Some concerts are free of charge.

The new foyer contains Denmark's longest saltwater aquarium which houses sharks, rays and over 1600 fish. Though the foyer is open all day, there is a charge to enter just to see the aquarium.

MUSEUM

Musik Historisk Museum

Åbenrå 30; map p.138 B4

This niche museum has a collection of vintage instruments.

SEE ALSO MUSEUMS AND GALLERIES P.91

Choral Music

Copenhagen has a strong tradition of choral music that predates classical music and inspires most young people to become members of choirs. Today most choirs are connected to the church.

COMPANIES

Danish National Choir and the Danish National Chamber Choir

www.dr.dk

Above: the Copenhagen Opera House hosts opera, classical music and ballet performances on two stages.

Founded in 1932, the company's repertoir now ranges from Bach passions to brand new works by Danish composers Nørgard and Pärt.

Musica Ficta

Gammeltoftsgade 16; tel: 35 38 44 83; www.ficta.dk

Named after the latin term, 'feigned music', which was used to describe a musician's practice of adding accidentals in early music to avoid 'forbidden' harmonic and melodic intervals, this company, established by international conductor Bo Holten, explores and interprets early Danish vocal music. They do not have a regular venue but perform in churches throughout Denmark. Check their website for performance information.

VENUES

Christianskirke

Strandgade 2; tel: 32 54 15 76; www.christianskirke.dk; bus: 1A, 2A, 15; map p.138 C1

Garnisons Kirken

Skt Annæ Plads 4; tel: 33 91 27 06; www.folkekirken.dk; bus: 1A, 15, 19; map p.139 C3

Holmens Kirke

Holmens Kanal; tel: 33 13 19 51; www.holmenskirke.dk; bus: 1A; map p.138 C2

Hosts about 50 concerts a year with many during Easter and Christmas time.

Kastelskirken

Kastellet; tel: 33 91 27 06; map p.135 E2

Opera

Royal Danish Opera

www.operaen.dk

Danish opera began by entertaining the Royal Court with Italian operas that were often produced by imported experts.

In the late 19th century, the company began to develop native works of international quality with Carl Nielsen *(see box left)* leading the way with *Saul and David and Mascarade*. But in many ways, the Royal Danish

Various concerts take place in Copenhagen's churches throughout the year and the vast majority of them are free – an admirable tradition. Ask in the tourist office for the concert programme, which is published every three or four months. Although it is written in Danish, the basic information will be perfectly understandable without any knowledge of the language.

One handy tip: from 5pm onwards, the Royal Theatre box office offers 50 per cent reductions on unsold tickets for events taking place that day.

Opera only came into its own with the opening of the new Opera House in 2005. Before this it had shared (cramped) space with the Royal Danish Theatre. The new building has allowed this always innovative company even more freedom to commission new productions of classics and promote young Danish composers.

Operahuset (Opera House)
Operaen Ekvipagemestervej 10; tel: 33 69 69 69 for tickets which are also available at the Royal Theatre's ticket office on Kongens Nytorv; www.operaen.dk; guided tours Sat and Sun at 9.30am and 4pm; map p.139 D3
Since it opened in 2005, the Opera House, designed by Henning Larsen, has been Copenhagen's landmark building and led a rejuvenation of the waterfront. Guided tours let you explore the interior and back stage areas. The restaurant opens three hours before the performance and reservations are suggested. The café is open daily.
SEE ALSO ARCHITECTURE P.26–7

Ballet

Royal Danish Ballet
Internationally acclaimed, and rightly so – it is one of Europe's oldest companies with a repertory going back 200 years.

Nowadays, the company experiments in modern dance as well, but its great tradition lies in Bournonville classics, such as *La Sylphide* and *The Dancing School*.

Det Kongelige Teater
Kongens Nytorv; tel: 33 69 69 69; www.kglteater.dk; ticket center to the left of the main entrance and open Mon–Sat 2–8pm; train: Kongens Nytorv, bus: 15, 19, 26, 1A, 999; map p.138 C3
The Royal Theatre provides a home for drama and ballet. While plays in Danish may not have much appeal for foreign visitors, it is definitely worth enquiring about tickets for ballet performances. Advance ticket sales Monday to Friday.
SEE ALSO LITERATURE AND THEATRE P.77

Modern Dance

Copenhagen has a thriving modern dance scene with dozens of companies operating throughout the city. Check at the tourist information office for more details. The list below is but a few companies operating around the year.

Dansescenen
Øster Fælled Torv 34, Østerbro; tel: 35 43 83 00; www.dansescenen.dk
The main venue for contemporary dance in Copenhagen with performers from home and abroad. Dansescenen does produce some of its own material, but its main function is to promote dance in the city.

Dansk Danse Teater
Folketeatret; Nørregade 39; tel: 33 12 18 45; www.danskdanseteater.dk; map p.138 A3
With the benefit of its own venue in the Folketeatret, Tim Rushton's company has established itself as one of Denmark's finest contemporary dance ensembles.

Kanonhallen
Østerfælled Torv 37, Østerbro; tel: 35 43 20 21; www.kanonhallen.net
A venue for touring international dance and theatre festivals, especially during the summer.

Jazz and Blues

Various clubs offer jazz of all persuasions every night until 2am or later. The capital's reputation as northern Europe's jazz centre is so great that many foreign stars now live in Denmark and appear at the top clubs. At smaller bars the jazz is sometimes free.

Copenhagen JazzHouse
Niels Hemmingsensgade; tel: 33 93 26 16; www.jazzhouse.dk; open for concerts only; map p.138 B3
As the city's top jazz venue, this club attracts talent from throughout Denmark and the best in touring internationals. It's located just off of Strøget and presents all kinds of con-

Below: the Royal Danish Ballet performs from September to June.

Above: Copenhagen is one of Europe's leading jazz centres.

temporary jazz from electronic to free improvisation. There are 3–5 performances per week.

La Fontaine
Kompagnistræde 11, parallel to Strøget; tel: 33 11 60 98; www.lafontaine.dk; Mon–Thur 7pm–2am, live music on Fri and Sat only 11pm–3am and Sun 9pm–1am; map p.138 B2
This legendary and intimate pub-like venue is Copenhagen's oldest Jazz house. The jam sessions on the weekends are the main attraction, but a high quality sound system also makes it worth visiting on the quieter weeknights.

Mojo Blues Bar
Løngangsstræde 21 C; tel: 33 11 64 53; www.mojo.dk; daily 8pm–5am; bus: 6A; map p.138 A2
This cramped, dingy bar packs in the punters as much as the artists, leaving the audience with little room to manoeuvre once things get going.

Cheap beer betwen 8 and 10pm eases the pain of the entry fee and crowds and there is live music every night of the week.

Contemporary Music

There are several venues for folk music in the town centre, near the university. Check *Copenhagen This Week* for more details. On summer Sundays free rock concerts are held in Fælled Park.

Vega
Enghavevej 40; tel: 33 25 70 11; www.vega.sk; open for performances only; bus: 3A, 20; map p.136 B2
The lush, 50s-style Vega is the youngest listed building in Copenhagen and the city's main venue for contemporary music. The top floor has a nightclub and the Ideal Bar is at street level. The concerts themselves take place in either old *(store)* or little *(lille)* Vega.
SEE ALSO NIGHTLIFE P.105

Music Shops

Copenhagen has the usual international chain stores for music, but the following specialist shops are also useful places to find information on what's on and who's the latest big name in town.

Accord
Vestergade 37; tel: 70 15 16 17; www.accord.dk; Mon– Thur 10am–6pm, Fri until 7pm, Sat 10am–4pm, Sun noon–5pm; map p.138 A2
What started as a mecca for second-hand classical music collectors has now broadened its horizons to include all musical tastes, DVDs and video games. There is another store in Nørrebro. **Nørrebrogade 88–90; tel: 70 15 16 17; Mon–Fri 10am– 8pm, Sat until 5pm, Sun noon–6pm; bus: 5A, 350S; map p.134 B2**

Danmusik
Vognmagergade 7; tel: 33 15 78 88; www.danmusik.dk; Mon–Thur 10am–5.30pm, Fri until 6pm, Sat 11am–2pm; map p.138 B3
Specialises in Danish classical composers; also stocks books and sheet music.

Jazz Cup
Gothersgade 107; tel: 33 15 02 02; www.jazzcup.dk; Mon–Thur and Sat 10am–6pm, Fri until 7pm; map p.134 A4
A relaxed and welcoming jazz CD store, with friendly and well-informed staff.

Sex Beat Records
Studiostræde 18; tel: 33 12 82 92; www.sexbeatrecords.dk; Mon–Thur 11am–6pm, Fri until 7pm, Sat until 3pm; map p.138 A2
Indie rock/metal specialists, selling both new and used CDs; very knowledgeable staff and the best place for info on gigs; tickets sold here.

Below: the Jazz Cup hosts weekly live jazz performances.

Nightlife

Copenhagen's nightlife is generally quite young, relaxed and evolves fairly quickly, although some of the best venues have been around for years. Increasingly, the division between bar, café, restaurant and club is becoming more blurred, and many places where mums and small children can be seen taking a break during the day turn into an altogether different beast at night – with a trendy crowd, a cocktail menu, and late-night opening hours. On Friday and Saturday nights, clubs don't start filling up until midnight and stay open until five or six in the morning.

Lounges & DJ cafés

Aura

Rådhusstræde 4; tel: 33 36 50 60; www.restaurantaura.dk; Tue–Thur 6pm–midnight, Fri–Sat 6pm–3am; bus: 6A; map p.138 B2

Eat, drink and be merry with the young and lively crowd at this restaurant/DJ bar hybrid in sophisticated surroundings.

Boutique Lize

Enghave Plads 6, end of Istedgade, Vesterbro; tel: 33 31 15 60; Wed 8pm–midnight, Thur 8pm–2am, Fri–Sat 8pm–4am; map p.136 B2

On trendy and quickly evolving Istedgade, this café has a great selection of mixes from 45DKK and has recently become considered the best cocktail bar in town, at least for now. Sip your drink to the sounds of the likes of KISS and REM.

For the latest information about entertainment, music, venues and up coming events in Copenhagen, check out: www.aok.dk and click on Aok in English.

Café Ketchup

Pilestræde 19, tel: 33 32 30 30; Mon–Thur noon–midnight, Fri noon–2am, Sat 11am–4am; map p.138 B3

Trendily decked out in chrome and leather in a modern bistro-type style, this was one of the first hybrid café-bar-restaurants that pushed back the furniture for dancing into the night. It's classy and attracts a beautiful crowd, but not as relaxed or as reasonably priced as some.
SEE ALSO CAFÉS AND BARS P.29

Ideal Bar

Enghavervej 40, Vesterbro; tel: 33 25 70 11; www.vega.dk; Wed 10pm–4am, Thur 7pm–4am, Fri–Sat 7pm–5am; bus: 3A; map p.136 B2

Attached to Vega in Vesterbro – a sweaty, studenty crowd bops in among the beers.

Stereo Bar

Linnésgade 16A; tel: 33 13 61 13; www.stereobar.dk; Wed–Sat 8pm–3am; map p.138 A4

A funky, trendy, black-walled bar popular with students and a media crowd, with DJs playing an eclectic mix of music in the basement club.

Above: cocktails for the ladies.

Dance Clubs

Club Mambo

Vester Voldgade 85; tel: 33 11 97 66; Thur 9pm–2am Fri–Sat 9pm–5am; admission charge; bus: 6A, 12, 26, 29, 33; map p.138 A2

Just by city hall, this is a great place for salsa and other Latin dancing. It's popular with very good local dancers and expats, but if you are not so good take advantage of the free lessons at 9pm on Thur and 10pm Sat–Sun before everything really hots up.

Park Café & Nightclub

Østerbrogade 79, Østerbro; tel: 35 42 62 48; www.park.dk; café

Left: as trendy as principals of *hygge* will allow.

opens at noon, nightclub Fri–Sat 11pm–5am, Thur 11pm–4am; minimum age 18 on Thur, 20 on Fri, 22 on Sat; bus: 1A, 14; map p.135 C4

Dress up for this popular, mainstream nightclub, home to several dance floors in funky, pseudo-Renaissance surroundings with chandeliers, velvet and plenty of gilt decoration. Music is pop and house rather than cutting edge, but makes for a fun evening.

Rust

Guldbergsgade 8, Nørrebro; tel: 35 24 52 00; www.rust.dk; Wed–Sat 9pm–5am; entrance charge (free on Thur with student ID); over-21s only for nightclub and live bands after 11pm; map p.134 B2

Rust is an imtimate and busy venue and has been in the vanguard of late-night clubbing for 20 years. Its appeal and ability to attracts up-and-coming bands shows no sign of abating. Late night disco with café and three bars.

Søpavillonen

Gyldenløvesgade 24; tel: 33 15 12 24; www.soepavillonen.dk; 9pm–5am; entrance charge; bus: 12, 67, 68, 66, 2A, 250S; map p.134 B1

With an entrance requirement of over 25, this is really a club for the thirtysomethings in a lovely, white lakeside pavillon dating from 1896. It has a restaurant, three bars and spacious dance floor. Live tribute/jam bands play from 10pm and a DJ kicks in from midnight, playing a mix of 70s and 80s disco, with elements of Latin, classic rock and Danish pop. To avoid queues, it's advisable to get there before 11pm.

Stengade

Stengade 18, Nørrebro; tel: 35 36 09 38; www.stengade30.dk; Tue–Wed 9pm–2am, Thur–Sun 9pm–5am; bus: 3A; map p.134 B2

This venue has been going for 30 years and has always had a rough, underground edge to it. Music ranges from rock to hip hop, reggae and jazz. Check out the website for events; reggae on RubA'-Dub Sundays are popular.

Vega

Enghavevej 40, Vesterbrø; tel: 33 25 70 11; www.vega.dk; nightclub Fri–Sat 11pm–5am; DJ from 10pm; Lille VEGA concerts start 9pm; Store VEGA concerts start 8pm; free before 1am, entrance charge after 1am; concert tickets vary on the band c. 50DKK–400DKK; bus: 3A; map p.136 B2

The undisputed king of the nightclubs, with the best live music, the coolest and trendiest scene and the top DJs. The venue, an old trade union building that holds 2,000, is split into three parts, Store Vega, which holds big concerts and events, Lille Vega, the site for weekend clubbing, and Ideal Bar – a cosy lounge area with live music or DJs at the weekends.

SEE ALSO MUSIC AND DANCE P.103

Below: at night Rådhuspladsen is the central hub for night buses.

Palaces

The Golden Age for grand, palatial architecture was during the reign of Christian IV (1588–1648), who is renowned for having been a prolific builder. The king's crowning glory was the exquisite Rosenborg Palace, built in 1617 in the Dutch Renaissance style – the only royal palace never to have had a fire. Here, and in and around Frederiksstaden and Slotsholmen, are the best preserved neighbourhoods containing Copenhagen's most magnificent historic buildings. Further afield, Kronborg Slot in Helsingør and another lovely Renaissance creation, Frederiskborg Slot, are well worth a visit.

The Amalienborg complex is named after a former palace on the site that was built by Queen Sophie Amalie in the 17th century. It burnt down during a theatrical performance for Christian V, on 19 April 1689.

Amalienborg Palace

Amalienborg Plads, Bredgade; www.ses.dk; museum in Christian VIII's Palace open Jan–Apr and Nov–Dec: Tue–Sun 11am–4pm; May–Oct: daily 10am–4pm; guided tours of Christian VII's Palace July–Sept: Sat and Sun in English at 1 and 2.30pm and in Danish at 11.30am; entrance charge; map p.139 C4/D4

The octagonal square, overlooked by four ornate Rococo palaces – initially occupied by four aristocratic families – was always intended to be the centrepiece of Frederiksstaden. When the second Christiansborg Palace on Slotsholmen burnt down in 1794, Christian VII moved his residence to Amalienborg as a temporary residence, but he and his family liked the building so much they never left.

The Royal Architect, Nikolaj Eigtved, designed the palaces, which were completed in the middle of the 18th century. The colonnade was built when the royals first moved in to link Christian VII's palace (to the right of the palace square) with that of Crown Prince Frederik (on the left), where Queen Margarethe II now lives. This made it easier for Frederik, who had been ruling in all but name since 1784, to get his father Christian VII, who had failing mental health, to sign official documents.

Clockwise from the Sound, the palaces are Christian IX's palace, home to the queen and her husband Prince Consort Henrik, Christian VII's palace, which is used for receptions and to house royal guests, Christian VIII's palace and Frederik VIII's palace (with a clock on the façade), which is now home to Crown Prince Frederik and his Australian wife Princess Mary *(see page 17)*.

Below: Christian VIII's palace is home to the Amalienborg Museum.

Left: Amalienborg Palace is considered today to be one of the finest Rococo ensembles in Europe.

Above: keeping watch at Christiansborg Slot.

Traditionally, the royal family's rooms have been shared out among several palaces. The palace known as Christian VIII's palace, on the right as you face the Marble Church is the **Amalienborg Palace Museum**. At weekends in July and August you can visit some of the living quarters in Christian VII's Palace that are usually not open to the public. There is an English tour at 1pm and Danish tours at 11.30am and 2.30pm. You can also go on a guided tour of the Bel–étage of Christian VIII's Palace on Wednesdays and Sundays every second week (ie weeks one and three each month) at 11.30am, 1pm and 2.30pm.

Dominating the centre of the square is a statue of Frederik V.

SEE ALSO AMALIENBORG P.16 AND MUSEUMS AND GALLERIES P.82

Christiansborg Slot

Christiansborg Slotsplads, Slotsholmen; tel: 33 27 55 0004; www.ses.dk; state apartments open May–Sept: tours in English at 11am and 3pm; June–Aug: tours also at 1pm; Oct–April: tours in English Sun 3pm; Folketinget Prince Jørgens Gard (Parliament Yard and Parliament) free access to visitors' gallery during parliamentary sessions; tours Mon–Sun from 10am–4pm on the hour, except noon; entrance charge; map p.138 B2

Christiansborg Palace is the sixth castle to be constructed over Bishop Absalon's original 12th-century edifice, the ruins of which can be visited in the basement. The palace's dark granite façade, like many of the other buildings on Slotsholmen, creates a rather gloomy and melancholy impression. Small wonder then that the royal family prefers to live in Amalienborg Palace *(see previous page)*. In fact, quiet outdoor retreats on Slotsholmen are few and far between. The complex is home to the Danish Parliament *(Folketing)*, Danish Supreme Court, Royal Reception Chambers *(see below)*, Royal Stables, Theatre Museum, Thorvaldsen Museum and the Tøjhusmuseet (Arsenal Museum). These all have varying opening times, so try to plan your day to take most of them in.

SEE ALSO MUSEUMS AND GALLERIES P.97, 98

ROYAL RECEPTION CHAMBERS

It is the proximity of the country's political base that requires the Queen to maintain a presence in Christiansborg. In accordance with established protocol, she invites guests to the Royal Reception Chambers. Meetings with foreign ambassadors take place in the Audience Room, while guests of the State dine in

Below: Christiansborg Slot is the centre of Danish power.

Annual performances of Hamlet have been held at Kronborg Slot since 1937 when Laurence Olivier, playing the lead role, met, fell in love (and later married) his leading lady, Vivien Leigh, who played Ophelia (see www.hamletsommer.dk).

Above: a reminder of past warriors at Kronborg.

the Red Hall. Highly interesting are the 11 new tapestries in the Banqueting Hall by artist Bjørn Nørgard depicting 1,000 years of Danish history; it is he who is also responsible for the new mermaid sculpture and accompanying triumphal arch and figures in the harbour *(see page 81)*. The tapestries were presented to Queen Margrethe on her 50th birthday and were completed in the year 2000. If these rooms are not in use, they are open to the public during the day.

Frederiksborg Slot

The Museum of National History at Frederiksborg Castle, DK-3400 Hillerød; tel: 48 26 04 39; www.frederiksborgmuseet.dk; castle open Apr–Oct: daily 10am–5pm; Nov–Mar: 11am–3pm; gardens (excluding Baroque garden) all year, all times; Baroque garden open daily Nov–Feb: 10am–4pm, Mar–Apr: until 7pm; May–Oct: until 9pm; entrance charge; S-tog: Hillerød, and then bus: 701 or 702; map p.24

After Rosenborg, Frederiksborg Palace, situated 35 km northwest of Copenhagen near Hillerød is probably the finest royal palace on Sjælland, and Christian IV's finest architectural achievement.

At the start of the 17th century, Christian IV transformed his father's castle into a grand Renaissance-style castle, standing astride three tiny islands in Hillerød's town lake. The Dutch Renaissance style, with its red bricks, bright sandstone and arching gables, is immortalised here. Some sections of the sandstone adornments were gilded and painted. Highlights include the 'Rose' or Knight's room decorated with gilded leather, a splendid becherubbed Baroque chapel and the ornate Great Hall with minstrels' gallery.

Frederik VII was the last monarch to reside at Frederiksborg. When a fire damaged the main block in 1859, he ordered it to be rebuilt, but restricted finances slowed down progress and, when Frederik died in 1863, work stopped completely.

There is a formal French garden west of the palace – the only Danish royal garden to escape updating in the romantic style in the 19th century. The park that leads to a delightful lake called Esrum Sø, has a distinctive collection of sculptures. The gardens open daily at 10am, closing at different times depending on the season.

There is also the **National History Museum** in the palace, which contains Denmark's national portrait gallery.

Below: even today, Kronborg evokes the intrigue and royal plots of Shakespeare's Hamlet.

Kronborg Slot

Helsingør; tel: 49 21 30 78; www.kronborgslot.dk; www.kronborg.com; May– Sept: daily 10.30am–5pm; Oct and Apr: Tue–Sun 11am–4pm; Nov–Mar: Tue–Sun 11am–3pm; guided tours in English in the Casemates at noon and 1.30pm, in the Castle 2pm; entrance charge; S-tog: Helsingør; map p.24

Helsingør, just 7km north along the coast from Louisiana, is the setting for Kronborg, the 'Castle of Elsinore' for Shakespeare's *Hamlet*, written in 1601/2.

The castle is on Unesco's World Heritage list. Originally built by King Erik of Pomerania in 1420 when he introduced the 'Sound Dues' – fees to be paid to the Danish crown by all ships passing through to the Baltic.

Kronborg has been rebuilt several times, Erik's chilly strategic fortress castle called Krogen was transformed into a Renaissance palace between 1574–85 by Frederik II and rebuilt in 1639 by Christian IV, after it was decimated by fire in 1629. It was captured and pillaged by the Swedish in 1658. After they left in 1660, the castle was refortified with a new series of ramparts and was the strongest fortress in Europe.

It became a prison in the 17th century and then an army barracks from 1785–1922. When you see the casements (dungeons) where many soldiers were billetted you'll wonder what the difference was.

SHAKESPEARE'S MARK

Krongborg Slot has been the setting for many international productions of *Hamlet*. Visitors can see the richly decorated King and Queen's Chambers. The chapel and the 62m long Great Hall, where English actors from the Globe theatre put on plays, are also well worth viewing.

FIGHTING SPIRIT

Down in the dungeon is the statue of Holger Danske, a slumbering Danish Viking chief who, according to legend, will awake when the country is in danger and fill Danes with his fighting spirit. His name was used as a codeword by the Danish Resistance during World War II. The castle also has a maritime museum on the first floor.

Above: Rosenborg's treasury is home to the Danish crown jewels.

Rosenborg Slot

Oster Volgade 4a, Kongens Have; tel: 33 15 32 86; Jan–Apr: Tue–Sun 11am–2pm, treasury 11am–4pm; May, Sept–Oct: daily 10am–4pm; June–Aug: daily 10am–5pm; Nov–Dec: Tue–Sun 11am–2pm; entrance charge; map p.139 B4

Lovely Rosenborg Slot was built as the royal residence for Christian IV (1577–1648), instead of Copenhagen Castle, which he found rather dark and gloomy. He ran the affairs of state from Frederiksborg, but he really wanted to live somewhere more suited to his tastes for grand festivals and splendour.

So, in 1605 he ordered work to start on a palace just outside the city walls. It was 1624, after several alterations and enlargements, before Christian declared himself content with the outcome: Rosenborg Slot. Christian had commissioned highly-regarded architects from the Netherlands, and their work was a masterpiece of Dutch Renaissance. Constructed from red bricks, the façade was decorated with light sandstone. There are 24 rooms over three floors; get the English guide book for detailed information as it is not labelled in English.

SEE ALSO ROSENBORG SLOT AND AROUND P.14

Below: originally Rosenborg was secured by a moat with a drawbridge and surrounded by a magnificent rose garden, hence the name.

Pampering

Any holiday should involve a bit of tender loving care and though Copenhageners have always liked their saunas, hotels have only recently begun to offer spa holidays of the standard most Europeans would expect. The city can now claim two world-class facilities in the Arndal and Rosenborg spas – elite retreats for those who can afford the luxury. If you are looking for a more reasonably priced indulgence, DGI-Byens has opened one of the finest swimming facilties in Europe, complete with spa treatments and kiddie attractions that cater for the whole family.

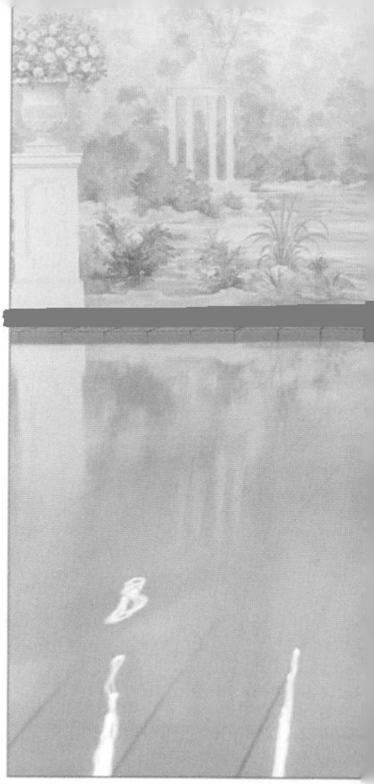

Independent Spas

Arndal Spa

Hotel d'Angleterre, Kongens Nytorv 34; tel: 33 37 06 68; www.arndalspa.dk; Mon–Fri 7am–9pm, Sat 8am–8pm, Sun 8am–7pm; train: Kongens Nytorv, bus: 15, 19, 26, 1A, 999; map p.138 C3

Based in the five-star Hotel d'Angleterre, Arndal is one of the city's finest spas. In addition to their heated swimming pool, saunas, whirlpool and normal gym facilities, their wellness centre offers an extensive list of massages and facial treatments, including special massages for pregnant women, hot stone massage, acupuncture, body scrubs and wraps, a facial for men that will ease the pain of daily shaving, aromatherapy, waxing and bubble baths. Treatments start at about 500DKK, but facilities are free for hotel guests.

Mirage Spa

H.C. Andersens Boulevard 10; tel: 33 33 95 00; www.miragespa.dk; Mon–Wed 10am–7pm, Thur–Sat 10am–11pm, Sun 10am–6pm; train: Vesterport, bus: all Rådhuspladsen buses; map p.138 A2

Just off the traffic, congestion and noice of Rådhuspladsen, the Mirage has a lot of chaos to overcome before it can provide any relaxation. Treatments are in private rooms and include a chocolate massage for two, a hot stone massage, facials and waxing treatments.

Ni'mat

Købmagergade 41; tel: 33 15 89 55; www.nimat.dk; Mon–Sat 10am–9pm, Sun 10am–5pm; map p.138 B3

Ni'mat is a unique wellness centre based around Thai food and massage. A typical package consists of a body massage, outdoor bubble bath with champagne and a three-course dinner with wines and coffee. Other a la carte options include a scalp or hot stone massage.

Rosenborg Spa

Kronprinsessegade 20; tel: 33 32 30 05; www.rosenborgspa.dk; Mon–Fri 11am–11pm, Sat 10am–11pm, Sun noon–7pm; map p.138 B4

A classically luxurious spa, housed in a restored 19th-century house, complete with chandeliers and glowing candlelight. Come here for the ultimate treat, with your own private bathing room, where you can sip champagne and let the bubbles get to work.

Above: Ni'mat's hot stone massage helps improve circulation.

Hotel Spas

Copenhagen Admiral Hotel

Tolbodgade 24–28, tel: 33 74 14 14; www.admiral.dk; map p.139 D3

The Admiral is currently constructing a new wellness centre for its guests. At time of writing, it was yet to be completed. Check their website for further details.

DGI-Byens Hotel
Tietgensgade 65; tel: 33 29 81 40; www.dgi-byen.dk; Mon–Thur 6.30am–midnight, Fri 6.30am–7pm, Sat and Sun 9am–5pm; ticket office shuts one hour before closing and the pool 30 minutes before closing; train: Hovedbanegård, bus: 1A, 65E; map p.138 A1
For most tourists, the swim facilities at DGI-Byens will be a unique experience. The admission fee is for as long as you like and includes access to their super-ellipse pool for the serious swimmers, the climbing and diving pool, the warm spa pool and a water playground for the kids.

Their spa facilities include a wet and dry sauna, cold tub, and lounge away from the bustle of the pool. Treatments include a mud or seaweed body pack, foot rubs, bubble baths and facials.

One spa is devoted to a theme each day. Themes include Finnish sauna, Native American Sweat Lodge, Roman and Turkish baths. You must book in advance for these sessions.

Radisson SAS
Hammerichsgade 1; tel: 38 15 65 00; www.royal.copenhagen.radissonsas.com; train: Vesterport or Hovedbanegård, bus: 6A, 26; map p.137 C3
Everytime you look at the Radisson SAS you cannot help but feel that time has moved on and it has been left behind. The same is to be said for their health and fitness facilities. The large fitness centre and dry/steam saunas would have seemed innovative 20 years ago, but for such a key hotel, you would hope they would have developed better services by now.

Left: a moment of peace at the Arndal Spa in the Hotel d'Angleterre.

Health Clubs and Pools

Copenhagen Havnebadet
Havnefronten Islands Brygge; daily during summer; bus: 34; map p.137 D2/E2
Copenhageners are rightfully proud of the cleanliness of their harbour. The Islands Brygge baths opened in July 2002, 50 years after swimming in the harbour was banned due to pollution.
SEE ALSO ENVIRONMENT P.44–5; PARKS, GARDENS AND BEACHES P.112

Frederiksberg Svommehal
Helgesvej 29; tel: 38 14 04 04; Mon–Fri 7am–9pm, Sat 7am–4pm, Sun 9am–4pm
An excellent and fun indoor pool with loads of extras: mammoth slide, salt bath, solarium, massage room and children's pool.

Vesterbro Fitness Centre and Swimming Baths
Angelgade 4; Tel: 33 22 05 50; www.fritidkh.dk; Mon 10am–9pm, Tue–Thur 7am–7pm, Fri 7am–6pm, Sat–Sun 9am–2pm; train: Enghaven; map p.136 A2
A superb new swimming pool and indoor gym opened recently as part of Copenhagen's redevelopment scheme for Vesterbro.

Below: a luxurious massage at the Asian-themed Ni'mat.

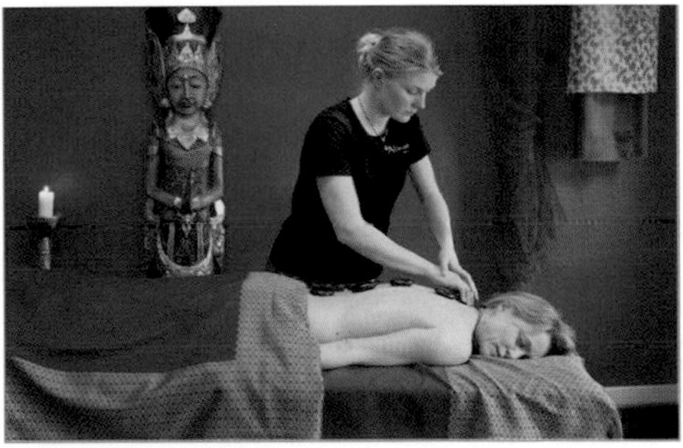

Parks, Gardens and Beaches

Copenhagen has every right to be proud of its open spaces, which are an important part of city life, especially in summer. Nearly all the parks have royal connections. In addition, the city has a vibrant outdoor social life, with plenty of tree-lined squares, terraced cafés and the grassy banks of its reservoirs to the west. Whether you want active entertainment, a gentle stroll in a formal garden, frisbee on the lawn, sunbathing or a swim, there are plenty of places for you to choose from.

Assistens Kirkegård

Kapelvej 2, entrances on Jagtvej and Nørrebrogade; tel: 35 37 19 17; www.assistens.dk; daily Nov–Feb: 8am–4pm, Mar–Apr: 8am–6pm, May–Aug: 8am–8pm; bus: 5A, 18, 350S; map p.134 A2

Although it lies off the beaten track in the Nørrebro district, Assistens Kirkegård, which is both a cemetery and a park, is included in many organised tours. Famous Danes, including Søren Kierkegaard, Christen Købke and Hans Christian Andersen, are buried here.

During the summer, the park is popular with picnickers, sunbathers, joggers and mothers with buggies.

SEE ALSO COPENHAGEN'S SUBURBS P.22 AND MONUMENTS AND FOUNTAINS P.81

Beaches

In the summer, the closest 'beach' is the man-made 'floating' city pool at Islands Brygge, where part of the Sound has seen cordoned off and swimming facilities provided. Further out of town, Amager Strandpark is popular and if you are looking for something more natural, head out to Klampenborg, where you can combine the beach with funfairs or museums if you feel so inclined.

Amager Strandpark

tel: 33 66 35 00; www.amager-strand.dk; Mar–Oct; train: Lergravsparken and 15 min walk; bus: 12, 77, 78; map p.22

5km from the centre, you will find a 2-km lagoon, sandy beaches and changing rooms in this luxury beach park.

Right: the city centre beaches, like Islands Brygge pictured here, have Blue Flag status.

SEE ALSO COPENHAGEN'S SUBURBS P.23

Bellevue Beach

Strandvejen 340, Klampenborg; train Klampenborg; map p.24

A lively beach 10km out of town with plenty to do in the way of games and sailing. The left end is nudist and predominantly gay.

Havnebadet

Islands Brygge; tel: 23 71 31 89; June–Aug/Sept; daily 11am–7pm; bus: 34; map p.137 D2/E2

Popular harbour city pool.

SEE ALSO ENVIRONMENT P.44–5; PAMPERING P.111

Botanisk Have

Gothersgade 128; tel: 35 32 22 40; www.botanic-garden.ku.dk/eng; summer 8.30am– 6pm; winter 8.30am–4pm; free; bus: 350s; map p.138 A4

The Botanical Gardens, just to the north of Gothersgade, are a delightful open space for a relaxing stroll, with plenty of benches, bridges, flowerbeds and glasshouses, though it's not the place to expect to run about. Some 10 hectares of land contain a variety of

Left: Frederiksberg's Chinese pavillion dates from the 19th century.

plant life, including herbs, shrubs and rock gardens. Many of the plants are native to northern Europe, but some are exotic and come from further afield.

The impressive conservatory, opened in 1874 with the rest of the Botanisk Have, contains a marvellous collection of tropical and subtropical flora. There is a café just behind the conservatory, which serves refreshments during the summer. The small Botanisk Museum is only opened for special exhibitions

Fælledparken

Bus: 15, 3A; map p.134–5 C4

Out in Østerbro near the stadium, this is Copenhagen's largest park and a nice place for a wander or to come to play games. It was originally common ground outside the city walls where cattle grazed and public executions took place. There is also a shallow outdoor pool for kids in summer.

Frederiksberg Have

Main entrance Frederiksberg Runddel; tel: 33 92 63 00; www.ses.dk; Dec–Jan: 7am–5pm; Feb and Nov: 7am–6pm; Mar: 7am–7pm/9pm; May–Aug: 7am–10pm; Sept: 7am–9pm; Oct: 7am–7pm/6pm; Chinese island Jun–Aug: Sun 2–4pm; free; bus: 18, 26; map p.18

After the centrally located Kongens Have (King's Garden) next to Rosenborg Slot, the Copenhageners' favourite park is the spacious Frederiksberg Have.

Inspired by many journeys to France and Italy, Frederik IV had the gardens laid out symmetrically in Baroque style. Frederiksberg Palace, built in 1703, overlooks the park from a hill in the grounds.

The gardens were redesigned in an English style at the end of the 18th century, and a system of canals replaced the original moats, so that summer visitors could enjoy a relaxing boat trip through the park. Crocuses, lilies, rhododendron, roses and lavender keep Frederiksberg Have in colour throughout the summer months, but more flowerbeds, huge trees, a fountain, artificial caves and little waterfalls add to its appeal.

On an island in the lake stands a pretty Chinese pavilion, where in the 19th century Frederik VI took afternoon tea with his family.

Below: tropical plants fill the conservatory at the Botanisk Have.

Two of the nicest outdoor activities in Copenhagen are to take a harbour tour *(see page 133)* and to hire a bike, which is the most common means of transport and unlikely to put you in any danger as the roads and the Danes are so bike-friendly *(see p.132)*.

Above: the formal gardens at Kongens Have are a popular park with Copenhageners.

An icerink is set up for skating every winter at the main entrance to Frederiksberg Have. Skates can be hired by the hour.
SEE ALSO PALACES P.108

Jægersborg Dyrehave

Dyreshavesbakken, Klampenborg; train Klampenborg; map p.24

Bakken Hill, in the Klampenborg suburb, forms the southern edge of what used to be the royal hunting grounds, Jægersborg Dyrehave. Christian V, was a keen hunter, and after his coronation in 1670, he enlarged the grounds so that prey could be rounded up and driven towards the hunters. Forestry workers and hunters throughout Denmark were obliged to catch red deer and bring them to Jægersborg Dyrehave. The monarch's passion for hunting proved fatal – he died in a hunting accident in 1699.

In 1756 Frederik V opened up the woodland to the public. Many of the trees, mainly beeches and oaks are more than 200 years old.

Dyrehave, now the biggest recreational area within greater Copenhagen, is criss-crossed by a network of footpaths, bridle paths and wide tracks, blissfully traffic-free.

During the summer you can take a ride through the forest in an (expensive) horse-drawn carriage. It is also the site of the Bakken funfair.
SEE ALSO CHILDREN P.34

Right: the reservoirs at the edge of the city centre provide a large expanse of undeveloped land near the heart of the city.

Kongens Have (Kings Garden)

Entrances on Gothersgade, Kronprinsessegade and Øster Voldgade; 6am–dusk; free; bus: 6A, 184, 185, 150S, 173E, 350S; map p.138 B4

Surrounding the 17th-century Rosenborg Palace, this park was converted into an English-style garden in 1820. Just over the road from the lovely, but more formal Botanical Gardens *(see page 112)*, Kongens Have, with its tall, old trees, statues, lawns and shady walks, is now an important breathing space in the densely populated city. It lends itself to all sorts of activities from picnicking on the lawn, sunbathing and chilling out to playing frisbee, cricket or football. Over two million people visit the park every year.
SEE ALSO PALACES P.109

Playgrounds

All of Copenhagen's parks (except the Botanical Gardens) are ideal spaces for kids to let off steam, but the following, in particular, have excellent play areas: Østre Anlæg, behind the National Museum and the Hirschsprungske Gallery, has three great playgrounds and lots of space for ball games.

Kongens Have can also offer sandpits, wooden

Above: the reservoirs are home to many species of birds.

climbing frames and puppet theatre in summer.

Reservoirs

Five reservoirs split central Copenhagen city from Nørrebro and Østerbro. Visitors are most likely to come across Skt Jorgens Sø, Peblinge Sø and Sortedam Sø, which run from behind the Tycho Brahe Planetarium as far as the Statens Museum for Kunst. They are popular places to jog, cycle and watch the world go by. There are also a few cafés along the Nørrebro bank side.

Tivoli

Vesterbrogade 3; tel: 33 15 10 01; ticket booking 33 15 10 12; www.tivoli.dk; mid-Apr–mid-June, mid-Aug–mid-Sept: Sun–Thur 11am–11pm, Fri 11am–12.30am, Sat 11am–midnight; mid-June–mid-Aug: Sun–Thur 11am–midnight, Fri–Sat 11am–12.30am; 12–21 Oct: daily 11am–11pm; mid-Nov–Dec: Mon–Thur 11am–10pm, Fri 10am–11pm/midnight, Sat 10am–11pm; entrance charge; bus: 6A, 26; map p.138 A1/A2

Founded in 1843 outside the city walls, Tivoli is as popular now as it has ever been with over five million visitors every year.

Ignore the cynics, this is a great day or night out whether you go on the rides or not.

In terms of rides, there is plenty of choice. Among other stomach-churning options, there are four roller coasters: one travels at speeds of up to 80mph, while the Dragon moves in several directions at once. Himmelskibet, new in 2006, is the tallest carousel in the world, and twirls its riders along at a height of 80m.

For kids, a Viking-ship merry-go-round, flying aeroplanes and miniature classic cars, an old-fashioned trolley bus ride or a traditional carousel are among several rides to choose from.

For the even fainter of heart the dragon boats on the lake, the pantomime theatre, the Tivoli boys guard and trees and lakes lit with Chinese lanterns have a romantic appeal.

To go on any of the rides you need to either buy a multi-ride pass (200DKK over-12s), which lasts all day, or separate tickets (15DKK) – rides need up to four tickets each.

If you have a Copenhagen card and just wish to wander, this will let you in for free.

There is also plenty of musical and dramatic entertainment available; the concert hall is one of the best in Copenhagen offering ballet and opera (buy tickets ahead of time) and the open-air stage sees loud, free rock and pop concerts every Friday night; the pantomime theatre is free, as are the many musical groups playing on bandstands throughout the park.

If you get peckish, there are 32 restaurants to choose from, ranging from budget to very expensive, or bring a sandwich and sit on a bench watching the world go by.

There are disabled access and facilities and free wheelchairs – see website for details – and for families with babies and young children, free nappies and changing facilities.

SEE ALSO CAFÉS AND BARS P.28; MUSIC AND DANCE P.100 AND RESTAURANTS P.116–7

Zoo

Frederiksberg Have; map p.18

Not solely the exclusive right of the kids, this is a super zoo in nice surroundings, open until 10pm on summer evenings.

SEE ALSO CHILDREN P.35

Below: day or night, the attractions at Tivoli are popular with all ages.

Restaurants

Danish cooking is as cosmopolitan as anywhere in northern Europe and Copenhagen reflects this, sporting 10 Michelin-starred restaurants, as well as over 2,000 eating places serving just about any type of cuisine you can think of – but be warned that prices (especially for bottles of wine and other alcohol) can be very high. However, many restaurants have fixed price menus and the more courses you have, proportionately the less expensive your meal becomes. If you are on more of a budget, eat in a café where a couple of unpretentious courses will set you back 150–200 DKK.

Tivoli & Rådhuspladsen

DANISH

Copenhagen Corner

Rådhuspladsen, Vesterbrogade 1A; tel: 33 91 45 45; www.remmen.dk; daily 11.30am–midnight; €–€€; bus: all Rådhuspladsen buses; map p.138 A2

This brightly decorated restaurant overlooking City Hall serves excellent French/Danish cuisine with specialities, including very good smørrebrød and fried veal, garlic entrecôte and a herring plate of three types of spiced and marinated herring.

Friggaden

Tivoli; tel: 33 15 92 04; www.bojesen.dk; same hours as Tivoli; €€; bus: 6A, 26; map p.138 A1/A2

It is not necessary to leave a tip in restaurants as it is usually part of the bill. If you do leave something, 5 per cent of the bill is perfectly acceptable, even in expensive restaurants, and in cheaper places, rounding up the bill is fine. Not leaving a tip is not considered bad manners.

The traditional Danish menu here (including lovely salads) is good, but the real reason for eating here is to partake of your iron rations on deck (especially nice on a clear day or evening), in splendour in the captain's cabin or down in the bowels of this fantastic replica sailing ship, where warlike canons have been replaced by tables and the ship's cook works wonders in his galley kitchen. Three courses will cost 375DKK or go à la carte.

SEE ALSO PARKS, GARDENS AND BEACHES P.115

EUROPEAN

Alberto K

Radisson SAS Royal Hotel, Hammerichsgade 1; tel: 33 42 61 61; www.alberto-k.dk; Mon–Sat 6pm–midnight; kitchen closes 10pm; €€€€; train: Vesterport, Hovedbanegård, Bus: 6A, 26; map p.137 C3

High above the rest of the city, on the 20th floor of this iconic Arne Jacobsen hotel, this stylish gourmet restaurant has fabulous views and is considered one of the best in Denmark.

Above: even the humblest café will give attention to detail.

It specialises in Italian-Danish fusion cuisine (choose from between four and seven courses), with offerings such as duck with foie gras, pistachio nuts and cumquats, scallop carbonara with pancetta, quail egg and parmesan and king crab or woodland pig. Menus range from 555–745DKK without wine.

The Paul

Tivoli; tel: 33 75 07 75; www.thepaul.dk; during Tivoli's seasons; evening menu €€€€, lunch €€€; bus: 6A, 26; map p.138 A1/A2;

This is Tivoli's Michelin-starred restaurant, housed in a lovely, romantic 19th-century, glass-walled conservatory-type building. The food, designed with loving care and artistic flourish by Devon-born Englishman Paul Cunningham, is

Left: there is more to summer at Tivoli than thrill rides and fairy lights; it is home to some of the city's best restaurants.

international with a dollop of mediterranean inspiration and lots of fresh ingredients. The atmosphere is relaxed with a stylish homey feel with bright accessories and knick knacks scattered throughout.

Paul Cunningham's desk stands at the end of the restaurant, the power house where he designs the look of what you see on your plate.

The six course lunch and supper menus change regularly and there are wine menus (same price as the food menus) to match.

SEE ALSO PARKS, GARDENS AND BEACHES P.115

ITALIAN

Café Ultimo

Tivoli; tel: 33 75 07 51; Sun–Thur 11am–midnight, Fri–Sat 11am–12.30am; €€–€€€; bus: 6A, 26; map p.138 A1/A2

This pretty, white glass structure not far from Tivoli's lake dates from 1883 and was originally built as a dance hall.

It is now an Italian restaurant offering such delicacies as pan-fried *foie gras* with pear chutney and rucola tossed in truffle oil as well as a good selection of pasta dishes and pizzas.

STEAKHOUSES

Hereford Beefstouw

Tivoli, Vesterbrogade 3; tel: 33 12 74 41; Mon–Sat 11.30am–3pm, 5.30pm–10.30pm, Sun 5pm–10.30pm; €–€€; bus: 6A, 26; map p.138 A1/A2

Serving juicy steaks cooked to order and tasty seafood dishes, this is the flagship of a restaurant chain with a difference: it invests part of its profits in quality art, which adorns its walls. Definitely one for beer and beef-lovers, especially as the microbrewery Apollo takes pride of place in the centre of the restaurant and offers a new beer each month. Booking is recommended.

Rio Bravo

Vester Voldgade 86; tel: 33 11 75 87; www.riobravo.dk; Mon–Sat 11.30pm–5am, Sun 5pm–5am; €€; map p.138 A2/B1

This popular place is a firm favourite among late-night revellers. It's a no-nonsense, cowboy-style steakhouse, with pub-like decor, where even the seats at the bar are saddles.

Strøget and Around

DANISH

Det Lille Apotek

Store Kannikestræde 15; tel: 33 12 56 06; www.det-lille-apotek.dk; Mon–Sat 11am–midnight, Sun noon–midnight; €–€€; map p.138 B3

Below: a lads' night out by candlelight.

Prices for an average three-course meal without wine:

€	under 250DKK
€€	250–400DKK
€€€	400–550DKK
€€€€	over 550DKK

Above: Krogs Fiskrestaurant is housed in an 18th-century building with early 20th-century décor and has great views of Slotsholmen across Gammel Strand.

The 'Little Pharmacy' is Copenhagen's oldest cellar restaurant, with crooked walls, leaded windows and furnished with antiques, not to mention claims that many writers, including Hans Christian Andersen and Ludvig Holberg were clients.

The food is predominantly Danish, with a good selection of hearty fish and meat dishes. If you want to go for a truly traditional dish, have the roasted pork with boiled and sugar-browned potatoes, pickled cabbage and gravy. If this is a bit heavy, there is a wide selection of tender steaks as well. A popular haunt for students. Go à la carte or the monthly menu (you get a choice from two starters, main courses and puddings) offers two courses for 195DKK or three for 235DKK.

Kobenhavner Kafeen

Badstuestræde 10; tel: 33 32 80 81; daily 10am–midnight; €–€€; map p.138 B2

This small, cosy restaurant has an old-time atmosphere generated, not least, by the traditional Danish dishes on offer: roast pork and cabbage, *frikadeller*, grilled plaice, a highly recommended Danish cold table and the daily Copenhagen Plate offering marinated salmon, herring, shrimp, meatballs, vegetables and new-baked bread for 150DKK.

Krogs Fiskerestaurant

Gammel Strand 38; tel: 33 15 89 15; www.krogs.dk; Mon–Sat 6–10.30pm; €€€€; map p.138 B2

Possibly the best – and priciest – fish restaurant in town. Krogs serves everything fishy from bouillabaise to eel, in varied, imaginative dishes. You'll probably need to book ahead.

Peder Oxe

Gråbrødretorv 11; tel: 31 11 00 77; www.pederoxe.dk; Sun–Wed 11.30am–10.30pm, Thur–Sat 11.30am–11pm; €–€€; map p.138 B3

Nicely decorated with a light interior and a Portuguese-tile butcher's counter, Peder Oxe is situated in an old house in a square dating from 1238. You can go for a quick lunch (help yourself from the excellent and copious salad bar as many times as you like or have smørrebrød) or something more hearty, such as spring lamb, beef steak, dover sole or a burger. If you have a sweet tooth, try out the dessert tapas, which gives you a taste of ten different deserts.

Restaurant Gråbrødretorv 21

Gråbrødretorv 21; tel: 33 11 47 07; www.graabrodre21.aok.dk; daily for lunch and dinner; €€€; map p.138 B3

Eating here is like eating in a rather splendid Danish home in one of Copenhagen's oldest squares. Unsurprisingly, Danish cuisine is the speciality. It is well prepared and presented. A delightful restaurant, whether you eat in the charming dining rooms or outdoors.

Slotskaelderen

Fortunstræde 4; tel: 33 11 15 37; open 10am–5pm; €–€€; map p.138 B2

You can chomp on the best open sandwiches in Copenhagen here or choose from the Danish menu, in this intimate, historic restaurant, dating from 1910, which is popular with politicians from the nearby parliamaent.

Be warned that although a restaurant may appear to stay open late, its kitchen is likely to shut a couple of hours before closing time. If in doubt, ring to check – you are unlikely to be able to order food much later than about 10pm in most places.

Sorgenfri
Brolæggerstræde 8; tel: 33 11 58 80; daily 11am–9pm; €; map p.138 B2
This centrally located frokost restaurant is tucked in a basement just to the north of Christiansborg Slot. It's not posh, but for a very Danish fast-food eaterie, it has good smørrebrød, beer and akvavit, which it has been doling out to the locals for 150 years.

Tyvenkokkenhansk oneoghendeselsker
Magstræde 16; tel: 33 16 12 92; www.tyvenkokkenhansk oneoghendeselsker.dk; Mon–Sat 6pm–2am; €€€–€€€€; map p.138 B2
Named after Peter Greenaway's *The Thief, the Cook, his Wife and her Lover* (which, if you've seen this film about a cannibal, the name may give you indigestion even before you've sat down). A shame, because this restaurant has a very romantic setting, with its speciality an appropriately huge, seven-course menu, boldly composed and inspired by many cuisines including Danish. Try, for instance, couscous with cardamom sauce or scallops with pear.

Victor
Ny Østergade 8; tel: 33 13 36 16; www.cafevictor.dk; Mon–Wed 8am–1am, Thur–Sat 8am–2am, Sun 11am–11pm; €€; map p.138 B3
Open all day long, Victor offers everything from coffee, wine and snacks to a traditional Danish lunch with smoked salmon or herring or a French dinner. The interior is decorated by Denmark's leading artists. Lunch prices start from 75DKK and dinner from 125DKK.

EUROPEAN

Restaurationen
Møntergade 19; tel: 33 14 94 95; www.restaurationen.com; Tue–Sat 6pm–midnight; €€€€; map p.138 B3
Multiple award-winning Restaurationen has won just about every star that magazine and food writers have to give, including the Michelin and Wine Spectator award of excellence. Its distinctive fixed menu (600DKK), based on Danish, French and Italian cuisine, is revised every week, with dishes based on fresh, seasonal produce. Its decor is traditional with contemporary touches.

Riz Raz
Kompagnistræde 20; tel: 33 15 05 75; www.rizraz.dk; daily 11.30am–midnight; €; map p.138 B2
This attractive, busy mediterranean restaurant is very popular with the locals, especially the young (the price may have something to do with it) and offers an excellent vegetarian buffet with every known vegetable and preparation known to man. There are a few meat dishes available too.

Above: Italian, Lebanese and Moroccan influences inspire Riz Raz's buffet.

FRENCH

Kong Hans Kælder
Vingårdstræde 6; tel: 33 11 68 68; www.konghans.dk; Mon–Sat 6pm–midnight; €€€€; map p.138 B3/C3
The Gothic arches in this building – Copenhagen's oldest – date back over a thousand years. The building itself is mentioned in medieval texts and was not only part of a vineyard, but also, probably, the site of Copenhagen's first royal mint. (And in the 19th century, Hans Christian Andersen lived in its garret.)

Now another Michelin-starred, expensive treat, you would be hard pushed to find such splendid surroundings

Below: the prices in Victor's café are a bit lower than in its restaurant and the atmosphere there is more relaxed.

Prices for an average three-course meal without wine:	
€	under 250DKK
€€	250–400DKK
€€€	400–550DKK
€€€€	over 550DKK

Prices for an average three-course meal without wine:	
€	under 250DKK
€€	250–400DKK
€€€	400–550DKK
€€€€	over 550DKK

elsewhere. The food is French based with an emphasis on simplicity and fresh ingredients and the menu offers such delicious dishes as sautéed langoustine with tagliatelle, shii-ta-ke mushrooms and scallions, *foie gras* and ducks' legs with quinces, barberries and cloudberry wine jelly, monkfish with ragout of lobster, chestnuts and pickled ceps and filet of beef in crouton with beer and oxtail sauce.

L'Alsace
Ny Østergade 9, on corner with Pistolstræde; tel: 33 14 57 43; www.alsace.dk; Mon–Sat 11.30am–midnight; €–€€; map p.138 B3
Tucked away towards the bottom end of Strøget, this cosy gourmet restaurant specialises in dishes from Alsace (with an emphasis on fresh fish but the hearty meat dishes and pig's knuckles are available too). It opens onto a charming cobbled courtyard, surrounded by ochre-painted, higgledy-piggledy 17th-century houses. Inside the walls are hung with a variety of striking artworks. The three-course lunch menu is a very reasonable 252DKK although service can be patchy. Elton John and Queen Margrethe have both eaten here.

Restaurant Pierre Andre
Ny Østergade 21; tel: 33 16 17 19; open Tue–Fri noon–midnight, Sat 6pm–midnight; kitchen open noon–2pm, 6pm– 9.30pm; €€–€€€; map p.138 B3
This is an intimate, terracotta-walled restaurant offering delicious French gourmet food that won a Michelin star just one year after its opening in 1996. There are three set menus: a three-course menu that changes every day, a six-course option and a nine-course extravaganza. Take your time!

St Gertrude's Kloster
Hauserplads 32d; tel: 33 14 66 30; daily 5–11pm; €€€€; map p.138 B3
This lovely restaurant can be found within the atmospheric walls of a 14th-century monastery, where you begin with an aperitif in the leather-book-lined library before repairing to the candlelit vault to eat fabulous food based on medieval recipes, including *foie gras* that melts on the tongue. Its wine cellar contains some 39,000 bottles. Very expensive, but what a meal and what a place!

Above: the streets around Strøget are filled with restaurants, cafés and traditional *smørrebrød* delis.

ITALIAN
San Giorgio
Rosenborggade 7 (near the Kultorvet); tel: 33 12 61 20; www.san-giorgio.dk; Mon–Sat 6–11pm; €€–€€€; map p.138 B4
Nicely decorated with white-washed walls, dark wood furniture, chandeliers, candles and crisp white tablecloths, San Giorgio offers authentic Italian cuisine – very much more than pizza and pasta. Three fixed menus give you a choice on price.

TURKISH
Ankara
Krystalgade 8–10; tel: 33 15 19 15; www.restaurant-ankara.dk; Mon–Sat 1pm–midnight; €; map p138 A3
Extensive Turkish buffet adapted for Danish tastes. Inexpensive wines and coffees; a belly dancer provides entertainment.

VEGETARIAN
Den Grønne Kaelder
Pilestræde 48; tel: 33 93 01 40; Mon–Sat 11am–10pm; €; map p.138 B3
One of Copenhagen's few vegetarian restaurants, this is

Below: Nyhavns Færgekro is renowned for its herring buffet.

an excellent place for a wholesome vegetarian lunch or supper. Choose from salads and warm dishes including vegetable hash with tomatoes, rosemary and walnuts. There is a good selection of vegan options too and if you like your beer, Czech and organic beer are both on offer.

Govindas Vegetarian Restaurant

Nørre Farimagsgade 82; tel: 33 33 74 44; www.govindas.dk; Mon–Fri noon–9pm; Sat 1–7pm (buffet closes 30 mins earlier); bus: 14, 40, 42, 43; €; map p.138 A4

This small and simple vegetarian restaurant (run by the Hare Krishna movement) is conveniently located close to the Botanical Gardens. It offers a daily though limited fixed menu of vegetarian and vegan options.

Kongens Nytorv and Nyhavn

DANISH

Cap Horn

Nyhavn 21; tel: 33 12 85 04; www.caphorn.dk; daily 9am–1am, kitchen open 9am–11pm; €€; map p.139 C3

This is one of several restaurants along Nyhavn that gets very busy owing to its appealing location. Sit out under an umbrella (or a heater!) on the dockside or cuddle up inside by the open fire, in the wood-beamed interior. Lunch is usually Danish and supper international with dishes ranging from pasta to smoked duck, fresh lobster, tuna or fallow deer.

> If you pay your bill with an international credit card, especially one such as Barclaycard, Diners or American Express, you may be charged an additional fee. This is quite common in Denmark and often happens in small shops as well.

Above: mornings are a great time to enjoy Nyhavn's scenery without facing the crowds.

Fyrskibet

Nyhavn 61; tel: 33 11 93 33; www.fyrskibet.com; summer Mon–Sat 10.30am–11pm; €€; map p.139 C3

Until 1978, this lighthouse ship saw active service. Now, it is a floating restaurant berthed at the foot of Nyhavn and makes for a lovely atmospheric evening, especially when the fairy-lights go on. Have a drink on deck before eating in the glass-sided cabin. The menu is Danish and fish dishes are a speciality. There are also vegetarian options.

Nyhavns Færgekro

Nyhavn 5; tel: 33 15 15 88; www.nyhavns-faergekro.dk; daily 11.30am–11.30pm; €–€€; map p.139 C3

Like Cap Horn, another recommended restaurant along Nyhavn, Færgekro is housed in an 18th-century building. It's unpretentious and serves particularly good traditional food. There's seating indoors and outside, which is lovely in summer, but don't expect to be alone overlooking the water and the boats. The fixed price menu at 165DKK is very reasonable.

EUROPEAN

E-go

Hovedvagtsgade 2; tel: 33 12 79 71; www.egocph.dk; Mon–Thur 11.30am–midnight, Fri 11.30am–2am, Sat 10am–2am; €€–€€€; map p.138 C3

Classic French cuisine and Danish lunch, carefully prepared and nicely presented in a trendy interior with a corrugated roof and interesting purple lighting. The staff are very helpful, the food good and, owing to its late opening, this is a popular place for a cocktail before heading out clubbing into the night.

Kommandanten

Ny Adelgade 7; tel: 33 12 09 90; www.kommandanten.dk; Mon–Sat 5.30–10pm, normally shuts for much of July and for a week at the end of December; €€€€; map p.138 C3

This attractive, Michelin-starred restaurant, is housed over two floors in a historic 17th-century building that is decorated by master florist Tage Andersen and was formerly owned by the city's commander who supervised the gateway from here (hence the name). The food is predominantly inspired by Denmark, France and Italy and you can choose from the seven-course fixed menu (changes bi-weekly) or go à la carte, with dishes such as

Above: be sure to try Danish specialities.

halibut with gnocchi and fennel, rabbit with lentils and bacon or marinated salmon with oysters and parsley.

Zeleste

Store Strandstræde 6; tel: 33 16 06 06; www.zeleste.dk; daily 10am–1am, kitchen open 10.30am–10.30pm; €–€€; map p.139 C3

Just off Nyhavn and away from the crowds, the large, cheerful plastic shrimp that heralds the entrance of this charming little restaurant is perhaps not indicative of what you will find within, namely a pretty whitewashed interior, a cobbled courtyard for summer eating and delicious food. The menu is limited to three to five interesting choices for each course but changes regularly offering such dishes as lobster, wild boar with garlic butter, parmesan-encrusted Argentine steak and pan-fried cod with almond citrus butter. If you want to be sure of a table, it's best to book as this place is popular with the locals, especially for its well-rated brunch (95DKK).

Prices for an average three-course meal without wine:

€	under 250DKK
€€	250–400DKK
€€€	400–550DKK
€€€€	over 550DKK

INDONESIAN

Restaurant Bali

Kongens Nytorv 19; tel: 33 11 08 08; daily noon–midnight; €; train: Kongens Nytorv, bus: 15, 19, 26, 1A, 999; map p.138 C3

This Indonesian restaurant on the corner of Kongens Nytorv has a tropical ambience with plenty of Balinese decoration. Specialities include *rijstaffel* and a selection of delicious, delicately-spiced meat and vegetable dishes.

Rosenborg and Around

DANISH

Ida Davidsen

Store Kongensgade 70; tel: 33 91 36 55; www.idadavidsen.dk; Mon–Fri 10am–4pm; €; bus: 1A, 15, 19; map p.139 C4

This family-run, traditionally decorated frokost restaurant in Frederiksstaden has been serving up delicious smørrebrød since 1888 when the first shop opened in Nørrebro, offering 177 different ingredients. You can now choose from 250 – the most popular is still 'the old showman', a piece with salmon, freshly marinated lumpfish caviar, crayfish tails, Greenland shrimp, lime and dill mayonnaise.

EUROPEAN

Kokkeriet

Kronprinsessegade 64; tel: 33 15 27 77; www.kokkeriet.dk; Tue–Sat 6pm–1am; €€€€; map p.138 B4

This charming, relaxed modern restaurant boasts one Michelin star and a monthly changing six-course menu (650DKK) offering beautifully presented, interesting food combinations such as king crab with cabbage and quail's egg, cod roe and cucumber in rape oil, glazed sweetbread salsify and vadouvan, ham and langoustine mushroom and cracklings, fried foie-gras, calf's cheek and lobster, marsh lamb with carrots and goat's milk and Kiwi with white chocolate and liquorice. There is a matching, (expensive) wine menu. You can eat à la carte if you prefer and if you are inspired, you can arrange to take lessons from the chef!

Meet the Danes is an excellent organisation that arranges for visitors to have dinner with the locals. The food is usually traditional and the conversation lively, and lasting friendships have been formed. Tel: 23 28 43 47, info@meetthedanes.dk, www.meetthedanes.dk.

Restaurant Godt

Gothersgade 38; tel: 33 15 21 22; Tue–Sat 5.30pm–10pm, closed July and last weekend in December; €€€–€€€€; bus: 350S; map p.138 B3

Godt means 'good', an understatement for this small, family-run 20-seat restaurant. The cuisine is European with one daily, three- to five-course menu; the wine list is mainly French though expanding its range. They have one Michelin star, so reservations are advised and don't

Below: pickled herring and chilled *akvavit – bon appetit.*

be surprised if the friendly English chef wanders through to talk to you.

JAPANESE
Umami
Store Kongensgade 59; tel: 33 38 75 00; www.restaurantumami.dk; Mon–Fri noon–3pm, Sun– Thur 6–10pm, Fri–Sat 6–11pm; €€€€; bus: 1A, 15, 19; map p.138 C4
This stylish Japanese-French fusion restaurant is a popular celebrity haunt. In addition to sushi, Umami features dishes such as deep-fried squid and prawns with avocado, jalapeños and tamari sauce, ribeye tataki with deep-fried lotus and ponzu dressing, guinea fowl breast teriyaki with Japanese pickles, ginger- poached duck breast with gyoza, sesame and garlic or grilled veal tenderloin with wasabi.

Above: Umami is fiendishly cool and seriously expensive.

Amalienborg and Around

DANISH
Lumskebugten
Esplanaden 21; tel: 33 15 60 29; www.lumskebugten.dk; Mon–Fri 11.30am–10pm, Sat 5–10pm; €€–€€€; map ref p135 E2
Formerly a sailor's tavern dating from 1854, this charming restaurant by Churchill Park is very much more salutary than it would have been in days of yore. The sawdust and the ladies of the night have long gone and smart clients (including the Queen), friendly staff, a light cream-walled interior and an upmarket but homey Danish menu (set or à la carte) with fine wine have taken their place.

Restaurant Amalie
Amaliegade 11; tel: 33 12 88 10; weekday lunchtime; €€–€€€; map p.139 C3
A secret known only to the locals, this tiny, classic basement restaurant is in great demand so you need to book ahead, especially around Christmas when it is even more popular. It doesn't have a star, but Michelin recommends it nonetheless. It specialises in traditional Danish fare, including smørrebrød.

Below: sip a cocktail in Umami's ground-floor bar before heading upstairs to sup on sushi.

FRENCH
Le Sommelier
Bredgade 63–65; tel: 33 11 45 15; www.sommelier.dk; Mon–Thur noon–2pm, 6–10pm, Fri noon–2pm and 6–11pm, Sat 6– 11pm, Sun 6–10pm; €€€; bus: 1A, 15, 19; map p.139 C4
French in name and French in style, both in terms of the menu and the decor, with a large bar and dining area covered in French posters. Le Sommelier prides itself on its wine list (reputedly, the largest cellar in Denmark and not always as expensive as you might expect) and offers forty wines by the glass. Its two-course lunch menu costs a reasonable 260DKK while the three-course evening menu is 365DKK. The menu offers dishes such as coquelet with olives, piement and sage, tenderloin of beef with Madeira sauce, truffle and celery purée, *foie gras* poached in consommé with cherries and fried lobster with soft polenta and lemon butter.

Vesterbro and Frederiksberg

DANISH
Restaurant Klubben
Enghavevej 4; tel: 33 31 40 15; daily 11am–10pm; €; bus: 3A; map p.136 B2
This pub is a tad too rough and ready to tempt many tourists if they are not already

Above: even the simplest lunch uses the finest ingredients.

Above: preparing a welome at Noma.

in the know. However, if you are happy on wobbly tables with plastic table cloths and occasional beery looking locals, this place offers generous portions of traditional home cooking such as *frikadeller* with creamed cabbage and beetroot or the traditional Danish plate of herring.

EUROPEAN
Formel B
Vesterbrogade 182, Vesterbro; tel: 33 25 10 66; www.formelb.dk; Mon–Sat 6pm–1am, last table reservation at 10pm; €€€€; bus: 6A; map p.136 A3
A charming Michelin-starred restaurant where you can relax in an uncluttered interior decorated in restful shades of white, chocolate and taupe. Eat à la carte or, for 700DKK, sit down to six fabulous set courses (not including wine). The menu changes every two weeks and offers dishes such as Danish cod with watercress, dandelion and cod roe, monkfish with snails, mushrooms and basil, tenderloin of veal and escalope of *foie gras* with kale and giblets and everything is locally sourced for maximum quality and freshness. In summer, there is a terrace where you can eat out.

Many restaurants, especially the more expensive ones, change their menus on a weekly or monthly basis. If you want to be sure of the menu before you go, check online or ring to enquire. Vegetarians are usually well catered for.

FRENCH
Trois Cochons
Værnedamsvej 10, Vesterbro; tel: 33 31 70 55; www.cofoco.dk; Mon–Sat noon–3pm, Mon–Sun 5.30pm–midnight; €; bus: 6A, 26; map p.136 B3
Housed in a former butchers – the white tiles still adorn the walls – this charming French bistro with Danish overtones, complete with chandeliers, candles and rattan screens, offers good food at reasonable prices and is pretty and romantic in the evening. After lunch you can check out the gourmet food shops along the same road.

ITALIAN
Fiasco
Gammel Kongevej 176, Frederiksberg; tel: 33 31 74 87; Tue–Sat 5.30–10pm; €€; bus: 14, 15; map p.136 A4
This rustic Italian restaurant is very popular with the locals who like the unpretentious atmosphere, the borderline gourmet dishes and the reasonable prices. In the summer, you can eat al fresco in the courtyard, fulfilling yet more of your Italian fantasies.

VIETNAMESE
Lê Lê
Vesterbrogade 56, tel: 33 22 71 34; daily noon–10pm; €€; bus: 6A, 26; map p.136 C3
A unique, Vietnamese restaurant makes the best use of its fresh ingredients.

Christianshavn and Holmen

DANISH
Noma
Strandgade 93, Nordatlantens Brygghe, Christianshavn; tel: 32

Below: cafés and restaurants line the canals of Christianshavn and become crowded when the sun comes out.

96 32 97; www.noma.dk; Tue–Fri noon–1.30pm, Mon–Sat 6–10pm; €€€€; map p.138 C1
One of Copenhagen's newest gourmet restaurants and its only establishment to receive two Michelin stars, Noma is housed in an 18th-century warehouse near the docks. It takes its inspiration, both in terms of decor and cuisine, from Denmark, Iceland, Greenland and the Faroe islands from whence it imports its fresh ingredients daily. For the experience without the top-end expense, come in for the three-course lunch menu (295DKK). In the evening, a seven-course menu is on offer, which at 685DKK is rather good value.

Viva
Langebro Kajplads 570 (by Langebro bridge); tel: 27 25 05 05; Mon–Sat 11.30am–3pm, Sun 11.30am–4pm, Mon–Thur 5.30–10pm, Fri–Sat 5.30–10.30pm, Sun 5.30–9pm. Bar open until midnight/1am; €€€; bus: 5A, 12, 33, 40, 250S; map p.138 B1
Jump aboard Viva's stylish ship restaurant with a view of the Black Diamond and dive into their sea of creative hors d'oeuvres. The menu is predominantly fish and shellfish.

Above: Noma's candlelit, seven course dinner features the best in Scandinavian atmosphere and cuisine.

ITALIAN
Era Ora
Overgaden neden Vandet 33B; tel: 32 54 06 93; www.era-ora.dk; Mon–Sat noon–3pm and 7pm–1am (kitchen closes 11.30pm); €€€–€€€€; map p.139 C1
This friendly Michelin-starred, stylish Italian restaurant on the banks of the canal has a calming Italianate beige and white interior and a pretty summer courtyard. Era Ora has been serving innovative Italian cuisine here since 1983 and is one of the best restaurants in the city.

L'Altro
Torvegade 62; tel: 32 54 54 06; www.laltro.dk; Mon–Sat 5.30pm–12am (kitchen closes at 10pm); €€–€€€€; train: Christianhavns, bus: 350S, 2A, 19, 47; map p.139 C1
This unpretentious Italian restaurant is run by the same excellent team as Era Ora *(see above)*, is very popular and has been described by locals as 'Era Ora for the poorer'. it may not be quite that if you have a blow out, but the lower end of the set menus at 250DKK is very reasonable for this Umbrian-Tuscan home cooking, served in a relaxed and homely atmosphere.

Below: Lê Lê's healthy Vietnamese cuisine is very popular with the younger crowd.

Copenhagen's Suburbs

Kaffesalonen
6 Peblinge Dosseringg, Nørrebro, tel: 35 35 12 19; €–€€; map p.134 B1
This is one of a couple of charming small restaurants on the banks of Pebblinge Sø, just over the Louise bridge. The food is fairly casual but good – burgers, salads, etc. – but its charm lies in its location where you can sit out on the river watching the swans of a summer evening. Service can be a tad slow and you order from the bar.

Prices for an average three-course meal without wine:

€	under 250DKK
€€	250–400DKK
€€€	400–550DKK
€€€€	over 550DKK

Shopping

Shopping in Copenhagen is a unique pleasure, and the city's pedestrian precincts and spacious squares add to ease with which you can seek out those special purchases. Characterful shops in the side streets and arcades around the Strøget area specialise in everything from antiques to avant-garde furniture, while chic department stores such as Magasin du Nord offer the very best in Danish fashions. If you make purchases in tax-free stores, you will be able to reclaim your sales tax, a valuable bonus in a city that isn't the cheapest, but where quality is very high.

Shopping Areas

STRØGET

Depending on what you are looking for, and how much time you have, Strøget and the streets to north and south are the best places to begin.

Strøget itself is a pedestrian-only shopping street made up of four streets starting at Rådhuspladsen with Frederiksberggade, which leads into Nygade Vimmelskaftet, Amagertorv, Østergade, and ends in Kongens Nytorv square.

Starting at Rådhuspladsen, it becomes progressively more expensive and upmarket – so look for bargain bins at one end and designer labels at the other. Most of the shops that you find along here will belong to a chain of one sort or another, with the more independent shops found in the streets nearby. But that said, you will find ceramics, silver and crystal, superb home furnishings and interiors stores, the city's leading furriers, antiques shops, department stores, clothing shops and souvenir outlets side-by-side with a varied selection of restaurants and bars.

If you are short on time, check out the department stores **Illums Bollighus** (for household goods) and **Magasin du Nord** (on Kongens Nytorv) as well as **Royal Copenhagen** for its world famous china.

In the smaller streets branching off (and running parallel to) Strøget are an eclectic array of workshops belonging to young potters, silversmiths, numerous antiques shops, and many boutiques.

SEE ALSO STRØGET AND AROUND P.8

Illums Bolighus
Amagertorv 10; map p.138 B3
SEE ALSO DANISH DESIGN P.42

Magasin du Nord
Kongens Nytorv 13; www.magasin.dk; Mon–Thur 10am–7pm, Fri 10am–8pm, Sat 10am–5pm; train: Kongens Nytorv, bus: 1A, 15, 19, 26, 999;

Below: Magasin du Nord on Kongens Nytorv is the city's biggest department store.

Left: Magasin du Nord features mostly international brands.

To claim back tax, non-EU members must spend over 300DKK in a 'tax-free' store and receive a form to show with the receipt, on leaving Denmark. They can then apply for their discount on www.globalrefund.com.

map p.138 C3
Royal Copenhagen
Amagertorv 6; map p.138 B3
SEE ALSO DANISH DESIGN P.41

BEYOND KONGENS NYTORV

On the opposite side of Kongens Nytorv, and convenient for those visiting Amalienborg and the Marble Church, are **Bredgade** and **Store Kongensgade**, both lined with boutiques, galleries and more antiques shops. **Kronprinsessgade**, near Kongens Have, is Copenhagen's Bond Street and expensive.
SEE ALSO ROSENBORG AND AROUND P.14–5; AMALIENBORG AND AROUND P.16–7

TOWARDS THE SUBURBS

Away from the centre, heading towards Nørrebro, **Nansengade** has a reputation for good street gear and Nørrebro and Vesterbro are also good for browsing at the cheaper, younger and often more individual end of the market.

If you are looking for second-hand goods, Nørrebro is particularly good – though if you think you might fit into any of Helena Christiansen's cast-offs, check out her mum's second-hand shop, **Yo-Yo** in Christianshavn.
SEE ALSO VESTERBRO AND FREDERIKSBERG P.18–9; COPENHAGEN'S SUBURBS P.22–3

Yo-Yo
Sankt Annæ Gade 31; Wed–Fri 1–5.30pm; map p.139 D1

Opening Hours

Shops are generally open Monday–Friday 9am or 10am– 5.30pm or 7pm, and from 9am–1pm or 2pm on Saturday. However, shopping hours have been extended, permitting stores to open from 6am–8pm if they so choose – most don't, but you can count on the department stores not to close before 5pm and some of the shops around Strøget also stay open longer.

A small number of shops (often food shops) are closed on Monday or Tuesday.

Certain stores stay open longer, including bakers, florists, smørrebrød shops and kiosks. In addition, late-night (until 10pm or mid-night) and Sunday shopping is possible at Central Station, with banks open for foreign exchange and a post office.

Antiques

Quality antiques shops are concentrated mainly in the **Bredgade**, **Store Kongensgade**, **Kompagnistræde**, **Farvergade**, **Læderstræde** **Ravnsborgade** (Nørrebro) and **Nordre Frihavnsgade** (Østerbro) areas. Illums *(see above)* also has an antiques market on the second floor. But the largest destination is in **Amager**.

Green Square
Strandlodsvej 11B, Amager; tel: 32 57 59 59; www.green-square.dk; Mon–Thur 10am–5.30pm, Fri 10am–6pm, Sat 10am–4pm

Below: Illums on Strøget features the best in Danish fashion and design.

Above: shop and ride.

Scandinavia's largest antiques warehouse. Over 10,000sq m in size it has an eclectic mixture including Spanish, Chinese and Danish antiquities.

Clothing and Fashion

Knitwear comes Nordic-style, often highly patterned, warm, and, in some cases, expensive. There are knitwear shops all over the city; the **Sweater Market** claims to be Europe's largest sweater store.

For shops specialising in retro clothing and memorabilia from the 1950s to the 1970s, have a look around **Ravnsborgade** in Nørrebro and **Nordre Frihavnsgade** in Østerbro.

If you are looking for Danish women's wear, check out established designers **Sand** and **Munthe plus Simonsen** and **Bruuns Baazar** (for men and women).

For younger designers who haven't quite hit the big time, visit the design cooperative **Montre** in Vesterbro and **Designer Zoo**, which covers everything from clothing to homeware and jewellery.

For women of a generous size check out **Søstrene Nielsen** near Rosenborg, which sells clothes from all over the world in sizes 44–56 (European).

Bruuns Bazaar
Kronprinsessegade 8–9; www.bruunsbazaar.com; map p.138 B4; **Østergade 52**; map p.138 B3

Designer Zoo
Vesterbrogade 137, Vesterbro; map p.136 A3/B3
SEE ALSO DANISH DESIGN P.40–1

Montre
Halmtorvet 19; map p.137 C3

Munthe plus Simonsen
Grøneggade 10; tel: 33 32 03 12; www.muntheplussimonsen.com; map p.138 B3

Sand
Østergade 40; www.sand-europe.com; map p.138 B3

Søstrene Nielsen
Christian IXs gade 1; map p.138 B3

Sweater Market
Frederiksberggade 15, Strøget; map p.138 B3

Household Goods

Crystal glassware and porcelain products are especially good buys, offering top-quality design matched with supreme craftsmanship. Of the numerous shops offering fine porcelain and crystal, **Skandinavisk Glas** has a wide range of Scandinavian brands.

Danish and other Scandinavian knives and tableware are of the highest standard, and **Zwilling J.A. Henckels A/S** has by far the widest and most interesting array. **Bodum** has a great selection of tea- and coffee-making paraphernalia.
SEE ALSO DANISH DESIGN P.40–3

Bodum
Østergade 10, www.bodum.com; map p.138 D3

Skandinavisk Glas
Ny Østergade 4; map p.138 B3

Zwilling J.A. Henckels A/S
Vimmelskaftet 47; map p.138 B3

Below: the Royal Copenhagen Porcelain company produces dinnerware fit for a king (or queen).

Souvenirs and Luxuries

Amber jewellery is offered everywhere, particularly in stores along Strøget. The local 'gem' (actually a fossil resin from the southern Baltic) may be cheaper here than at home, but beware, the quality can vary tremendously. The **House of Amber** is a respectable outlet.

Silver is another Danish speciality, dominated by the name **Georg Jensen** *(see page 43)*. Silver in Denmark is quality-controlled and should always be hallmarked.

If you are interested in clocks and watches, the owner of **Gullacksen Ure** is the third generation of an old watchmaking family, and his shop offers a wide collection of international brand-name watches, clocks, barometers and hygrometers, as well as museum pieces on the walls.

If you like hand-made goods, visit **Gustus** for fabulous hand-blown glass at reasonable prices – from Christmas decorations to beautiful vessels and chandeliers.

For the committed handbag connoisseur, **Jane Burchard** offers a treasure trove of beautiful, Baroque-style cloth handbags and for affordable kitsch, girly presents, check out **Akimbo**.

SEE ALSO DANISH DESIGN P.40–3

Akimbo
Nyskenstraede 3

House of Amber
Ravhuset, Kongens Nytorv 2; train Kongens Nytorv; bus 1A, 15, 19, 26, 999; map p.138 C3

Gullacksen Ure
Frederiksberggade 8; map p.138 A2

Gustus
Istedgade 67b, Vesterbro; bus 10; map p.136 C3

Above: there are only so many plates they can make at the Royal Copenhagen Porcelain company.

Jane Burchard
Købmagergade 7; map p.138 B3

Markets

For a current list of markets, see the weekly publication *Copenhagen This Week*. Those listed below are held on a regular basis.

Frederiksberg
Smallegade; Sat 8am–2pm; map p.136 A4
Popular with the locals.

Gammel Strand
Sat–Sun 8am–2pm; map p.138 B2
This canal-side market includes good-quality antiques and, thanks to numerous open-air cafés, it makes a good spot to linger at the weekends.

Below: market time on Israel Plads.

Israel Plads
Sat 8am–2pm; map p.138 A3/A4
Typical flea market with a variety of goods including fruit and vegetables.

Food and Drink

Copenhagen has some excellent food stores. For organic bread, pâtisserie, wine, chocolate and oil check out one of the Emmerys stores *(see page 54)*; for more chocolate specialists *see page 53–54*, and if you can't get to one of those, the royal chocolate concession at Illums on Strøget is very good.

All the department stores are in fact generally worth a visit for their upmarket grocery stores. If you go a little further afield, Værnedamsvej in Vesterbro has an excellent reputation as 'gourmet' street, where you can find quality butchers, greengrocers, wine and cheese shops.

Akvavit, the local spirit, usually flavoured with caraway seed, is cheaper than imported spirits. You will also find good prices at the airport duty-free store.

SEE ALSO FOOD AND DRINK P.52–5; VESTERBRO AND FREDERKSBERG P.18–9

Transport

Getting to Copenhagen is easy, with many airlines offering daily flights, and direct rail services from Sweden and Germany. Access from the airport is also very straight forward. The train is a great option: not only will you arrive right in the city centre, but it's also the least polluting form of transport, which will win you friends with the eco-conscious Danes. From London's Waterloo station you are less than 24 hours away from the city. There are also good ferry services to Copenhagen – from Britain by ferry you arrive at Esbjerg on Jutland three hours' drive away.

Arriving by Train

Trains arrive daily from Germany, Britain and Sweden. Hovedbanegården, the central station, is situated opposite Tivoli and the Tourist Office. Buses for onward journeys leave either from outside the station or the nearby Rådhuspladsen. The S-trains leaving from the central station run on a separate network.

For European rail enquiries contact Danish or German Rail or DFDS Seaways

Danish Rail (DSB)
tel: 70 13 14 16 (international travel); www.dsb.dk/english

German Railways
Tel: 0870 243 5363 (UK); www.bahn.de

The Man in Seat 61
www.seat61.com
The website all 'slow travellers' should know by heart is The Man in Seat 61. It provides regularly updated, detailed routes for rail travel between European cities. There are two routes to Copenhagen from London, both take about 24 hours and involve an overnight train.

Arriving by Boat

Copenhagen is easily accessible by sea. There are a number of different routes available. Most ferries operate from the new ferry terminal in Copenhagen, north of the cruise-ship harbour, and close to Nordhavn train station.

There are ferries direct to Copenhagen from Poland, Sweden and Norway. Ferries from the UK arrive at Esbjerg and from Germany at Rostock and Rønne.

DFDS Seaways
www.dfds.co.uk; (UK) tel: 08702 520 524, (Oslo) tel: 33 42 30 00, (Copenhagen) tel: 33 42 30 00;

Polferries (Swinoujscie)
tel: 33 13 52 23

Port of Copenhagen Ltd
PO Box 2083, Nordre Toldbod 7, DK-1013 Copenhagen K; tel: 33 47 99 99; www.cphport.dk

Arriving by Bus

Eurolines
tel: 08705 143 219 (UK); www.eurolines.com
Though still a greener option than a short-haul flight, this is no easy route. The trip from London takes over 22 hours and does not provide the comfort of the train. The prices are cheaper than either train or plane, but the savings are not as much as you'd expect considering the hardship of the journey. If travelling from Germany or Scandinavia this is a very good value option. Buses stop at Copenhagen's central station.

Above: waiting times are displayed for the major bus routes (such as the 2A pictured here).

Arriving by Plane

Copenhagen Airport,
tel: 32 31 32 31; www.cph.dk; map p.22

Left: though Sweden and Denmark have been politically independent for nearly five centuries the Øresund bridge has brought them closer together than ever before.

The bus, Metro and S-tog (suburban train) all use the same tickets, so you can transfer between services without buying a new one. The cheapest option is to buy a discount clip card of ten tickets. Alternatively, if you have a CPH Card, local travel is free.

Copenhagen Airport is situated some 12km east of the city centre on Amager island. A rail shuttle service links Kastrup and Copenhagen's central station. The fast train link leaves from Track *(Spor)* 2 (located beneath Terminal 3), three times every hour; journey time is about 12 minutes.

An airport bus service runs every 15 minutes to Hovedbanegården (Central Station), takes 25 minutes and costs 35DKK, slightly more than the train (27DKK).

There is also a regular bus service, 250S, which departs from outside Terminals 1 and 3 every 15 minutes between 5.30am–midnight, takes 35 minutes (a bit longer than the airport bus, but less than half the price, at 16.50DKK).

There is a taxi rank at terminal 3. A taxi to the centre will cost between 170–220DKK depending on the time and includes tax and tip.

Arriving by Car

Most British drivers to Denmark arrive either by ferry direct from the UK or from Germany, and then either on the motorway from Hamburg in the west, or by car ferry across the Femer Bælt from Puttgarden to Rødby.

The E47 covers the last 165km to Copenhagen. Boats leave Puttgarden throughout the day every half hour and the journey takes just under an hour. You don't normally have to wait very long, except on busy summer weekends. Traffic can also be heavy at these times on the main road border crossing north of Flensburg.

Both the Storebælt bridge/tunnel (Funen–Sjælland), and the Øresund bridge (Malmö–Copenhagen) levy a toll.

Below: much of the city's modern bus fleet employ carbon-free technology.

Getting around by Bus

The bus network covers practically every destination in Copenhagen and must be the best way to get around until the metro devlops a more comprehensive network; although in the centre, everything is so close you might as well walk.

Nearly all buses stop at either Rådhuspladsen or the Central Station. Passengers enter at the front of the bus and alight at the rear. For ticket purposes, greater Copenhagen is split into zones and the cost of your journey depends on the number of zones you go through, regardless of where you end up. The most expensive zone you pass through determines the cost of your journey.

Individually bought tickets have a time limit of an hour for two zones (adult 19DKK/child 9.50DKK) and you must clip your ticket when you get on. A journey taking in 8 zones would cost 66.50DKK/38DKK and the time limit would be two hours.

All discount cards are available from manned stations and from Movia ticket

To minimise your energy impact, you can measure your travel usage and gain carbon emission credits. More information is available at www.carbonresponsible.com and www.climatecare.org

offices. You can buy discount cards for two or three zones from most vending machines at stations. You must keep tickets and discount cards throughout the journey and present them to ticket inspectors on request.

Alternatively, a 24-hour travel card (110DKK; 55DKK) or a Copenhagen Card might be more suitable. If you are not sure, just tell the driver where you want to go. When catching the night bus or the metro between 1am and 5am, you must pay double fare.

S-train

The S-train connects Copenhagen and other towns on Sjælland. Within the city, it runs underground. Tickets are available at all S-stations.
SEE MAP ON INSIDE BACK COVER

Metro

Tel: 70 15 16 15; Mon–Fri 8am–6pm; www.m.dk; bus and metro planner: www.dsb.dk

The trains run every 3–6 minutes from 5am–1am daily with special night services at weekends.

Work is continuing on Copenhagen's new Metro system, which opened in 2002. The system is due to extend out to Copenhagen Airport by 2007. All the stations are made of steel and glass in stunning examples of Danish design. The trains are fully automated and unmanned.

The main route runs from Frederiksberg, over Nørreport to Kongens Nytorv, under the inner harbour to Christianshavn and the university at Amager. It connects with the S-train at Nørreport Station and with buses as well. To find out which lines are now running, pick up a map from any tourist office or station.
SEE MAP ON INSIDE BACK COVER

Cycling

The Danes are avid cyclists; bicycles enjoy equal status with cars on Copenhagen's roads, and consequently they usually make rapid and relatively safe progress.

When using the cycleways, keep to the right and always use lights at night or risk an instant 500DKK fine.

If you don't have your own bike, hire a bike or, in summer, use a City Bike. These are available between April and November at 110 stands around the inner city. Cyclists put a 20-krøner coin into a slot to unlock a bike, and it's theirs for as long as they like. When the bike is returned to a stand, the 20-krøner is refunded. The bikes may only be used within the old ramparts of the city, but this is where most of the sights are located. Pick up a City Bike Map from the Tourist Information Office, at Vesterbrogade 4a, oppposite the entrance to Tivoli.

Bike rental varies from 60–75DKK per day. Deposits 200–500DKK.

City Safari
Strandgade 27B, Christianshavn; tel: 33 23 94 90; www.citysafari.dk; map p.139 D2
Offers tours, on bikes of course, throughout the city.

Kobenhavns Cykelbørs
Gothersgade 157; tel: 33 14 07 17; www.cykelboersen.dk; Mon–Fri 8.30am–5.30pm, Sat 10am–1pm; map p.138 A4

Kobenhavns Cykler
Reventlowsgade 11 (behind the main station); tel: 33 33 86 13; www.copenhagen-bikes.dk; open also Sun in summer 10am–1pm; map p.137 C3

Harbour Buses

Daily 6am–6/7pm, every 10 mins; Adults 30DKK, children 25DKK; clip cards or Copenhagen card accepted

The 901 and 902 harbour buses run regularly between Den Sorte Diamant (The Black Diamond) near Slotsholmen and Gefion Springvandet near the Little Mermaid, zigzagging between the two shores and taking 20 mins. There is a suggestion that these may not be retained but no decision had been made at time of printing.

Below: Copenhagen's Metro system is the latest addition to the city's transport scheme.

Harbour Tours

One of the best ways of seeing the city is on a boat cruising the main harbour and the canals around Slotshomen and Christianshavn.

DFDS Canal Tours

Tel: 32 96 30 00; www.canaltours.com; ticketoffices at Nyhavn 2, map p.138 C3; and Gammel Strand 26, map p.138 B2

DFDS's 50-minute guided tours are the most popular. Prices are 60DKK (25DKK for children). They also offer dinner cruises that last two hours and cost about 600DKK.

The Netto Boats

tel: 32 54 41 02; www.netto-baadene.dk

The open-top Netto Boats take a 60-minute guided tour of the harbour and the canals but cost significantly less, at 30DKK (15DKK for children).

Above: on sunny summer days, water buses make a great alternative for getting about and seeing the waterfront.

Car Hire

Driving around Copenhagen is not a practical option; parking is very expensive and busy streets are likely to make your journey time extremely long. If you do hire a car, you must be over 20 and hold a valid licence.

Danes drive on the right and speed limits are 110 or 130kph on motorways, 80kph on other roads and 50kph in a built-up area. Wear a seat belt at all times.

You must also use dipped headlights at all times. Beware of cycle lanes on both sides of the road in towns.

Car hire companies operating in Denmark include:

Europcar

tel: 0845 758 5375; www.europcar.com

Hertz

tel: 08708 44 88 44; www.hertz.co.uk

Taxis and Rickshaws

Taxis can be identified by the sign on the roof with the word FRI, meaning 'free'. Most drivers speak English and often some German. They can give you receipts and you can pay with a credit card. The basic fare for a taxi is19DKK; 11DKK for each 1km thereafter Mon–Fri 7am– 4pm; 14DKK per 1km Fri–Sat 11pm–7am; 12.1DKK per 1km at all other times.

Cyclo rickshaws are available for short rides around town and can be found at Stork Fountain, Nyhavn, Tivoli and Rådhuspladsen. Prices vary. Negotiate first.

Amager Øbro Taxi

tel: 32 51 51 51

Kobenhavns Taxa

tel: 35 35 35 35

Minibuses/handicap

tel: 35 39 35 35

Taxa-motor

tel: 38 10 10 10

Below: in the mostly pedestrianised area around Strøget, rickshaws are the only transport option to rest your feet.

Walking

Copenhagen is an ideal city to explore on foot. It is very compact, with a well-preserved old-town area of winding cobbled streets, stuccoed houses and a network of canals, and almost everything is easily accessible. Despite the fact that the reliable public transport system is superb, walking around Copenhagen is, in reality, the best way to discover this city's inestimable charms. However, if you are heading over to Nørrebro or down to Frederiksberg, it's worth hopping on a bus to save time and shoe leather.

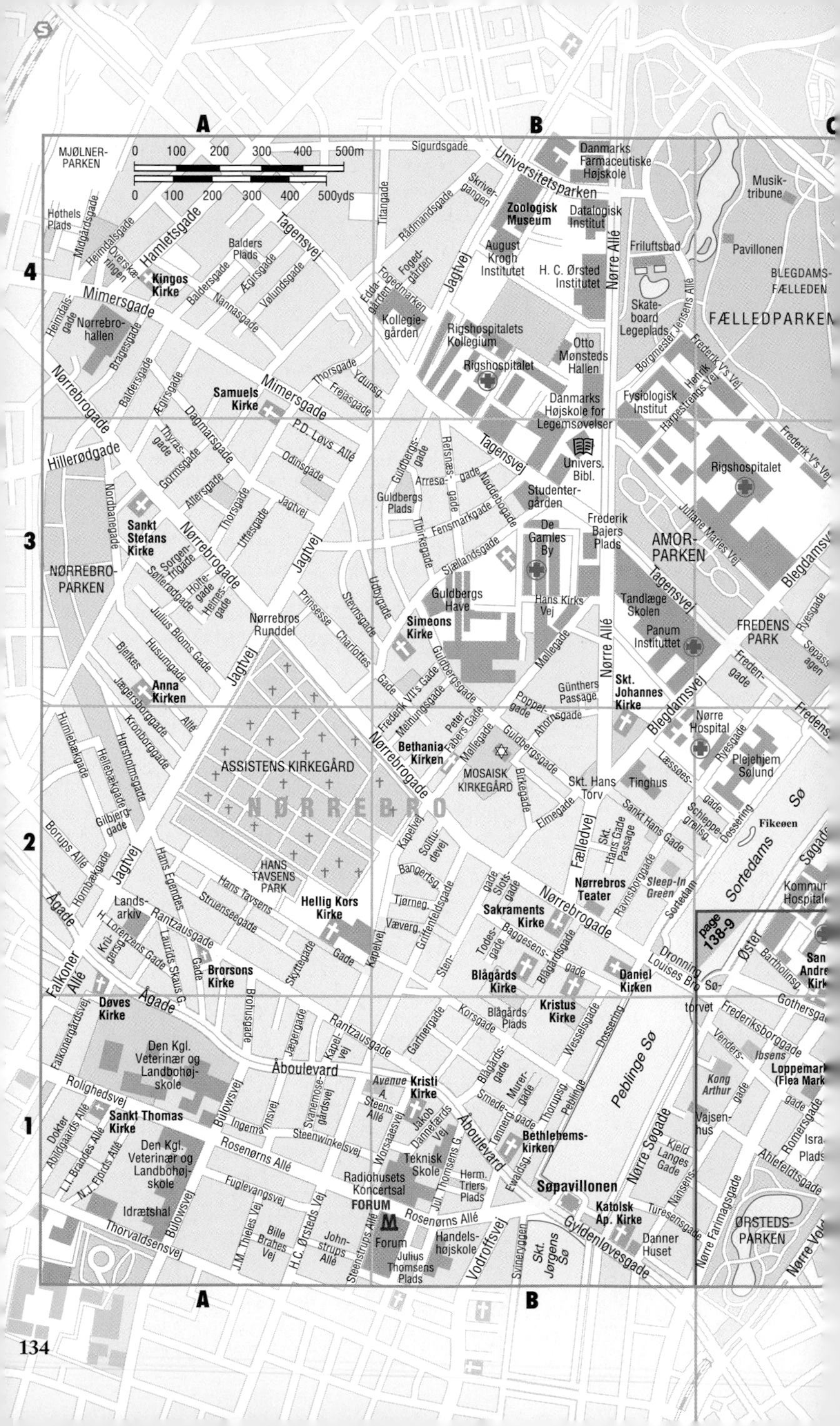
A
B
C
1
2
3
4
0 100 200 300 400 500m
0 100 200 300 400 500yds
MJØLNER-PARKEN
Høthels Plads
Midgårdsgade
Heimdalsgade
Overskæringen
Hamletsgade
Kingos Kirke
Balders Plads
Tagensvej
Ægirsgade
Vølundsgade
Baldersgade
Nannasgade
Mimersgade
Heimdalsgade
Nørrebrohallen
Bragesgade
Nørrebrogade
Samuels Kirke
Thorsgade
Ydunsg.
Frejasgade
P.D. Løvs Allé
Dagmarsgade
Thyrasgade
Gormsgade
Odinsgade
Hillerødgade
Nordbanegade
Altersgade
Uffesgade
Jagtvej
Sankt Stefans Kirke
NØRREBROPARKEN
Sorgenfrigade
Søllerødgade
Holtegade
Heimesgade
Nørrebros Runddel
Prinsesse Charlottes Gade
Julius Bloms Gade
Husumgade
Bjelkes Allé
Anna Kirken
Jægersborggade
Kronborggade
Humlebækgade
Hellebækgade
Hørsholmsgade
ASSISTENS KIRKEGÅRD
NØRREBRO
Gilbjerggade
Borups Allé
Hornbækgade
Ågade
Landsarkiv
Hans Egedes Gade
HANS TAVSENS PARK
Hans Tavsens Gade
Struenseegade
Hellig Kors Kirke
H. Lorenzens Gade
Krügersg.
Rantzausgade
Laurids Skaus G.
Brorsons Kirke
Skyttegade
Falkoner Allé
Døves Kirke
Ågade
Brohusgade
Jægergade
Kapelvej
Falkonergårdsvej
Den Kgl. Veterinær og Landbohøjskole
Aboulevard
Rolighedsvej
Bülowsvej
Ingemannsvej
Svanemøsegårdsvej
Avenue
Kristi Kirke
Sankt Thomas Kirke
Dokter Abildgaards Allé
L.I. Brandes Allé
N.J. Fjords Allé
Steenwinkelsvej
Rosenørns Allé
A. Steens Allé
Worsaaesvej
Jakob Dannefærds Vej
Teknisk Skole
Fuglevangsvej
Radiohusets Koncertsal
FORUM
Idrætshal
Thorvaldsensvej
J.M. Thieles Vej
Bille Brahes Vej
H.C. Ørsteds Vej
John-strups Allé
Steenstrups Allé
Forum
Julius Thomsens Plads
Jul. Thomsens G.
Herm. Triers Plads
Handelshøjskole
Vodroffsvej
Sigurdsgade
Titangade
Rådmandsgade
Skrivergangen
Universitetsparken
Danmarks Farmaceutiske Højskole
Zoologisk Museum
Datalogisk Institut
August Krogh Institutet
H. C. Ørsted Institutet
Nørre Allé
Friluftsbad
Skateboard Legeplads
Musik-tribune
Pavillonen
BLEGDAMSFÆLLEDEN
FÆLLEDPARKEN
Eddagården
Fogedgården
Fogedmarken
Kollegiegården
Rigshospitalets Kollegium
Rigshospitalet
Otto Mønsteds Hallen
Borgmester Jensens Allé
Frederik V's Vej
Henrik Harpestrengs Vej
Fysiologisk Institut
Danmarks Højskole for Legemsøvelser
Guldbergsgade
Refsnæsgade
Arresøgade
Nøddebogade
Univers. Bibl.
Guldbergs Plads
Tibirkegade
Fensmarkgade
Studentergården
Frederik Bajers Plads
De Gamles By
Sjællandsgade
AMORPARKEN
Juliane Maries Vej
Tagensvej
Blegdamsvej
Udbygade
Stevnsgade
Guldbergs Have
Hans Kirks Vej
Simeons Kirke
Tandlæge Skolen
Panum Instituttet
FREDENS PARK
Ryesgade
Søpassagen
Fredensgade
Frederik VII's Gade
Meinungsgade
Møllegade
Günthers Passage
Skt. Johannes Kirke
Poppelgade
Ahornsgade
Peter Fabers Gade
Bethania Kirken
MOSAISK KIRKEGÅRD
Birkegade
Skt. Hans Torv
Tinghus
Nørre Hospital
Plejehjem Sølund
Læssøesgade
Schleppegrellsg.
Sankt Hans Gade
Dossering
Fikeøen
Sortedams Sø
Søgade
Kommunehospital
Elmegade
Fælledvej
Skt. Hans Gade Passage
Kapelvej
Solitudevej
Bangertsg.
Tjørneg.
Væverg.
Griffenfeldsgade
Slotsgade
Nørrebros Teater
Ravnsborggade
Sleep-In Green
Sortedam
Sakraments Kirke
Todesgade
Baggesensgade
Blågårdsgade
Dronning Louises Bro
page 138-9
Øster Søgade
Bartholinsg.
Sankt Andreas Kirke
Gade
Sten-
Blågårds Kirke
Daniel Kirken
Blågårds Plads
Kristus Kirke
Korsgade
Wesselsgade
Dossering
Søtorvet
Gothersgade
Frederiksborggade
Rantzausgade
Gartnergade
Blågårdsgade
Murergade
Smedegade
Thorupsg.
Peblinge
Peblinge Sø
Vendersgade
Ibsens
Kong Arthur
Loppemarked (Flea Market)
Tømmerg.
Ewaldsg.
Bethlehemskirken
Nørre Søgade
Kjeld Langes Gade
Vajsenhus
Israels Plads
Rømersgade
Ahlefeldtsgade
Åboulevard
Søpavillonen
Nansensg.
Katolsk Ap. Kirke
Turesensgade
Nørre Farimagsgade
ØRSTEDSPARKEN
Nørre Voldgade
Svineryggen
Skt. Jørgens Sø
Gyldenløvesgade
Danner Huset

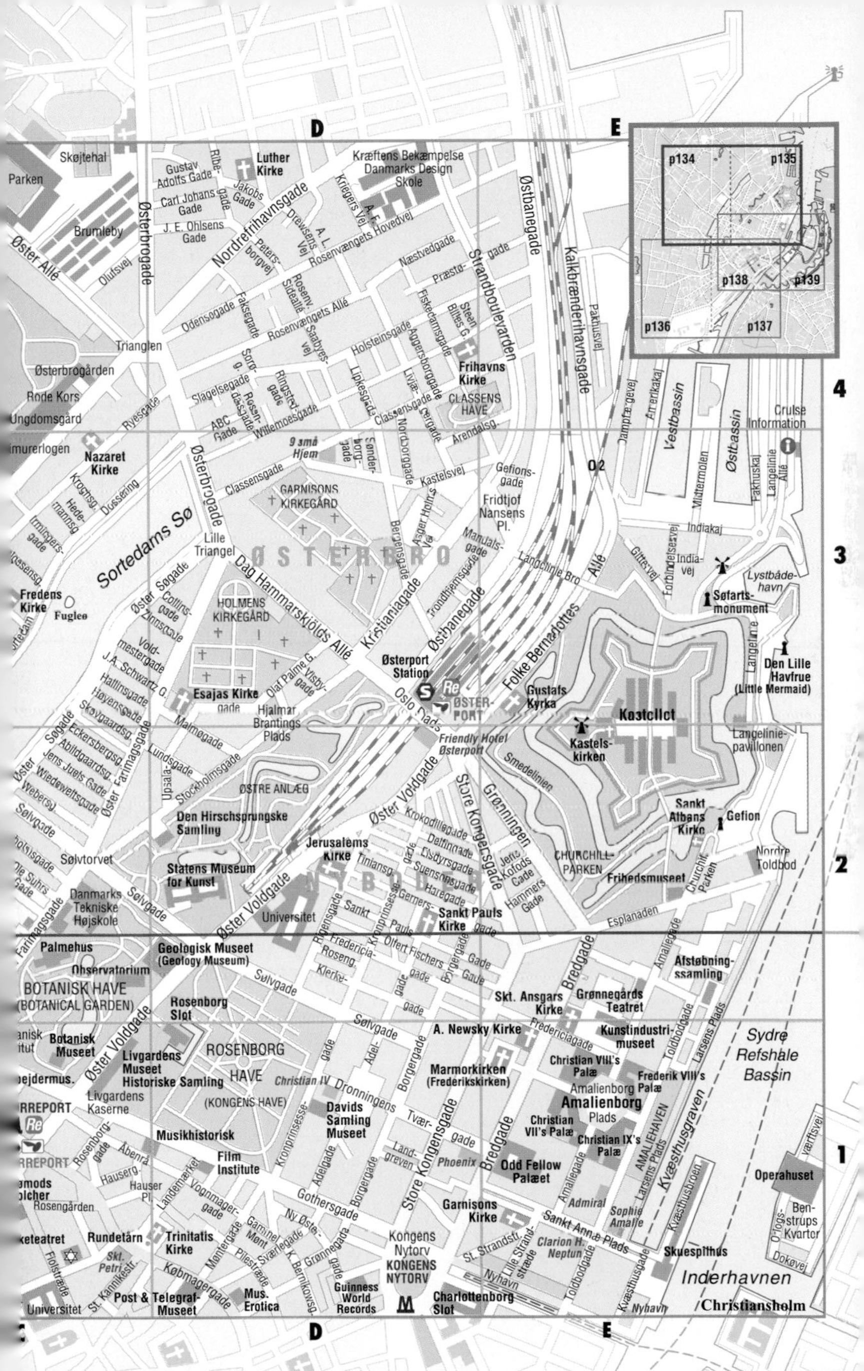
D
E
p134
p135
p138
p139
p136
p137
Skøjtehal
Parken
Gustav Adolfs Gade
Ribe-gade
Luther Kirke
Kræftens Bekæmpelse
Danmarks Design Skole
Carl Johans Gade
Jakobs Gade
J. E. Ohlsens Gade
Nordrefrihavnsgade
Drewsens Vej
Kriegers Vej
A. F.
A. L. Rosenvængets Hovedvej
Brumleby
Østerbrogade
Øster Allé
Olufsvej
Peters-borgvej
Rosenv. Sideallé
Næstvedgade
Strandboulevarden
Østbanegade
Kalkbrænderihavnsgade
Præstø-gade
Steen Billes G.
Odensegade
Faksegade
Rosenvængets Allé
Saabyes-vej
Holsteinsgade
Fiskedamsgade
Aggersborggade
Pakhusvej
Trianglen
Sorø-g.
Ringsted-gade
Lipkesgade
Frihavns Kirke
Østerbrogården
Slagelsegade
Rosen-dalsgade
Livjægergade
Classensgade
CLASSENS HAVE
Røde Kors Ungdomsgård
Ryesgade
ABC Gade
Willemoesgade
Nordborggade
Arendalsg.
Dampfærgevej
Amerikakaj
Vestbassin
Østbassin
Cruise Information
Frimurerlogen
Nazaret Kirke
9 små Hjem
Sønder-borg-gade
Gefions-gade
Kastelsvej
Middelmolen
Pakhuskaj
Langelinie Allé
Krogsg.
Hede-mannsg.
Dosseringen
Classensgade
GARNISONS KIRKEGÅRD
Fridtjof Nansens Pl.
Indiakaj
Irmingersgade
Sortedams Sø
Lille Triangel
ØSTERBRO
Bergensgade
Asger Holms Vej
Manddals-gade
Langelinie Bro
Gittervej
Forbindelsesvej
India-vej
Lystbåde-havn
Fredens Kirke
Fugleø
Øster Søgade
Collins-gade
Dag Hammarskjölds Allé
HOLMENS KIRKEGÅRD
Kristianiagade
Trondhjemsgade
Østbanegade
Allé
Søfarts-monument
Zinnsgade
Vold-mestergade
J.A. Schwartz G.
Folke Bernadottes
Langelinie
Den Lille Havfrue (Little Mermaid)
Østerport Station
Olaf Palme G.
Visby-gade
Hallinsgade
Højensgade
Esajas Kirke
Skovgaardsg.
Gustafs Kyrka
Kastellet
Hjalmar Brantings Plads
Oslo Plads
ØSTER-PORT
Kastels-kirken
Langelinie-pavillonen
Søgade
Eckersbergsg.
Abildgaardsg.
Jens Juels Gade
Wiedeweltsgade
Webersg.
Øster Farimagsgade
Malmøgade
Lundsgade
Upsalagade
Stockholmsgade
Friendly Hotel Østerport
Smedelinien
ØSTRE ANLÆG
Øster Voldgade
Store Kongensgade
Grønningen
Den Hirschsprungske Samling
Krokodillegade
Delfingade
Elsdyrsgade
Suensonsgade
Haregade
Sankt Albans Kirke
Gefion
Sølvgade
Sølvtorvet
Jerusalems Kirke
Tigergade
Jens Kofods Gade
CHURCHILL-PARKEN
Churchill Parken
Nordre Toldbod
Statens Museum for Kunst
NYBODER
Frihedsmuseet
Danmarks Tekniske Højskole
Øster Voldgade
Universitet
Rigensgade
Sankt Pauls Gade
Kronprinsessegade
Gerners-gade
Hammers Gade
Sankt Pauls Kirke
Esplanaden
Farimagsgade
Palmehus
Geologisk Museet (Geology Museum)
Fredericia-gade
Rosengade
Olfert Fischers Gade
Borgergade
Klerkegade
Observatorium
BOTANISK HAVE (BOTANICAL GARDEN)
Sølvgade
Bredgade
Amaliegade
Afstøbning-samling
Rosenborg Slot
Skt. Ansgars Kirke
Grønnegårds Teatret
Toldbodgade
Larsens Plads
Botanisk Museet
Sølvgade
A. Newsky Kirke
Fredericiagade
Kunstindustri-museet
Sydre Refshale Bassin
ROSENBORG HAVE
Øster Voldgade
Livgardens Museet
Historiske Samling
Adelgade
Borgergade
Marmorkirken (Frederikskirken)
Christian VIII's Palæ
Frederik VIII's Palæ
Amalienborg Plads
Amalienborg
Christian IV Dronningens Tværgade
Livgardens Kaserne
(KONGENS HAVE)
Davids Samling Museet
Christian VII's Palæ
Christian IX's Palæ
AMALIEHAVEN
Kvæsthusgraven
Musikhistorisk
Store Kongensgade
Bredgade
Land-greven
Phoenix
Odd Fellow Palæet
Kvæsthusbroen
Operahuset
Rosenborg-gade
Åbenrå
Hauserg.
Hauser Pl.
Film Institute
Kronprinsessegade
Adelgade
Borgergade
Vognmager-gade
Landemærket
Gothersgade
Garnisons Kirke
Admiral
Larsens Plads
Sophie Amalie
Sankt Annæ Plads
Ben-strups Kvarter
Rosengården
Rundetårn
Trinitatis Kirke
Møntergade
Gammel Mønt
Ny Øste-gade
Sværtegade
Pilestræde
K. Bernikowsg.
Grønnegade
Kongens Nytorv
KONGENS NYTORV
St. Strandstr.
Lille Strand-stræde
Clarion H. Neptun
Toldbodgade
Skuespilhus
Dokøvej
Inderhavnen
Skt. Petri
Fiolstræde
St. Kannikestr.
Post & Telegraf-Museet
Købmagergade
Mus. Erotica
Guinness World Records
Charlottenborg Slot
Nyhavn
Kvæsthusgade
Nyhavn
Christianshølm
Universitet
4
3
2
1

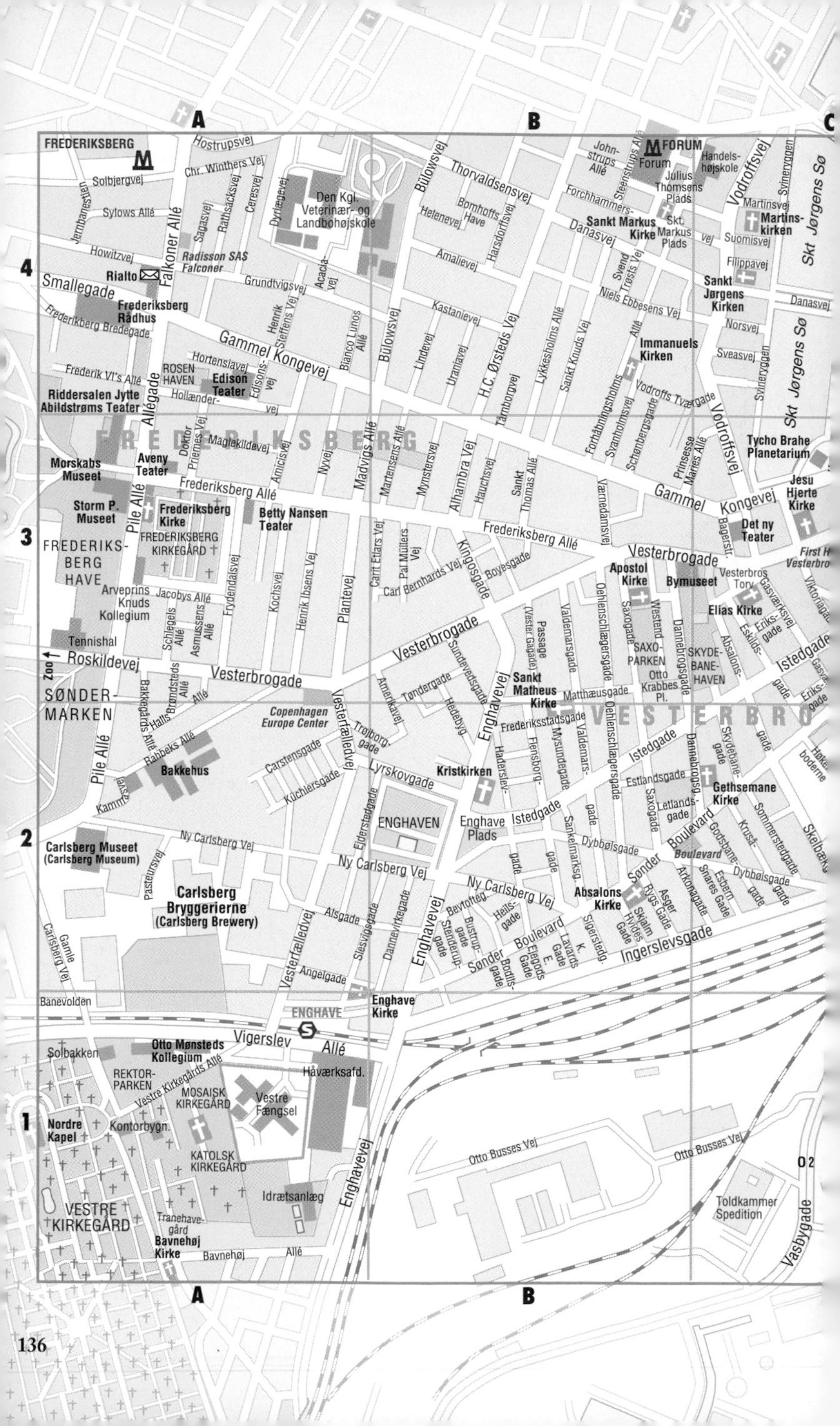

A
B
C
1
2
3
4
FREDERIKSBERG
FREDERIKSBERG
VESTERBRO
Hostrupsvej
Chr. Winthers Vej
Solbjergvej
Sylows Allé
Jernbanestien
Howitzvej
Falkoner Allé
Sagasvej
Rathsacksvej
Ceresvej
Dyrlægevej
Den Kgl. Veterinær- og Landbohøjskole
Radisson SAS Falconer
Rialto
Smallegade
Frederiksberg Rådhus
Frederikberg Bredegade
Grundtvigsvej
Acacia-vej
Henrik Steffens Vej
Gammel Kongevej
Hortensiavej
ROSEN HAVEN
Edison Teater
Edisons-vej
Frederik VI's Allé
Hollænder-vej
Allégade
Riddersalen Jytte Abildstrøms Teater
Bianco Lunos Allé
Bülowsvej
Thorvaldsensvej
Bomhoffs Have
Helenevej
Harsdorffsvej
Amalievej
Kastanievej
Lindevej
Uraniavej
H.C. Ørsteds Vej
Tårnborgvej
Lykkesholms Allé
Sankt Knuds Vej
John-strups Allé
Steenstrups Allé
FORUM
Forum
Julius Thomsens Plads
Handels-højskole
Vodroffsvej
Svineryggen
Forchhammers-vej
Danasvej
Sankt Markus Kirke
Skt. Markus Plads
Martinsvej
Martins-kirken
Suomisvej
Filippavej
Svend Trøsts Vej
Niels Ebbesens Vej
Sankt Jørgens Kirken
Danasvej
Norsvej
Sveasvej
Skt Jørgens Sø
Immanuels Kirken
Allé
Vodroffs Tværgade
Forhåbningsholms Allé
Svanholmsvej
Schønbergsgade
Prinsesse Maries Allé
Tycho Brahe Planetarium
Maglekildevej
Doktor Priemes Vej
Amicisvej
Nyvej
Madvigs Allé
Martensens Allé
Mynstersvej
Alhambra Vej
Hauchsvej
Sankt Thomas Allé
Værnedamsvej
Gammel Kongevej
Jesu Hjerte Kirke
Det ny Teater
Bagerstr.
Morskabs Museet
Aveny Teater
Frederiksberg Allé
Storm P. Museet
Pile Allé
Frederiksberg Kirke
FREDERIKSBERG KIRKEGÅRD
Betty Nansen Teater
Frederiksberg Allé
FREDERIKS-BERG HAVE
Carit Etlars Vej
Pal Müllers Vej
Carl Bernhards Vej
Kingosgade
Boyesgade
Vesterbrogade
Apostol Kirke
Bymuseet
Vesterbros Torv
Gasværksvej
Viktoriagade
First Hotel Vesterbro
Arveprins Knuds Kollegium
Jacobys Allé
Schlegels Allé
Asmussens Allé
Frydendalsvej
Kochsvej
Henrik Ibsens Vej
Plantevej
Oehlenschlægersgade
Valdemarsgade
Passage (Vester Gade)
Saxogade
Westend
Dannebrogsgade
Elias Kirke
Eriks-gade
Eskilds-
Tennishal
Zoo
Roskildevej
Vesterbrogade
Sundevedsgade
SAXO-PARKEN
Otto Krabbes Pl.
SKYDE-BANE-HAVEN
Absalons-
Istedgade
SØNDER-MARKEN
Bakkegårds Allé
Halls Allé
Brøndsteds Allé
Copenhagen Europe Center
Vesterfælledvej
Amerikavej
Tøndergade
Hedebygade
Enghavevej
Sankt Matheus Kirke
Matthæusgade
Frederiksstadsgade
Haderslev-
Flensborg-
Mysundegade
Valdemars-
Skydebane-gade
Høkerboderne
Rahbeks Allé
Bakkehus
Kammas
Carstensgade
Küchlersgade
Trøjborg-gade
Lyrskovgade
Kristkirken
Istedgade
Estlandsgade
Letlands-gade
Gethsemane Kirke
Eiderstedgade
ENGHAVEN
Enghave Plads
Istedgade
Sankelmarksg.
gade
Dybbølsgade
Boulevard
Sønder Boulevard
Godsbane-gade
Krusågade
Sommerstedgade
Skelbækgade
Carlsberg Museet (Carlsberg Museum)
Ny Carlsberg Vej
Ny Carlsberg Vej
Pasteursvej
Carlsberg Bryggerierne (Carlsberg Brewery)
Absalons Kirke
Arkonagade
Esbern Snares Gade
Asger Ryes Gade
Skjalm Hvides Gade
Alsgade
Slesvigsgade
Dannevirkegade
Bevtoftg.
Bustrup-gade
Heils-gade
Stenderup-gade
Sønder Boulevard
Bodils-gade
Ejegods Gade
E.
Lavards Gade
K.
Sigerstedg.
Ingerslevsgade
Gamle Carlsberg Vej
Angelgade
Banevolden
ENGHAVE
Enghave Kirke
Vigerslev Allé
Solbakken
Otto Mønsteds Kollegium
REKTOR-PARKEN
Vestre Kirkegårds Allé
MOSAISK KIRKEGÅRD
Vestre Fængsel
Håværksafd.
Nordre Kapel
Kontorbygn.
KATOLSK KIRKEGÅRD
Enghavevej
Otto Busses Vej
Otto Busses Vej
Toldkammer Spedition
Idrætsanlæg
VESTRE KIRKEGÅRD
Tranehave-gård
Bavnehøj Kirke
Bavnehøj
Allé
Vasbygade
O2

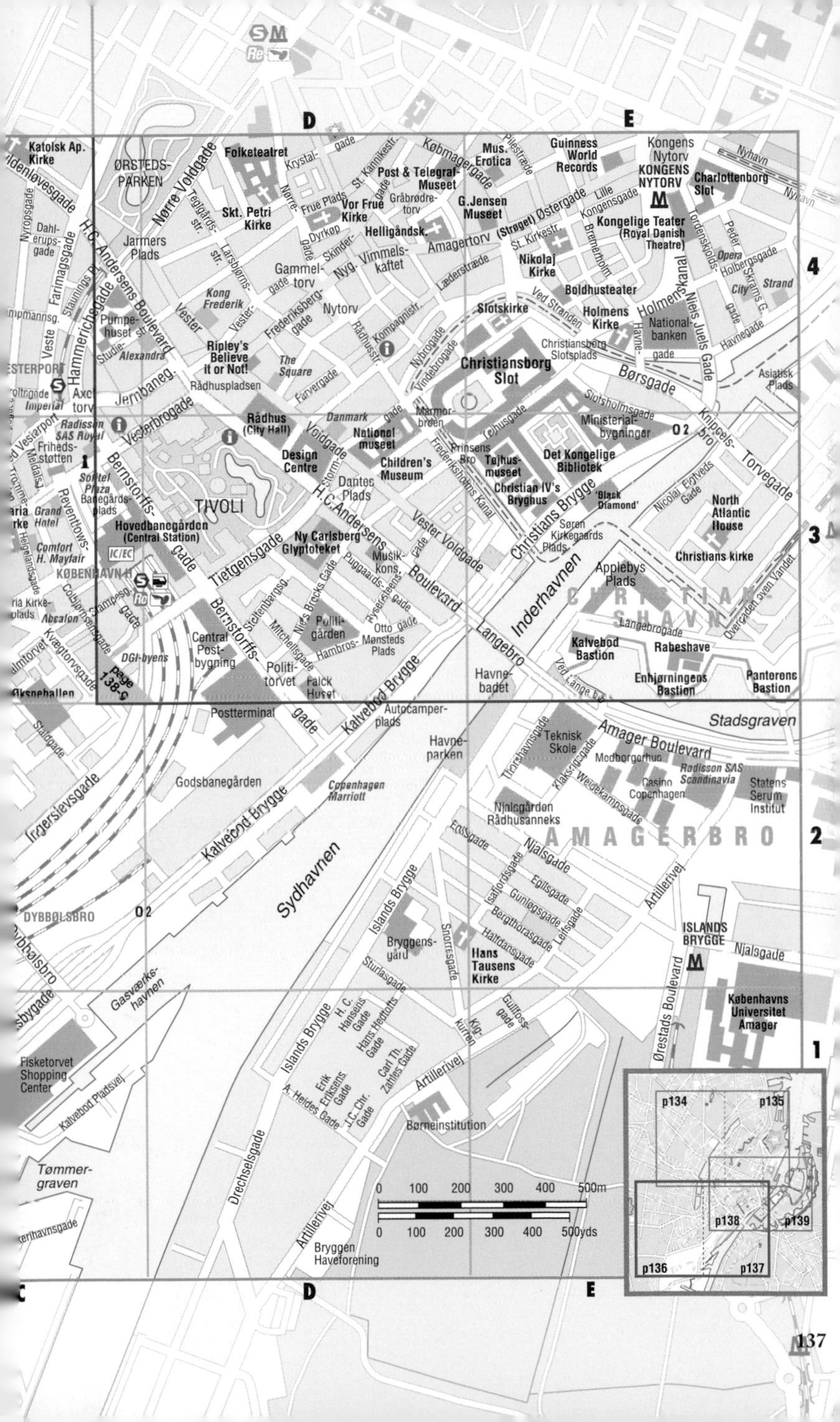

D
E
Katolsk Ap. Kirke
ØRSTEDS-PARKEN
Folketeatret
Krystal-gade
St. Kannikestr.
Købmagergade
Mus. Erotica
Pilestræde
Guinness World Records
Kongens Nytorv
KONGENS NYTORV
Charlottenborg Slot
Nyhavn
Nørre Voldgade
Nørre-gade
Post & Telegraf-Museet
G.Jensen Museet
Lille Kongensgade
Kongelige Teater (Royal Danish Theatre)
Frue Plads
Vor Frue Kirke
Gråbrødre-torv
(Strøget) Østergade
Skt. Petri Kirke
Teglgårds-str.
Dyrkøp
Helligåndsk.
Amagertorv
St. Kirkestr.
Bremerholm
Tordenskjolds-gade
Peder Skrams G.
Holbergsgade
H.C. Andersens Boulevard
Jarmers Plads
Larsbjørns-str.
Gammel-torv
Skinder-gade
Nyg.
Vimmels-kaftet
Nikolaj Kirke
Opera
City
Strand
4
Nyropsgade
Dahl-erups-gade
Farimagsgade
Staunings Pl.
Kong Frederik
Vester-
Frederiksberg-gade
Nytorv
Læderstræde
Boldhusteater
Ved Stranden
Holmens Kirke
Holmens Kanal
Niels Juels Gade
Nationalbanken
Havnegade
Hammerichsgade
Pumpe-huset
Studie-str.
Alexandra
Vester
Ripley's Believe it or Not!
The Square
Rådhusstr.
Kompagnistr.
Slotskirke
Christiansborg Slotsplads
Havne-gade
Vesterport
Jernbaneg.
Rådhuspladsen
Farvergade
Nybrogade
Vindebrogade
Christiansborg Slot
Børsgade
Asiatisk Plads
Axeltorv
Imperial
Vesterbrogade
Radisson SAS Royal
Rådhus (City Hall)
Danmark
Voldgade
Marmor-broen
Slotsholmsgade
Ministerial-bygninger
Knippels-bro
Torvegade
Vesterport
Frihedsstøtten
Bernstorffsgade
Design Centre
National museet
Children's Museum
Storm-gade
Prinsens Bro
Tøjhusgade
Tøjhus-museet
Det Kongelige Bibliotek
Sofitel Plaza
Banegårds-plads
TIVOLI
Dantes Plads
Frederiksholms Kanal
Christian IV's Bryghus
'Black Diamond'
Nicolai Eigtveds Gade
North Atlantic House
Grand Hotel
Reventlows-gade
Hovedbanegården (Central Station)
H.C. Andersens Boulevard
Ny Carlsberg Glyptoteket
Vester Voldgade
Christians Brygge
Søren Kierkegaards Plads
3
Comfort H. Mayfair
Helgolandsgade
IC/EC
KØBENHAVN H
Tietgensgade
Musik-kons.
Christians kirke
Puggaards-gade
Inderhavnen
Applebys Plads
CHRISTIAN-SHAVN
Absalon
Colbjørnsensgade
Stampesg.
Stoltenbergsg.
Niels Brocks Gade
Politi-gården
Fiskerstensgade
Otto Mønsteds Plads
Overgaden oven Vandet
Langebrogade
Kvægtorvsgade
Central Post-bygning
Bernstorffs-gade
Mitchellsgade
Hambros-gade
Langebro
Kalvebod Bastion
Rabeshave
DGI-byens
page 138-9
Politi-torvet
Falck Huset
Kalvebod Brygge
Havne-badet
Ved Langebro
Enhjørningens Bastion
Panterens Bastion
Øksnehallen
Postterminal
Autocamper-plads
Stadsgraven
Teknisk Skole
Amager Boulevard
Staldgade
Havne-parken
Thorshavnsgade
Modborgerhus
Radisson SAS Scandinavia
Statens Serum Institut
Casino Copenhagen
Weidekampsgade
Ingerslevsgade
Godsbanegården
Copenhagen Marriott
Njalsgården Rådhusanneks
Kalvebod Brygge
AMAGERBRO
2
Egilsgade
Njalsgade
Artillerivej
Sydhavnen
Isafjordsgade
Gunløgsgade
Bergthorasgade
Leifsgade
DYBBØLSBRO
Islands Brygge
Snorresgade
Halfdansgade
ISLANDS BRYGGE
Njalsgade
Dybbølsbro
Bryggens-gård
Hans Tausens Kirke
Sturlasgade
Ørestads Boulevard
Gasværks-havnen
Københavns Universitet Amager
Islands Brygge
H. C. Hansens Gade
Hans Hedtofts Gade
Gullfoss-gade
Kigkurren
1
Fisketorvet Shopping Center
Kalvebod Pladsvej
Erik Eriksens Gade
A. Heides Gade
J.C. Chr. Gade
Carl Th. Zahles Gade
Artillerivej
Børneinstitution
p134
p135
p138
p139
p136
p137
Tømmer-graven
Drechselsgade
0 100 200 300 400 500m
0 100 200 300 400 500yds
Artillerivej
Bryggen Haveforening
C
D
E

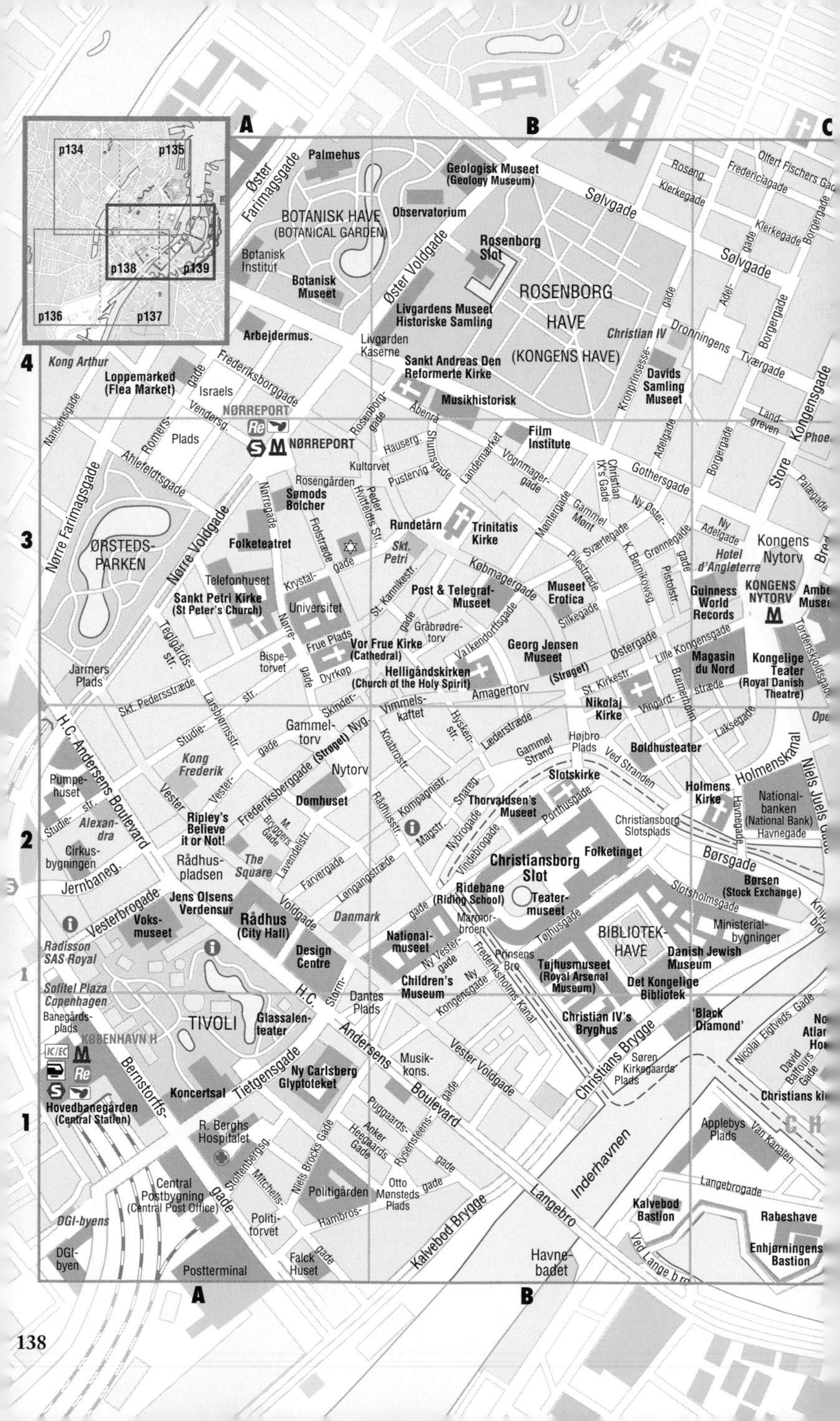

A
B
C
p134
p135
p138
p139
p136
p137
Palmehus
Geologisk Museet
(Geology Museum)
Øster Farimagsgade
BOTANISK HAVE
(BOTANICAL GARDEN)
Observatorium
Botanisk Institut
Botanisk Museet
Øster Voldgade
Rosenborg Slot
ROSENBORG HAVE
(KONGENS HAVE)
Livgardens Museet Historiske Samling
Livgarden Kaserne
Arbejdermus.
Sankt Andreas Den Reformerte Kirke
Musikhistorisk
Sølvgade
Roseng.
Klerkegade
Fredericiagade
Olfert Fischers Gade
Borgergade
Adel-gade
Dronningens Tværgade
Christian IV
Kronprinsessegade
Davids Samling Museet
Land-greven
Kongensgade
Adelgade
Borgergade
Store
Kong Arthur
Loppemarked
(Flea Market)
Israels Plads
Frederiksborggade
NØRREPORT
NØRREPORT
Nansensgade
Romersgade
Vendersg.
Ahlefeldtsgade
Nørre Farimagsgade
ØRSTEDS-PARKEN
Nørre Voldgade
Rosenborggade
Åbenrå
Hauserg.
Kultorvet
Pustervig
Shumsgade
Landemærket
Film Institute
Vognmagergade
Christian IX's Gade
Gothersgade
Ny Østergade
Rosengården
Sømods Bolcher
Nørregade
Fiolstræde
Peder Hvitfeldts Str.
Rundetårn
Trinitatis Kirke
Møntergade
Gammel Mønt
Sværtegade
K. Bernikowsg.
Grønnegade
Ny Adelgade
Hotel d'Angleterre
Kongens Nytorv
Folketeatret
Krystalgade
Skt. Petri
Købmagergade
Pilestræde
Museet Erotica
Pistolstr.
Guinness World Records
KONGENS NYTORV
Telefonhuset
Sankt Petri Kirke
(St Peter's Church)
Universitet
St. Kannikestr.
Post & Telegraf-Museet
Silkegade
Gråbrødretorv
Valkendorfsgade
Georg Jensen Museet
Østergade
Lille Kongensgade
Magasin du Nord
Kongelige Teater
(Royal Danish Theatre)
Tordenskjoldsgade
Teglgårdsstr.
Frue Plads
Vor Frue Kirke
(Cathedral)
Bispetorvet
Dyrkøp
Helligåndskirken
(Church of the Holy Spirit)
Amagertorv
(Strøget)
St. Kirkestr.
Nikolaj Kirke
Vingårdstræde
Bremerholm
Jarmers Plads
Skt. Pedersstræde
Larsbjørnsstr.
Skindergade
Vimmelskaftet
Hyskenstr.
Læderstræde
Gammel Strand
Højbro Plads
Ved Stranden
Boldhusteater
Laksegade
H.C. Andersens Boulevard
Studiestræde
Kong Frederik
Gammeltorv
Nytorv
Knabrostr.
Frederiksberggade (Strøget)
Nyg.
Slotskirke
Holmens Kirke
Holmenskanal
National-banken
(National Bank)
Havnegade
Niels Juels Gade
Pumpehuset
Alexandra
Vester Voldgade
Ripley's Believe it or Not!
Domhuset
Rådhusstr.
Kompagnistr.
Snareg.
Thorvaldsen's Museet
Porthusgade
Christiansborg Slotsplads
Cirkus-bygningen
M. Bryggers Gade
Lavendelstr.
Magstr.
Nybrogade
Vindebrogade
Folketinget
Børsgade
Rådhus-pladsen
The Square
Farvergade
Christiansborg Slot
Børsen
(Stock Exchange)
Jernbaneg.
Vesterbrogade
Jens Olsens Verdensur
Longangstræde
Ridebane
(Riding School)
Teater-museet
Slotsholmsgade
Voks-museet
Rådhus
(City Hall)
Voldgade
Danmark
Marmorbroen
Tøjhusgade
BIBLIOTEK-HAVE
Ministerial-bygninger
Radisson SAS Royal
Design Centre
National-museet
Ny Vestergade
Prinsens Bro
Tøjhusmuseet
(Royal Arsenal Museum)
Danish Jewish Museum
Det Kongelige Bibliotek
Sofitel Plaza Copenhagen
Children's Museum
Ny Kongensgade
Frederiksholms Kanal
Banegårdsplads
KØBENHAVN H
TIVOLI
Glassalen-teater
H.C. Andersens Boulevard
Stormgade
Dantes Plads
Christian IV's Bryghus
'Black Diamond'
Nicolai Eigtveds Gade
David Balfours Gade
Musik-kons.
Vester Voldgade
Christians Brygge
Søren Kirkegaards Plads
Bernstorffsgade
Koncertsal
Tietgensgade
Ny Carlsberg Glyptoteket
Hovedbanegården
(Central Station)
R. Berghs Hospitalet
Stoltenbergsg.
Niels Brocks Gade
Puggaardsgade
Anker Heegaards Gade
Rysensteensgade
Christians Kirke
Applebys Plads
Van Kanaten
Inderhavnen
Central Postbygning
(Central Post Office)
Mitchellsg.
Politigården
Otto Mønsteds Plads
Langebrogade
Langebro
Kalvebod Bastion
Rabeshave
DGI-byens
Politi-torvet
Hambrosgade
Kalvebod Brygge
Ved Langebro
Enhjørningens Bastion
DGI-byen
Postterminal
Falck Huset
Havne-badet
4
3
2
1

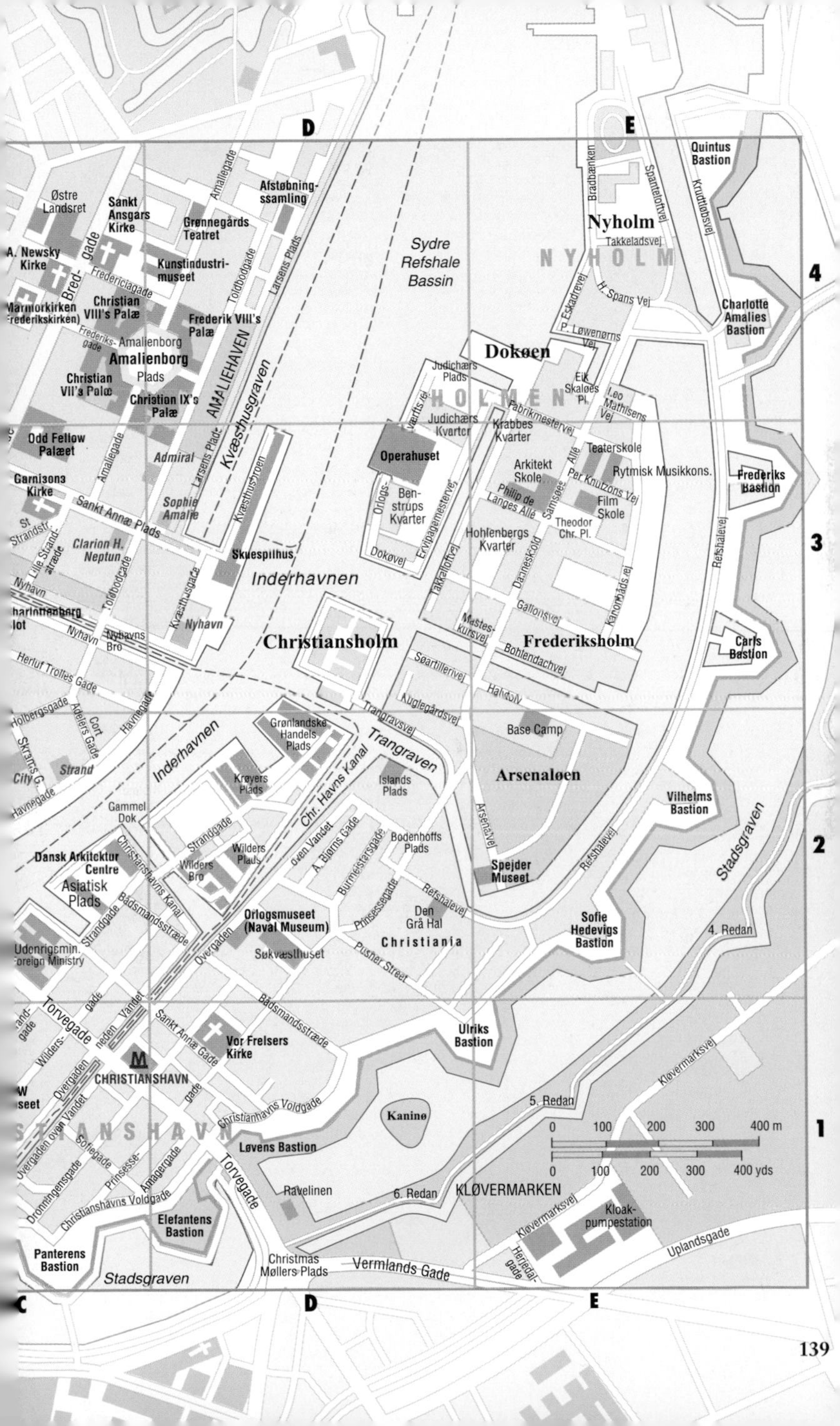
D
E
C
D
E
4
3
2
1
Østre Landsret
Sankt Ansgars Kirke
A. Newsky Kirke
Bredgade
Fredericiagade
Marmorkirken (Frederikskirken)
Christian VIII's Palæ
Frederiksgade
Amalienborg
Amalienborg Plads
Christian VII's Palæ
Christian IX's Palæ
Frederik VIII's Palæ
Kunstindustrimuseet
Grønnegårds Teatret
Amaliegade
Afstøbningssamling
Toldbodgade
Larsens Plads
AMALIEHAVEN
Kvæsthusgraven
Odd Fellow Palæet
Garnisons Kirke
Admiral
Sophie Amalie
Sankt Annæ Plads
St Strandstr.
Lille Strandstræde
Clarion H. Neptun
Kvæsthusbroen
Kvæsthusgade
Skuespilhus
Nyhavn
Charlottenborg Slot
Nyhavns Bro
Herluf Trolles Gade
Holbergsgade
Adelers Gade
Cort
Havnegade
Skt. Strand
City
Inderhavnen
Sydre Refshale Bassin
Christiansholm
Operahuset
Orlogsværftsvej
Benstrups Kvarter
Ervipagemestervej
Dokøvej
Judichærs Plads
Judichærs Kvarter
HOLMEN
Krabbes Kvarter
Dokøen
Fabrikmestervej
Nyholm
NYHOLM
Bradbænken
Spanteloftvej
Takkeladsvej
Eskadrevej
H. Spans Vej
P. Løwenørns Vej
Eik Skaløes Pl.
Leo Mathisens Vej
Quintus Bastion
Krudtløbsvej
Charlotte Amalies Bastion
Teaterskole
Rytmisk Musikkons.
Arkitekt Skole
Philip de Langes Allé
Per Knutzons Vej
Film Skole
Samsøes
Theodor Chr. Pl.
Hohlenbergs Kvarter
Takkelloftvej
Danneskiold
Kanonbådsvej
Galionsvej
Mastekursvej
Frederiksholm
Bohlendachvej
Frederiks Bastion
Refshalevej
Carls Bastion
Søartillerivej
Halvtolv
Kuglegårdsvej
Trangravsvej
Trangraven
Base Camp
Arsenaløen
Arsenalvej
Grønlandske Handels Plads
Krøyers Plads
Islands Plads
Chr. Havns Kanal
Gammel Dok
Strandgade
Wilders Plads
Wilders Bro
Dansk Arkitektur Centre
Asiatisk Plads
Christianshavns Kanal
Bådsmandsstræde
Overgaden oven Vandet
A. Bjørns Gade
Burmeistersgade
Bodenhoffs Plads
Prinsessegade
Den Grå Hal
Christiania
Pusher Street
Spejder Museet
Vilhelms Bastion
Stadsgraven
Sofie Hedevigs Bastion
4. Redan
Orlogsmuseet (Naval Museum)
Søkvæsthuset
Udenrigsmin. Foreign Ministry
Torvegade
Overgaden neden Vandet
Sankt Annæ Gade
Vor Frelsers Kirke
Ulriks Bastion
M
CHRISTIANSHAVN
Christianshavns Voldgade
STIANSHAVN
Sofiegade
Dronningensgade
Amagergade
Løvens Bastion
Kaninø
5. Redan
Kløvermarksvej
0
100
200
300
400 m
400 yds
Ravelinen
6. Redan
KLØVERMARKEN
Kloakpumpestation
Elefantens Bastion
Panterens Bastion
Stadsgraven
Christmas Møllers Plads
Vermlands Gade
Herjedalgade
Uplandsgade

Selective Index for Street Atlas

PLACES OF INTEREST

A. Newsky Kirke 139 C4
Afstøbnings. 139 D4
Amalienborg 139 C4
Amber Museet 138 C3
Anna Kirken 134 A3
Apostol Kirke 136 B3
Arbejdermus. 138 A3
Aveny Teater 136 A3
Bakkehus-museet 136 A2
Bethania Kirken 134 B2
Bethlehems-kirken 134 B1
B. Nansen Teater 136 A3
Blågårds Kirke 134 B2
Boldhusteater 138 B2
Børsen (Stock Exchange) 138 C2
Botanisk Museet 138 A3
Brorsons Kirke 134 A2
Bymuseet 136 B3
Carls Bastion 139 E3
Carlsberg Brewery 136 A2
Carlsberg Museet (Carlsberg Museum) 136 A2
Central Postbygning 138 A1
Charlotte Amalies Bastion 139 E4
Charlottenborg Slot 139 C3
Children's Museum 138 B2
Christian IX's Palæ 139 D4
Christian VII's Palæ 139 C4
Christian VIII's Palæ 139 C4
Christiansborg Slot 138 B2
Christiansholm 139 D3
Christianskirke 138 C1
Daniel Kirken 134 B2
Danish Jewish Museum 138 B2
Dansk Design Centre 138 A2
Dansk Arkitektur Centre 139 C2
Davids Samling Museet 138 B4
Den Hirschsprungske Samling 135 D2
Den Lille Havfrue (Little Mermaid) 135 E3
Det Ny Teater 136 C3
Domhuset 138 A2
Døves Kirke 134 A2
Edison Teater 136 A4
Elefantens Bastion 139 D1
Enghave 136 A1
Enhjørningens Bastion 138 C1
Esajas Kirke 135 D3
Film Institute 138 B3
Folketeatret 138 A3
Folketinget 138 B2
Fredens Kirke 135 C3
Frederik VIII's Palæ 139 D4
Frederiks Bastion 139 E3
Frederiksberg Kirke 136 A3
Frederiksberg Rådhus 136 A4
Frederikskirken (Marmorkirken) 139 C4
Frihedsmuseet 135 E2
Fugleø Island 135 C3
Garnisons Kirke 139 C3
Gefion 135 E2
Geologisk Museet 138 B4
G.Jensen Museet 138 B3
Grønnegårds Teatret 139 D4
Guinness World Records 138 C3
Gustafs Kyrka 135 E3
Hans Tausens Kirke 137 E1
Hellig Kors Kirke 134 A2
Helligåndskirken 138 B3
Historiske Samling 138 B4
Holmens Kirke 138 C2
Hovedbanegården 138 A1
Jerusalems Kirke 135 D2
Jesu Hjerte Kirke 136 C3
Kalvebod Bastion 138 B1
Kaninø 139 D1
Kastellet 135 E3
Kastels kirken 135 E2
Katolsk Ap. Kirke 134 B1
Kingos Kirke 134 A4
Koncertsal 138 A1
Kongelige Bibliotek 138 B2
Kongelige Teater (Royal Danish Theatre) 138 C3
Kristi Kirke 134 B1
Kristus Kirke 134 B2
Kunstindustrie Museet 139 D4
Livgardens Museet 138 B4
Loppemarked 138 A3
Løvens Bastion 139 D1
Magasin du Nord 138 C3
Morskabs Museet 136 A3
Museet Erotica 138 B3
Musik Historisk 138 B4
Nationalbanken 138 C2
Nationalmuseet 138 B2
Nazaret Kirke 135 C3
Nikolaj Kirke 138 B3
Nordre Kapel 136 A1
Nørrebros Teater 134 B2
Ny Carlsberg Glyptoteket 138 A1
Observatorium 138 B4
Odd Fellow Palæet 139 C3
Øksnehallen 137 C3
Operahusset 139 D3
Orlogsmuseet (Naval Museum) 139 D2
Østerport Station 135 D3
Panterens Bastion 139 C1
Post & Telegraf Museet 138 B3
Quintus Bastion 139 E4
Rådhus (City Hall) 138 A2
Rialto 136 A4
Riddersalen Jytte Abildstrøms Teater 136 A4
Ridebane 138 B2
Ripley's Believe it or Not! 138 A2
Rosenborg Slot 138 B4
Rundetårn 138 B3
Sakraments Kirke 134 B2
Samuels Kirke 134 A4
Sankt Albans Kirke 135 E2
Sankt Andreas Den Reformerte Kirke 138 B4
Sankt Ansgars Kirke 139 C4
Sankt Johannes Kirke 134 B2
Sankt Pauls Kirke 135 D2
Sankt Petri Kirke 138 A3
Sankt Stefans Kirke 134 A3
Sankt Thomas Kirke 134 A1
Simeons Kirke 134 B2
Skuespilhus 139 D3
Slotskirke 138 B2
Søfarts-monument 135 E3
Sofie Hedevigs Bastion 139 E2
Sømods Bolcher 138 A3
Søpavillonen 134 B1
Spejder Museet 139 E2
Statens Museum for Kunst 135 D2
Storm P. Museet 136 A3
Teater-museet 138 B2
Thorvaldsen's Museet 138 B2
Tøjhusmuseet 138 B2
Trinitatis Kirke 138 B3
Tycho Brahe Planetarium 136 C3
Ulriks Bastion 139 E2
Vilhelms Bastion 139 E2
Voksmuseet 138 A2
Vor Frelsers Kirke 139 D1
Vor Frue Kirke (Cathedral) 138 A3
Zoo 136 A3
Zoologisk Museum 134 B4

STREETS

Åbenrå 138 B4
Åboulevard 134 A1-B1
Adelgade 138 C4
Ågade 134 A1
Alhambra Vej 136 B3
Allégade 136 A4
Amager Boulevard 137 E2
Amagergade 139 D1
Amagertorv 138 B3
Amaliegade 139 C3-D4
Amalienborg Plads 139 D4
Andreas Bjørns Gade 139 D2
Arsenalvej 139 E2
Artillerivej 137 D1
Asiatisk Plads 139 C2
Bådsmandsstræde 139 D1-D2
Benstrups Kvarter 139 D3
Bergthorasgade 137 E2
Bernstorffsgade 138 A1
Blegdamsvej 134 C4
Bodenhoffs Plads 139 D2
Bohlendachvej 139 E3
Borgergade 138 C3-C4
Børsgade 138 C2
Borups Allé 134 A2
Bradbænken 139 E4
Bredgade 139 C3-C4
Bremerholm 138 B3
Bülowsvej 134 A1
Burmeistersgade 139 D2
Christian IX's Gade 138 B3
Christianhavns Voldgade 139 D1
Christians Brygge 138 B1
Christiansborg Slotsplads 138 B2
Christianshavns Kanal 139 D2
Christianshavns Voldgade 139 C1
Christmas Møllers Plads 139 D1
Cort Adelers Gade 139 C2
Dag Hammarskjölds Allé 135 D3
Danasvej 136 B4
Danneskiold Samsøes Allé 139 E3
David Balfours Gade 138 C1
Dokøvej 139 D3
Drechselsgade 137 D1
Dronning Louises Bro 134 B2
Dronningens Tværgade 138 C4
Dronningensgade 139 C1
Dybbølsbro 137 C2
Dybbølsgade 136 B2
Egilsgade 137 E2
Ekvipagemestervej 139 D3
Enghavevej 136 A1-B3
Eskadrevej 139 E4
Estlandsgade 136 B2
Fabrikmestervej 139 E4
Fælledvej 134 B2
Falkoner Allé 136 A4
Farvergade 138 A2
Fiolstræde 138 A3
Folke Bernadottes Allé 135 E3
Forchhammersvej 136 B4
Fredensbro 134 C2
Fredericiagade 138 C4/139 C4
Frederik Bajers Plads 134 B3
Frederiksberg Allé 136 A3-B3
Frederiksberggade 138 A2
Frederiksgade 139 C4
Frederiksholms Kanal 138 B2
Frederiksstadsgade 136 B2
Frydendalsvej 136 A3
Galionsvej 139 E3
Gammel Kongevej 136 A4-C3
Gammel Mønt 138 B3
Gammel Strand 138 B2
Gammeltorv 138 A2
Gothersgade 138 B3
Gråbrødretorv 138 B3
Grønnegade 138 B3
Grønningen 135 E3
Grundtvigsvej 136 A4
Guldbergsgade 134 B3
Gunløgsgade 137 E2
Gyldenløvesgade 134 B1/137 C4
Halfdansgade 137 E2
Halvtolv 139 E3
Hamletsgade 134 A4
Hans Christian Andersens Boulevard 138 A2-B1
Hans Christian Ørsteds Vej 136 B4
Hauserg. 138 B3
Havnegade 138 C2/139 C3
Henrik Ibsens Vej 136 A3
Henrik Spans Vej 139 E4
Herjedalgade 139 E1
Herluf Trolles Gade 139 C3
Hjalmar Brantings Plads 135 D3
Højbro Plads 138 B2
Holbergsgade 139 C2
Holmenskanal 138 C2
Hostrupsvej 136 A4
Howitzvej 136 A4

Hyskenstr. 138 B2
Ingerslevsgade 136 B2-C3
Israels Plads 138 A3
Istedgade 136 B2-C3
Jacobys Allé 136 A3
Jagtvej 134 A2-B5
Jarmers Plads 138 A3
Judichærs Plads 139 D4
Kalkbrænderihavnsgade 135 E4
Kalvebod Brygge 137 D4/138 B1
Kanonbådsvej 139 E3
Kingosgade 136 B3
Klerkegade 138 B4/138 C4
Kløvermarksvej 139 E1
Knabrostr. 138 B2
Knippelsbro 138 C2
Købmagergade 138 B3
Kompagnistr. 138 B2
Kongens Nytorv 138 C3
Kristen Bernikowsg. 138 B3
Kristianiagade 135 D3
Kronprinsessegade 138 B4
Krudtløbsvej 139 E4
Krystalgade 138 A3
Kuglegårdsvej 139 D3
Kultorvet 138 B3
Kvæsthusbroen 139 D3
Kvæsthusgade 139 D3
Læderstræde 138 B2
Laksegade 138 C2
Landemærket 138 B3
Landgreven 138 C3
Langebro 138 B1
Langebrogade 138 C1
Langelinie Bro 135 E3
Larsens Plads 139 D4
Lavendelstr. 138 A2
Leo Mathisens Vej 139 E4
Lille Kongensgade 138 B3
Lille Strand stræde 139 C3
Lille Triangel 135 D3
Løngangstræde 138 A2
Lyrskovgade 136 B2
M. Bryggers Gade 138 A2
Magstr. Snareg. 138 B2
Marmorbroen 138 B2
Masteskursvej 139 E3
Matthæusgade 136 B3
Mimersgade 134 A4
Møntergade 138 B3
Nicolai Eigtveds Gade 138 C1
Niels Ebbesens Vej 136 B4
Niels Juels Gade 138 C2
Njalsgade 137 E2
Nordrefrihavnsgade 135 D4
Nørre Allé 134 B3-B4
Nørre Farimagsgade 138 A3
Nørre Søgade 134 B1
Nørre Voldgade 138 A3
Nørrebrogade 134 A4-B2
Nørrebros Runddel 134 A3
Nørregade 138 A3
Ny Adelgade 138 C3
Ny Carlsberg Vej 136 A2
Ny Kongensgade 138 B2
Ny Østergade 138 B3
Ny Vestergade 138 B2
Nybrogade 138 B2
Nyhavn 139 C3
Nyhavns Bro 139 C3
Nytorv 138 A2
Oehlenschlægersgade 136 B2
Olfert Fischers Gade 138 C4
Ørestads Boulevard 137 E1
Orlogsværftsvej 139 D3
Oslo Plads 135 D3
Østbanegade 135 D3-E4
Øster Allé 135 C4
Øster Farimagsgade 135 C2
Øster Søgade 135 D3
Øster Voldgade 135 D2/138 B4
Østerbrogade 135 D4-D3
Østergade 138 B3
Otto Krabbes Pl. 136 B3
Overgaden neden Vandet 139 C1
Overgaden oven Vandet 139 C1-D2
P. Løwenørns Vej 139 E4
Palægade 138 C3
Peblinge Dossering 134 B1
Peder Hvitfeldts Stræde 138 A3
Peder Skrams Gade 139 C2
Per Knutzons Vej 139 E3
Philip de Langes Allé 139 E3
Pile Allé 136 A3
Pilestræde 138 B3
Pistolstr. 138 B3
Plantevej 136 A3
Porthusgade 138 B2
Prinsens Bro 138 B2
Prinsessegade 139 C1-D2
Pusher Street 139 D2
Pustervig 138 B3
Rådhuspladsen 138 A2
Rådhusstr. 138 B2
Rahbeks Allé 136 A2
Rantzausgade 134 A2
Refshalevej 139 D2-E3
Rosenborggade 138 B4
Roseng. 138 C4
Rosengården 138 A3
Rosenørns Allé 134 A1
Roskildevej 136 A3
Sankt Annæ Gade 139 D1
Sankt Annæ Plads 139 C3
Sankt Hans Gade 134 B2
Sankt Hans Torv 134 B2
Sankt Kannikestr. 138 B3
Sankt Kirkestr. 138 B3
Sankt Knuds Vej 136 B4
Sankt Strandstr. 139 C3
Shumsgade 138 B3
Silkegade 138 B3
Sjællandsgade 134 B3
Skindergade 138 B3
Slotsholmsgade 138 C2
Smallegade 136 A4
Søartillerivej 139 D3
Sofiegade 139 C1
Sølvgade 138 B4-C4
Sønder Boulevard 136 B2
Sortedam Dossering 134 C2
Spanteloftvej 139 E4
Steenstrups Allé 136 B4
Stockholmsgade 135 D2
Store Kongensgade 135 D2/138 C4
Strandboulevarden 135 E4
Strandgade 139 C1-D2
Strøget 138 B3
Sværlegade 138 B3
Svineryggen 136 C4
Tagensvej 134 A4-B3
Takkeladsvej 139 E4
Takkelloftvej 139 D3
Theodor Chr. Pl. 139 E3
Thorvaldsensvej 136 B4/134 A1
Tietgensgade 138 A1
Tøjhusgade 138 B2
Toldbodgade 139 C3-D4
Tordenskjoldsgade 138 C3
Torvegade 139 C1-D1
Trangravsvej 139 D2
Trianglen 135 D4
Universitetsparken 134 B4
Uplandsgade 139 E1
Værnedamsvej 136 B3
Valdemarsgade 136 B3
Valkendorffsgade 138 B3
Van Kanalen 138 C1
Vasbygade 137 C1
Ved Langebro 138 D1
Ved Stranden 138 B2
Ved Vesterport 137 C3
Vermlands Gade 139 D1
Vester Farimagsgade 137 C4
Vester Voldgade 138 A2
Vesterbrogade 136 A3-C3/138 A2
Vesterfælledvej 136 A2
Vestre Kirkegårds Allé 136 A1
Vigerslev Allé 136 A1
Vimmelskaftet 138 B3
Vindebrogade 138 B2
Vingårdstræde 138 B3
Vodroffsvej 136 C4
Vognmagergade 138 B3
Weidekampsgade 137 E2
Wilders Bro 139 D2
Wilders Plads 139 D2
Wildersgade 139 C1

PARKS

Amaliehaven 139 D4
Amorparken 134 B3
Assistens Kirkegård 134 A2
Bibliotekhave 138 B2
Botanisk Have (Botanical Garden) 138 A4
Churchill-Parken 135 E2
Enghaven 136 B2
Fælledparken 134 C4
Fredenspark 134 C3
Frederiksberg Have 136 A3
Frederiksberg Kirkegård 136 A3
Garnisons Kirkegård 135 D3
Hans Tavsens Park 134 A2
Holmens Kirkegård 135 D3
Kløvermarken 139 E1
Mosaisk Kirkegård 134 B2
Nørrebroparken 134 A3
Ørstedsparken 138 A3
Østre Anlæg 135 D2
Rektorparken 136 A1
Rosen Haven 136 A4
Rosenborg Have (Kongens Have) 138 B4
Saxoparken 136 B3
Skydebanehaven 136 C3
Sønder-Marken 136 A3
Tivoli 138 A1
Vestre Kirkegård 136 A1

Index

A

Akvavit **54**
Amager **22, 23, 69, 112, 127, 131, 132**
Amalienborg **10, 15, 16–7, 38, 62, 66, 80, 123, 127**
Andersen, Hans Christian **12, 19, 22, 31, 72–3, 77–9, 80, 81, 84, 112, 118**
Antiques **127–8**
Architecture **26-27**

B

Ballet **49, 102**
  Copenhagen International Ballet **49**
  Royal Danish Ballet **48, 102**
Beaches **23, 25, 44–5, 112**
Beer **54–5**
Bishop Absolon **8, 10, 58, 78–9**
Black Diamond *(see Sorte Diamant)*
Book Shops **76–7**
Børsen (Stock Exchange) **11, 26**
Blixen, Karen **25, 50, 73–4, 88–9**

C

Cafés and Bars **28–33**
Carlsberg Brewery **19, 78, 84**
Children **34–5**
  Playgrounds **114–5**
Chocolate **53–4**
Christiania **21, 61**
Christiansborg Palace **11, 59, 97**
Christianshavn **20–1, 32–3, 90, 124–5, 127, 132**
Churches **36–9**
  Alexandr Nevsky Kirke **36**
  Christiansborg Slotskirke **11, 36**
  Christian's Kirke **21, 36, 99**
  Domkirke **37**
  Garnison's Kirken **99**
  Grundtvig's Kirke **37, 43, 60**
  Helligåndskirken **37–8**
  Holmens Kirke **37–8, 101**
  Kastelskirken **101**
  Marmorkirken **17, 38**
  Nicolaj Kirke **30, 85**
  Old Synagogue **38**
  Roskilde Domkirke **24, 38, 81**
  St Alban's **38**
  Skt Ansgar's Kirke **38**
  Skt Petri Kirke **38**
  Trinitatis Kirke **39**
  Vor Frelsers Kirke **4, 21, 39**
  Vor Frue Kirke (St Mary's) **39**
Copenhagen Art Academy **59**

D

Danmarks Akvarium **34**
Dansk Arkitektur Center **85**
Design **40–3, 48**
  Casa **40**
  Dansk Design Centre **7, 40, 85–6**
  Designer Zoo **19, 125–6**
  Montana Mobile **41**
  Rosendahl **41**
DGI-Byen Swim Centre **34, 68, 111**

E

Embassy, British **46**
Embassy, United States of America **46**
Embassy, Canadian **46**
Emergencies **46**
Environment **44–5**
Experimental School of Art **61**

F

Festivals **48–9**
  Architecture and Design Days **48**
  Copenhagen Catwalk **48**
  Copenhagen Cooking **49**
  Copenhagen Distortion **48**
  Father Christmas Congress **48–9**
  Golden Days in Copenhagen **49**
Food and Drink **52–5, 129**
Film **48, 50–1**
  Copenhagen International Film Festival **49**
  Danske Filminstitut **51, 52**
  CPH:DOX (Festival) **49**
  Dogme 95 **50–1**
  Empire Bio **51**
  Gay and Lesbian Film Festival **49**
  Grand Teatret **51**
  Husets Biograf **51**
  Night Film Festival **48**
  Nordisk Film Kompagni **50**
Frederiksberg **18, 19, 67–9, 111, 113–4, 123–5, 129**
Frederiksborg Slot **25, 108**
Frederiksstaden **16, 38, 68, 121**
Furniture **42–3**

G

Gammeltorv **8**
Gay and Lesbian **56–7**
  Accommodation **57**
  Advice and Information **56**
  Travel Agency **57**
Grabrødretorv **11**

H

Health Clubs and Pools **111**
Helsingor **24–5, 108–9**
History **58–61**
Holmen **21, 32–3, 124–5**
Hotels **62–9**
Hovebanegård **6, 130**
Hygge **5**

J

Jacobsen, Arne **18, 19, 27, 30, 33, 40, 42, 43, 62, 63–4, 116**
Jewellery **43**

K

Kastellet **17, 26**
Kierkegaard, Søren **74–5**
Kobnhavns Radhus **6, 26–7**
Kongelige Bibliotek (Royal Library) **11, 75, 77**
Kongens Nytorv **12–3, 31, 65–6, 78–9, 121–2, 126–7**

L

Language **70–1**
Lighting **43**
Literature and Theatre **72–7**
  Hamlet Summer **48**
  Kongelige Teater (Royal Theatre) **13, 77, 102**
  Lille Teater **77**
  Ny Theater **77**
  Teatermuseet **11, 77, 99**
Lille Havefrue (Little Mermaid) **17, 72, 79**

M

Markets **129**
Money **46–7**
Monuments and Fountains **76–81**
  Bishop Absolon Statue **78**
  Caritas Fountain **8, 78**
  Carlsberg Elephants **78, 81**
  Christian V **12, 13, 78**
  Dragon's Leap Fountain **6, 79**
  Fiskerkone (Fishwife) **79–80**
  Frederick V **16, 80**
  Frederick VII **5, 80**
  Frihedstøtten **18, 80**
  Gefionspringvand **17, 80**
  Hans Christian Anderson statues **80**
  Lurblœserne (The Hornblowers) **6, 80, 81**
  Paradise Genetically Altered **81**
  Royal Tombs **24, 81**
Museums and Galleries **82–99**
  Amagermuseet **23, 82**
  Amalienborg Museum **83, 107**
  Arbejdermuseet (Workers' Museum) **29, 82**
  Arken **25, 83**
  Bakkehusmuseet **84**
  Charlottenborg Slot **84–5**
  Children's Museum **93**
  Cisternerne, Museet for Moderne Glaskunst **85**
  Contemporary Art Centre Nikolai, KBJ **30, 85**
  Dansk Arkitektur Center **21, 85**
  Davids Samling Museum **15, 86**
  Den Hirschsprungske Samling **15, 60, 86**
  Den Kongelige Afstøbningssamlingen **86**
  Experimentarium **34, 86–7**
  Frihedsmuseet **87**
  Geologisk Museum **87–8**
  Georg Jensen Museum **88**
  Guinness World Records Museum **34, 88**
  Jewish Museum **88**
  Karen Blixen Museet **25, 74, 88–9**
  Kobnhavns Bymuseet **19, 89**
  Kunstindustrie Museet **17, 41, 89–90**
  Little Mill **90**
  Louisiana Museum for Moderne Kunst **25, 90–1**
  Medicinsk Museum **91**
  Museum Erotica **91**
  Musik Historisk Museet **91**
  National Museum **34–5, 92–3**
  Ny Carlsberg Glypotek **7, 28, 94–5**
  Ørdrupsgaard **95–6**
  Orlogsmuseet **96**
  Oksnehallen **19, 95**
  Politihistorisk Museum **96**
  Post and Tele Museum **29, 96**
  Ripleys Believe it or Not! Museum **96**
  Royal Copenhagen Porcelain Museum **96**
  Slotsholmen Ruins **97**
  Stable Museum **97**
  Staten Museum for Kunst **15, 35, 97**
  Storm P Museum **97**
  Teckniksmuseum **25**
  Thorvaldsen's Museum **11, 98, 107**
  Tøjhusmuseet (Arsenal Museum) **11, 98, 107**
  Tyco Brahe Planetarium **18, 35, 98–9**
  Victorian House **99**
  Vikingskibsmuseet (Viking Ship Museum) **24, 99**
  Wonderful World of Hans Christian Andersen Museum **35, 99**
Music and Dance **100–3**
  Classical Music **100–1**
  Choral Music **101**
  Contemporary Music **103**
  Copenhagen Music Week **49**
  Copenhagen Summerdance **49**
  Cultural Harbour **49**
  Danish National Symphony Orchestra **100**
  Dansk Danse Teater **49, 102**
  Jazz and Blues **102–3**
  Jazz Festival **49**
  Modern Dance **102**
  Music Shops **103**
  Opera **101–2**
  Roskilde Festival **49**

N

Nightlife **104–5**
Norrebro **22, 33, 115**
Nyhavn **13, 31, 65–6, 121–2**

O

Opera *(See Music and Dance)*
Operahuset (Opera House) **21, 27, 61, 100, 101, 102**

P

Palaces **104–9**
  Amalienborg Palace **16, 97–8, 106–7**
  Christiansborg Slot **10–1, 107–8**
  Frederiksborg Slot **25, 108**
  Kronborg Slot **25, 108–9**
  Rosenborg Slot **14, 15, 109, 112**
Pampering **110–1**
Parks and Gardens **112–5**
  Assistens Kirkegard **22, 81, 112**
  Botanisk Have **112–3**
  Fælleparken **22, 113**
  Frederiksberg Have **19, 113–4**
  Jægersborg Dyrehave **34, 111**

Kongens Have **15, 109, 114**
Post **47**

R

Rådhus **6, 26–7**
Rådhuspladsen **6, 7, 28, 62–4, 116–7, 131**
Reading List **75–6**
Recycling **45**
Reservoirs **115**
Restaurants **116–25**
Rosenborg **14–5, 32, 66–7, 109, 122–3**
Roskilde **24, 38, 49, 99**
Royal Copenhagen Procelain **9, 41, 126, 127, 128, 129**
Royal Library *(see Kongelige Bibliotek)*
Rundetarn **27**

S

SAS Radisson (Hotel) **18, 19, 27, 63–4, 111, 116**
Saunas and Spas *(See Pampering)*
Shopping **126–9**
Clothing and Fashion **128**
Household Goods **128**
Souvenirs **129**
Sjælland **24–5**
Slotsholmen **10–1, 80, 97, 107–8**
Smørrebrød **52**
Sorte Diamant (Black Diamond) **11, 26, 100, 132**
Stock Exchange *(see Borsen)*
Stroget **8–9, 28–31, 64–5, 81, 117–21, 126–7**

T

Telephones **47**
Theatre *(see Literature and Theatre)*
Tivoli **6, 7, 28–31, 35, 44, 62–4, 100, 115, 116–7**
Tourist Office **47**
Transport **128–32**
Boat **130**
Bicycle **132**
Bus **130, 131–2**
Car **131**
Harbour Buses **132–3**
Harbour Tours **133**
Metro **132**
Plane **130–1**
S-tog **132**
Taxis and Rickshaws **133**
Train **130**
Walking **133**

V

Vesterbro **18–9, 32, 67–9, 96, 123–4, 127**
Vikings **24, 99**
Visa Regulations **47**

W

Wind Farms **44**

Z

Zoo Kobenhavn **35, 115**

Insight Smart Guide: Copenhagen
Compiled by: Antonia Cunningham
Edited by: Jason Mitchell
Photography by: **4 Corners images** 3br, 11b, 29b, 31t. 33b, 40/41t, 40cr, 54tr, cr& br, 97b, 103t&b, 104cr, 104/105t; **akg-images London** 59tc. 60bc, 88b; **Alamy** 9t, 12b, 19t, 28/29t, 30t &b, 32t, 33t, 36b, 41b, 42t, 45b, 46/47t, 52b, 52/53t, 53b, 61bc, 63b, 76b. 81b. 95b, 100/101t, 102b, 116/117t, 117b, 119b, 120t&b, 122t, 123t&b, 124Tl&tr, 125t&b, 128t, 130cr, 130/131t, 132b, 133t&b; **Bridgeman Art Library** 75t; **Corbis** 48b, 55b, 56b, 100b; **Antonia Cunningham** 5bl, 18, 39t, 85t; **Jerry Dennis/Apa** 5cl cr &br, 17b, 38t, 87b, 90t; **Getty Images** 35b, 48/49t, 61t; **Clare Griffiths** 2b, 114br; **Rudy Hemmingsen/Apa** 2/3t, 4t&b, 5c, 7t&b, 8b, 11t, 13t&b, 14, 15t&b, 16, 17t. 20, 21t&b, 23t. 24, 25t&b, 26, 27t&b, 28b, 34/35t, 34cr, 36/37t, 37b, 38b, 43b, 47b, 58t, 59bc &b, 61tc &b, 65b, 70/71t, 71b, 72cr, 72/73t, 76t, 77t&b, 78bl&br, 78/79t, 79b, 80b, 81t, 82b, 82/83t, 83b, 84t, 85b, 86b, 87t, 88t, 89t&b, 90cr, 93t, 96t, 97t, 98, 99, 101c, 105b, 106b, 106/107t, 107b, 108t&b, 109t, 112/113t, 113b114t, 115t&b, 116cr, 118tl, 121t, 124b, 126b, 126/127t, 127b128t, 129t&b, 1131b; **Laif/Camera Press** 19b, 44/45t, 62b, 64t&b, 66b, 110cr, 110/111t, 111b, 112b, 119t; **Photolibrary** 22b, 118tr; **Rex Features** 56/57t, 57b; **Ronald Grant Archive** 50/51t, 51b; **Jeroen Snijders/Apa** 93b; **Stockfood** 122b; **TopFoto** 60b, 72b, 74t&b, 75b, 109b; **Visit Copenhagen** 44cr; **Visit Denmark** 5cr, 58c; **Werner Forman Archive** 95t
Picture Manager: Hilary Genin
Maps: James Macdonald
Series Editor: Maria Lord

First Edition 2008

Printed in Singapore by Insight Print Services (Pte) Ltd

Worldwide distribution enquiries:
Apa Publications GmbH & Co. Verlag KG (Singapore Branch) 38 Joo Koon Road, Singapore 628990; tel: (65) 6865 1600; fax: (65) 6861 6438
Distributed in the UK and Ireland by:
GeoCenter International Ltd
Meridian House, Churchill Way West, Basingstoke, Hampshire RG21 6YR; tel: (44 1256) 817 987; fax: (44 1256) 817 988
Distributed in the United States by:
Langenscheidt Publishers, Inc.
36–36 33rd Street 4th Floor, Long Island City, New York 11106; tel: (1 718) 784 0055; fax: (1 718) 784 0640l

Contacting the Editors
We would appreciate it if readers would alert us to errors or outdated information by writing to:
Apa Publications, PO Box 7910, London SE1 1WE, UK; fax: (44 20) 7403 0290; e-mail: insight@apaguide.co.uk